GOD
CHRIST
CHURCH

GOD
CHRIST
CHURCH

A Practical Guide to Process Theology

Marjorie (Hewitt) Suchocki

CROSSROAD NEW YORK

For My Mother,
FAITH HEWITT DOWNS

1982

The Crossroad Publishing Company
575 Lexington Avenue, New York, NY 10022

Printed in the United States of America

Library of Congress Cataloging in Publication Data
Suchocki, Marjorie Hewitt.
God–Christ–Church.

1. Process theology.   2. Theology, Doctrinal.
I. Title.
BT83.6.S93   230′.044   81-22189
ISBN 0-8245-0464-X   AACR2

CONTENTS

Part IV WISDOM
CHRIST IN GOD: A PROCESS ECCLESIOLOGY

Part V POWER
THE KINGDOM OF GOD: A PROCESS ESCHATOLOGY

CONCLUSION

FOREWORD

WHAT will happen when feminist theologians turn their attention away from the discussion of woman and man and feminine and masculine and join in writing about God and human beings, the church and the wider world? Will their theology turn out, after all, to be much like that to which we are already accustomed, despite their powerful critiques? Or will it truly be theology in a new key?

God–Christ–Church provides us with the first important answer to this question. It presupposes feminist insights without articulating or labeling them. And it proceeds to speak of the great doctrines of the church from a perspective which is not emphasized. It is not theology about feminist issues, but it *is* feminist theology.

So what do we have? First, it is a *process* theology. That is not surprising since so much of the dualism and substantialism and hierarchicalism against which feminists rightly protest has also been rejected in process theology.

But, second, it is process theology with a difference. Much of process theology has been written in a style that is in tension with its content. It speaks of movement and flux, and the style suggests static structure. It opposes dualism too often by making hard and fast conceptual distinctions. It speaks of the unity of thought and feeling in a rhetoric that seeks to be purely rational. Marjorie Suchocki overcomes all that. Her style is appropriate to what she says. It moves and flows, and it unites thought and feeling.

The third point is continuous with the second but deserves separate treatment. Much of process theology has been written by academicians for academicians. We write too often with the possible criticisms of our colleagues in mind. Even those who write for lay readers frequently offer ideas that are correct but lack the

juices which give them life. Suchocki reaches out to that wider
circle to whom she would like to communicate, risking images and
illustrations and flights of poetry that might entice and draw them
in. Her writing embodies the Whiteheadian notion of lures for
feeling instead of sharing in the quest for an exactness which
Whitehead knew to be unreachable. Readers of this volume will
understand more than they will be able to articulate, for they will
have experienced Suchocki's process vision at the level of image
and feeling as well as concept.

The addition of "as well as concept" is important. At least in
Suchocki's case the introduction of image and feeling is not at the
expense of rigor of thought. That, I take it, is just the feminist
point. Men have too often thought that conceptual rigor is to be
attained by the exclusion of emotive elements. Whitehead certainly did not support that notion when he described our most high-
grade experience as "intellectual feelings." But process theologians have for the most part been children of the culture and unable
to embody the approach for which our doctrines called. Suchocki
shows that passion and insight and force of argument can go
together.

A reader unfamiliar with the literature in process theology might
suppose that the book summarizes ideas already worked out more
fully somewhere else. Of course, this is true in part. But the book is
not primarily an introduction to the thought of others. On the
contrary, it is *a* process vision of reality—the vision, namely, of
Marjorie Suchocki. The vision is deeply indebted to other process
thinkers, especially to Alfred North Whitehead. But it is Suchocki's vision, arising out of her Christian faith, her life experience, and her original speculation.

Much of process theology has so concentrated on the philosophical conceptuality which gives it its distinctiveness among theologies that it falls short of being fully theological. A glance at the
table of contents can assure the reader that this is not true of
Suchocki. She grasps the philosophical conceptuality accurately,
but it has been so fully internalized that she can move on quickly to
the world of specifically Christian concerns which marks theology.
Here her rootedness in Christian history coalesces with her personal life as a Christian struggling both to understand and live her
faith. The theological gestalt that results is very much her own, not
in the sense that it is idiosyncratic, but in the sense that it is
original.

I have located Suchocki's work within the tradition of process theology. Certainly it belongs there and is an important step in the development of that movement. Suchocki very explicitly identifies herself in this way. But in some respects such an identification is unfortunate. Too many people without examination rule out anything that comes from this stream of American Christian thought as unacceptable or irrelevant. Some of these people would find themselves deeply challenged and moved by Suchocki's christology, ecclesiology, and eschatology. Her original vision of the Trinity is certainly grounded in process thought, but it can speak also to Christians who are not oriented by this tradition. We must hope for a time when ideas and doctrines can be judged on their merits rather than by their sources.

To one who has worked for many years within the tradition of process theology, it is profoundly encouraging to learn that feminists can find it an organ suitable for their use. It is exciting to see that much of the deeper existential meaning of process thought becomes clear for the first time only as the concepts are put to this use. This book at once advances process theology and develops feminist theology. It can further Christian theology generally as well.

John B. Cobb, Jr.

ACKNOWLEDGMENTS

To work within the context of process theology is to be deeply aware of dependencies. "The many become one and are increased by one" is a process axiom. Many influences enter into the creation of every reality. In the vast network of dependencies and interdependencies, how can one hope to acknowledge all the significant influences which have aided one?

The first draft of this book was written in Paris in the summer of 1979. Pierre and Genevieve Cahour graciously shared their home with my friend, Barbara Mitchell, and myself. Each day Barbara betook herself to the archives of the Bibliothèque Nationale, and I confronted the typewriter. After my daily hours of either production or despair (broken, I confess, by creative wanderings to nearby Notre Dame and Luxembourg Gardens), Barbara returned with copious notes from her readings on French anarchy; we'd treat ourselves to French cuisine, and then meander through the wonderful streets of Paris until the late evening dusk had turned to dark. And in those evening walks Barbara patiently bore with my talking-out thoughts I wished so deeply to express, and I in turn took in reams of information about anarchy in France. Wonderful summer! My indebtedness to Barbara and the Cahours is woven into the fabric of this book.

I went to the other side of the world the following summer—to Claremont, California, teaching in the summer School of Theology, and revising the Parisian manuscript. Long conversations with my dear mentors-turned-colleagues-and-friends, John B. Cobb, Jr., and Jack Verheyden, helped me immensely in the work of revision. Both read the entire manuscript, and each gave generous hours of conversation and critique. I owe much to these friends.

My colleagues on the faculty of Pittsburgh Theological Seminary likewise contributed a strong influence, particularly in the writing of chapter 16, "The Kingdom and the Gospel." A small faculty discussion group comprised of Don Gowan, George Kehm, Jim Walther, Walt Wiest, and myself met regularly to hammer out issues in eschatology. Without the stimulation of their creative thinking, my own thoughts on the matter would be greatly impoverished.

Since I wanted to write for those who do not have a strong theological or philosophical background, various friends volunteered or were corralled into reading portions of the manuscript for its ability to communicate to such an audience. Gregory Tolliver, Nancy Crawford, Archie M. Haines, Virginia Elgin, and Nancy Romell each offered valuable advice.

Finally, a particular church group played a critical role in the decision to write the book at all. The Adult Seekers' Class from Covenant United Presbyterian Church in Butler, Pennsylvania asked me in my first year at Pittsburgh Theological Seminary to give them a six-week course in process theology. Their critical attentiveness and appropriation of process thought encouraged me to present this mode of theology in other churches as well, and eventually to put the material from these classes in book form. I am grateful to that inspiring class, as well as to those others in the churches who likewise interacted with me in the process of expressing Christian faith.

There is also the very essential matter of presenting a manuscript in typed form. I am grateful to Ruth Alexander, Mary Ellen Oman, and Nancy Fraker for their invaluable aid in this task.

"The many become one, and are increased by one." Without these many people, I could not have written this book. Interwoven with gratitude is the profound wish that I could have listened and responded even more appropriately, so that the manuscript would do justice to the quality of help I received. In a process world, final responsibility for the outcome rests with the subject who weaves the many influences together, becoming one. Gratitude and responsibility mingle in the process.

Marjorie Hewitt Suchocki

Part One

THEOLOGY IN A RELATIONAL WORLD

1

WHY A
RELATIONAL THEOLOGY?

EACH generation expresses anew the Christian conviction that God is for us. The immediate catalyst for these expressions may well be the profound conviction that God is a force for love, trust, and hope in a communal world. The conviction carries with it a drive for expression, and the expression itself contributes to the creation of communities of love, trust, and hope. God is for us: therefore we speak, create a tradition, and live as a community called the church.

Expressions of faith, however, must partake of more than traditional categories if they are to be creative of community in the world. Communication is necessary to community, and communication depends upon using thought patterns that constitute the "common sense" of a time. If ordinary perceptions of the world deal in categories of subject/object, then expressions of faith will also use that language. Otherwise, the "God for us" message will not address the reality of the subject/object world of one's interpreted experience, and how then will the message even be heard? Likewise, if the world is understood in terms of substance and accidents, faith must also incorporate those categories or find itself addressing a story world unrelated to the "real" world of everydayness. And if the dominant understanding of the world is through categories of interrelationship, process, and relativity, then this sensitivity must be picked up by the language of faith. Theology, as the way in which we interpret existence in a world where God is for us, will be expressed in relational language.

The importance of expressing theology through the thought patterns of an age is hardly new. Augustine, for instance, gave an enduring formulation of faith by drawing heavily upon the understanding of the world which had been fashioned by the third-century philosopher Plotinus. Working from his own unique study of Plato, Plotinus had powerfully set out the structure of existence; his thought provided a popular framework within which people could understand themselves in relation to the whole of reality. Augustine used Plotinian thought as a vehicle through which to express the faith which was his both through his personal redemptive experience and through his study of the Christian scriptures and tradition.

Centuries later Thomas Aquinas utilized the newly discovered teachings of Aristotle to provide a background within which to express the dynamics of faith. Christian experience, scriptures, and tradition spilled into the philosophy. "Philosophy is the handmaiden of theology," was the watchword of the day. By this it was indicated that philosophy did not dictate the content of faith, it was simply the tool through which faith was explicated systematically. A strong advantage of the method was the sense in which it allowed a unified vision of reality. The understanding of the natural world and the understanding of faith were compatible. The paralysis of a compartmentalized religion was avoided, and there was a vigor to Christian thought and life.

Augustine and Aquinas might be considered watershed figures in terms of shifting philosophical worldviews which became intermingled with Christian faith. But they are only two of the most outstanding examples of this dynamic. Implicitly or explicitly, positively or negatively, Christians tend to express faith in ways which are generally compatible with dominant understandings of the world.

Our own age is one which has seen profound changes. Darwin, Marx, Freud, and Einstein are familiar names to us. Each one has contributed to a shift in the way we see things. It is not simply a matter of understanding the details of what each man said, nor is it even necessary to speak of a general familiarity with the school of thought each man represents. Nor is agreement with the theories propounded by them the issue. Rather, the intellectual climate within which we all think has been changed. Even when we strive to repeat the thought patterns of a previous age, we must do so against the counterforce presented by the contemporary milieu. It is as if we view the world as a kaleidoscope, filled with shapes and colors which can be described in terms of a particular pattern. A period of time is like one particular viewing of the pattern. But then someone turns the kaleidoscope, and all of the pieces shift. There is familiarity and some continuity, for the colors are still there—but their tones seem somehow different in the altered positions, and while at first we try to see them still in their familiar form, we nevertheless find ourselves struggling to express the difference in the way of seeing. Finally we must recognize the newness of the pattern, and we reach toward a familiarity with the new which can be as assuring as that which we remember—or project—as belonging to the old. But the kaleidoscope will never repeat exactly the same pattern. Darwin, Marx, Freud, and Einstein have all turned the kaleidoscope of our world, changing the configurations of reality.

Christians remaining true to their tradition will take the kaleidoscopic shift of our time seriously, and engage in the task of expressing again the redemptive realities of Christian faith. A biblical understanding of the nature of God, of Christ, of the church, and of the kingdom of God can as truly be expressed in twentieth-century thought patterns as they could in sixteenth-, thirteenth-, or fifth-century forms. The proclamation of faith in terms that speak to the whole of reality depends upon the church's faithfulness to this task.

Process theology is a contemporary expression of Christian faith. The content of that faith is still formed through personal and historical interpretations of God's work. One's personal experience, seen and evaluated in light of biblical texts and a particular current within the great river of the long Christian history, forms the core of that faith. The philosophical vehicle through which this faith is expressed is that of Alfred North Whitehead, who formulated his particular understanding of reality as a result of his work in physics and mathematics. Not content to confine his data to these fields, he drew as well from areas such as history, sociology, and of course philosophy. He gave a particular priority to the data of religious experience. Therefore, even though his model of reality reflects his highly technical background, it ultimately rests upon a contemporary understanding of ordinary experience. In fact, the power of his insight is principally this connection with experience. Faith, too, follows from our experience of God's redemptive power. By using Whitehead's model of experience to express the realities of Christian faith, we push toward the rewards of deepening our own vision and action in the world through theological thought.

The process model can be introduced simply by illustrating the dynamics of existence through a fictional person whom I shall call Catherine. Imagine that Catherine is a stranger whom you have just met. When asked to tell something about herself, she replies first of all with her name, of course. She lives in Pittsburgh, is a historian, and teaches at the university. She is married, has two grown children, and is a member of a Presbyterian church. She loves hiking, listens to music often, and plays the piano. Somewhere in her busy schedule she finds time for some political activity, and always she seems to have time for her friends. In this brief introduction Catherine has described herself. Notice, however, that every element in her description involves a primary reference to that which is not herself. In order to describe herself, she must have reference to others.

Her name, Catherine, was chosen for her before her birth because of her parents' feelings about the name. Perhaps it was the name of a loved relative or friend, and feelings for that person were associated with hopes for the child. A name like Catherine could have been chosen because of its association with saints in the Christian tradition, in which case certain attitudes toward holiness could have been involved in the choice. Even if the name was chosen at random the very lack of anticipation through association is significant. A name, given at the beginning of existence, is full of meaning: that meaning enters into the shape of personal existence. We begin life with a borrowed significance.

To define oneself through a locality such as Pittsburgh is also to be defined through that which is not oneself. Localities bear their own characteristic stamp: a river town, pushing the edges of the east toward the midwest, steel and smoke, parks, hills and bridges, and, inevitably—alas—potholes in all the streets. The last is not at all insignificant for the illustration, for common frustrations turned to wry humor become binding qualities among inhabitants of a locality, marking them as "insiders," as those who share a place. To live in a town or city is to discover its own peculiar character, and in a sense to bear that character, so that the locality, while certainly more than oneself, enters into the reality of one's identity.

A historian is defined by a long tradition which precedes individual history; association with that discipline is defining in that it marks specific interests, shaping them still further. To teach in the field also indicates perseverence in following these interests into professional competence. Catherine's self-definition as a historian goes deeply into who she is, but it does so primarily by reference to that which is more than herself.

To define oneself in terms of marriage and motherhood most assuredly requires reference beyond oneself; husband and children are necessary if one is to be wife and mother. Further, the particularities of that husband and those children have very much influenced the particular way in which Catherine is a wife and mother; the others of intimacy strongly mark out who we are.

One could go through each element Catherine names, and see that who she is takes shape through her relation to that which is external to her. Her internal reality is understood through external reality: relationships beyond herself are necessarily involved in her self-constitution and her self-understanding. External reality becomes internal through relation.

Does this mean that Catherine's life is evidence of a determinism, as if she were the passive puppet of forces which are beyond her? Not at all, for she is not reducible to any one of those forces; in fact, just as they shape her, she shapes them.

Look again at the reality of her name, that definition of who she is that was given to her at her birth. In every moment of her life she makes the name her own, so that for those who love her, "Catherine" becomes a name associated with the warmth of her person and their relationship to her. The initial meaning of the name is simply given to her, but in the process of her living she invests the name with a meaning of her own making. She may actualize the intimations of the name, or fill the name instead with new meanings. She makes the name her own.

Likewise, her association with Pittsburgh will be either a positive or negative response to the city that will affect the totality of what the city is. She will represent the quality of that city to those who listen to her. In her political activities, she actively works to influence the government of the city, stamping it with her own individuality, even as it influences her with its corporate character.

As a historian, Catherine contributes to her discipline through her own scholarly work in research and teaching. Her students form their opinion of what history is partly through their experience with Catherine. The discipline of history, affecting Catherine, is not a finality but a continually moving process, having its own history. That ongoing history is shaped by the selectors and interpreters of history, the Catherines who study and write history, as well as by the ongoing activities of the world.

Through Catherine's influence on her family, her grown daughter, becoming a mother in turn, will pattern much of her own

motherhood by the model given her through Catherine. The external realities used to understand Catherine must themselves be
understood through her. Identity is more than the external
influences affecting one; identity is also one's influence on that
which is beyond oneself. Relationships, received and given, are
integral to who we are.

Thus far we see one person, Catherine, with many relationships—family, profession, locale. Given the multiplicity of
influences upon her, how do we account for Catherine's unity? The
question is important, for this unity constitutes the power of her
own influence upon the world. How can she have such unity? Why
is she not simply a will-of-the-wisp, now this, now that, blown
hither and yon by the bombarding power of external forces? What
must be the case to account for the unity of her being which results
in her own forceful influence on the many?

In order to account for relational existence, the one and the
many must be complemented by a third term, creativity. How else
can we understand the reality that many influences are unified,
producing one individual? Unification must be a process of feeling
many influences, evaluating them, and selectively integrating them
according to one's own purposes. This is creativity. This creative
process is the emergence of one from many. "One," "many," and
"creativity" are all essential terms for understanding relational
existence.

How all the influences affecting one shall be welded together
finally depends upon the person. Imagine Catherine studying history at the library. No matter how much importance her immediate
studies have for her, this importance must be balanced by her
sense of her students' needs in her next lecture. This sense of
student needs, however, does not obliterate Catherine's family
situation. Feelings of family are also present as she sits in the
library. Furthermore, the environment has an importance—air
conditioning, contrasting with her immediate memory of the walk
to the library through the sultry day with its summer heat, smog
level, and traffic noise; this, too, affects Catherine's studying.
Which influence will dominate? Does it not depend finally on
Catherine's own determination of the relative importance of each
influence, based upon her choice of immediate goals? This weigh-
ing of importance, this comparing of influences, this decisive
movement toward one response rather than another may finally
take place at subliminal levels of consciousness, but the process

nevertheless takes place, allowing Catherine to achieve her immediate goals. The process is a creative unification of reality according to a single purpose. This entirety constitutes Catherine at that particular moment. She *is* that purposeful, creative unification of the many into one.

Notice, however, that the very dynamics of relational existence require that Catherine be understood not as a single process of unification spanning many years, but as many different single processes succeeding one another serially. The reason for this is simply that no sooner does Catherine respond to relationships in one way then she has changed them all to some extent. Further, her own immediate past response constitutes new data for her present. She must then respond again to the changes, in a new process of creative unification.

Reconsider Catherine's situation in the library. Should she decide to daydream instead of focusing upon the studies immediately before her, she has lessened the relative importance of the other influences. Studies, students, family, environment: all are distanced in the daydreaming, their importance relatively diminished, perhaps even levelled for the moment. Catherine then suddenly decides to respond to her studies: she renews her attention, and begins to read. The Catherine-who-is-reading is not precisely the same as the Catherine-who-is-daydreaming, for the reader succeeds the daydreamer, and must renew her studies against the ennui set into force through her daydreaming. A new fact has been added to her world, and it constitutes the most influential relationship of all for Catherine: her own immediate past. She relates not only to studies, students, family, environment, but also to her own successive responses to all of them. How she has responded to each in the past is part of the data influencing her response in the present. If, however, her own past also constitutes an influential relationship for her present becoming, then her existence is continually in a state of flux; identity is constantly being created through a series of becomings. The continuity of the self must be provided through the successiveness of instances, and not through some unchanging endurance through time.

Thus far, we have considered existence as a series of instances of becoming. This becoming is through-and-through relational; relativity is therefore constitutive of existence, and not simply accidental to it. Becoming takes place in the creative response to the past; in this becoming, something new comes into existence. This new instance of reality is itself a force, demanding a future to succeed it, to incorporate it, along with the many other influences, which are also instances of existence, into a new unification of reality. Relation pushes existence into being; once having become, that new being likewise demands relation to a future. Relationships are the beginning and ending of each unit of existence.

Notice the implications which have arisen with regard to time. Catherine's present is made up of her own decisive response to the past, but once that response is made, it too becomes past, demanding its own future. The present holds the past and future together in a dynamism which determines the importance of the past. This dynamism also sets boundaries for what the future might become.

The issue of the future requires attention since, in this philosophical model, the future becomes the key to a notion of the universe that can only be coherent if it includes the existence of God. Power is located in the energy that comes relationally, in molding the many relations into one and in thrusting the force of that unification into the immediate future. But the future is more than the past. How do we account for the power of that "more than," if power must be rooted in a unification of relationships? The implications of this issue clarify the philosophical outlines of the doctrine of God, allowing formulation of a theological notion of God that can illumine our contemporary experience and the witness to the nature of God contained in biblical and church history.

This consideration of Catherine introduces the relational model of existence utilized by process theology. The process of integrating relationships produces reality. This process is dynamic, ever giving rise to new relations, new integrations, new realities. The terms "one," "many," and "creativity" become key terms for understanding this process. But relational reality is hardly exhausted by human existence. Process is not simply the prerogative of the human condition; process is fundamental to all reality. Change pervades existence and change is a function of relationality. If relationality is the key to change in human existence, and if human existence is not foreign to the world and the wider universe but is itself simply part of the larger realm, why should not relationality be the key to all change?

Consider the pervasiveness of change. The mountains that appear so enduring are in constant response to pressures within themselves and their environment, and they change: lifting higher into the sky, flowing down with the water into the sea. The ordinary solid things of our daily lives, like tables and chairs, are just as surely in motion, composed of atoms of energy bombarding each other, reacting, moving; only the connectedness of their activity creates the solidity which we utilize so happily as the enduring realities of tables and chairs. The sky above us changes more obviously to our perception, with droplets of moisture condensing, dispersing, falling; currents of wind, motion. Our own bodies are in a continual process of change, a total replacement of cells occurring within the space of but seven years. And yet within this flux of movement there is also continuity, bringing with it whispers of permanence. What is the nature of this reality? How is it to be understood? Given such overwhelming change, what is the basis of continuity? What must be the way of things, for such existence to be?

2

THE PROCESS MODEL

THE relational reality that became apparent by looking at Catherine will now be given a more precise expression in order to apply it to existence as a whole. Whitehead's model posits that the past, on a microscopic level, is an infinite number of units of energy, each of which is indivisible, smaller than an atom, small enough to be the basic building block of existence. Each such unit in the past is precisely itself, a creative unification of all its past influences. As each unit was completed, its spark of energy, no longer involved in self-creativity, pushed off of itself into a future. To put it differently, the creativity of the universe is an infinite and infinitesimal array of actualities, each unifying the universe from its own perspective. The energy of each unit utilized in becoming itself is not exhausted in that process, but bounces off that unit. It bombards the world as an effect of the completed unit. Energy, shaped to one thing in the moment, pushes for a repetition of that one thing in the future.

Whitehead's analysis of the internal dynamics of one such unit presupposes the existence of others. Just as the present reality of Catherine in the library presupposed studying, students, family, and environment, even so each unit of energy presupposes a multiplicity of influences from the past. The new form of unification will constitute the present. The illustration of Catherine will no longer do, since it masks the microscopic nature we need. That is, "students" cannot really be understood merely as one influence, since "students" is but a group name for many, many influences, simplified for convenience into the category, "students." In order to understand the very process of simplification wherein the many become one, it is necessary to go beneath the level of personal existence to microscopic existence. An analogy might be drawn through a newsprint photo. Just as the photograph may be seen either as the object presented or as a myriad compilation of small dots, even so the past may be viewed either in its large objective pattern or in the many discrete parts which lent themselves to making it a whole. Whitehead names the discrete parts *actual occasions*.* By the term "actual," he designates something concrete and real. By "occasion," he means that this reality is a "happening," an "event." Each unit of existence is an actual occasion, something for itself as well as for the larger group of which it is a part.

The process of becoming an actual occasion might be illustrated through a series of increasingly complex diagrams. The first simply designates three occasions:

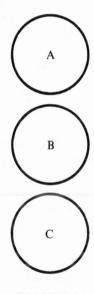

DIAGRAM I

The diagram may be taken further through recognition that each unit is a complex unification of its own many influences, having already undergone the process we are about to describe. Therefore, the components which make up the units of A, B, and C can

---

* Technical terms used in this chapter are italicized and explained as they are introduced. They are also defined in a Glossary at the back of the book. Whitehead's basic work, *Process and Reality*, has now appeared in a corrected edition prepared by David Griffin and Donald Sherbourne (New York: Free Press, 1978).

be illustrated like this:

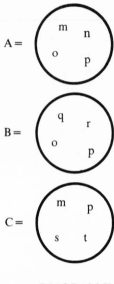

A =

B =

C =

DIAGRAM II

Each component represents some influence that has been incorporated into the final unification of the entity.

If, however, each of these three units of energy is completed,
each has an influence. Its influence is integrally related in content
to that which the unit became, which is to say that A pushes for a
repetition of precisely its own achievement of m-n-o-p in
unification. The creative energy, once utilized in self-becoming, is
now transitionally effective, pushing toward the becoming of another, as in Diagram III on the following page.

According to Whitehead, every unit of energy has a vectoral
effect; he calls this the *superjective* nature of the subject of existence. By this he simply means the manner in which it pushes
beyond itself—indicated by the arrow. A difficulty with the diagram emerges at this point, however. The superjective nature
indicated by the arrow is not simply "tacked on" to the unit: it is
the unit in the process of transmission. That which the actual
occasion is in itself, it becomes for others. Its subjectivity is offered to the world.

What are the dynamics of the becoming unit? Just as each past
occasion is a unification of *its* past, even so the becoming occasion

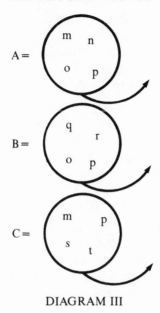

A =

B =

C =

DIAGRAM III

of existence must unify all of its past, simplified here to the occasions of A, B, and C. The combining of A, B, and C begins the production of a new subject.

A, B, and C are not necessarily amenable to combination. That is, each unit is precisely itself. If A is a creative unification of m-n-o-p then its influence for the future is going to be precisely that unification, and nothing else. Its transitional impulse of energy can only call for some kind of repetition of itself. The same is true for B, calling for repetition of its reality; and C, calling for its own unique determination of things. The power of the past, at its most basic level, is its call for conformity—but conformity, in the very nature of the case, is impossible. How can the new occasion repeat everything represented by A if in fact it must also take account of B and C? Even if it chooses to reenact A's achievement, it will nevertheless be different by virtue of the fact that, unlike A, it has had to negate B and C in the process. Since negation of B and C is not a component of A's actual achievement, the new occasion might choose to become similar to A, but it cannot be identical with A.

This principle can be illustrated by moving to the level of our own experience. Consider the power of habit, as seen for instance in the smoking of a cigarette. The act of smoking may not appear to be different between the first cigarette and the thousandth cigarette: in both cases, one picks up the cigarette, puts it in the mouth, lights the cigarette, and puffs. Yet for all the appearance of similarity, the two acts are not the same: the first cigarette will be smoked with the sensation of novelty, while the thousandth may be smoked almost automatically, attention being given, not to the cigarette, but perhaps to a conversation, or to the reading of a newspaper. Intervening between the two occasions are 998 repetitions of the act, each repetition making the power of influence that much greater, but each repetition adding something that the previous instance could not have. Despite the similarity between the 999th cigarette and the thousandth, the bare fact remains that the thousandth time must take account of the 999th time, whereas the 999th only had to take account of the 998 preceding it. The past calls for repetition; insofar as it succeeds, its power is reinforced. This power, however, is always qualified by an element of novelty, however slight, which must be introduced: the novelty is, in part, in the changed circumstances. This novelty provided by constant change is the wedge through which the power of the past may be broken; habit need not endure. No element of the past may be repeated in its entirely. Every element of the past must be modified.

To return to the model, the beginning of the new occasion is a feeling of the total past. Whitehead terms this beginning a *physical pole,* constitutive of each instant of becoming. Note that "physical" in this instance means a feeling of otherness. Physical does not here mean materiality or bodiness. Whitehead further breaks this physical pole down into the multiplicity of feelings of otherness which must be present, given the multiplicity of the past. Each feeling of otherness is called a *prehension* of the other, a taking into account of the other. The new occasion begins therefore at this physical pole, with feelings, prehensions, of A, B, and C.

If, however, A must be modified in terms of B and C, and likewise with B and C, each being modified in terms of the others, then a certain amount of contrasting must take place. The components of the past must be sifted in respect to each other; the comparabilities within them must be drawn out in order that unification may happen. Unification, after all, is a harmonization of the many into one; harmony cannot occur apart from some basic level of compatibility. The compatibility may be felt through some common element each possesses, or through the introduction of some new element which renders the past harmonious. In either case, selectivity occurs. This selectivity is the inner process of creativity essential to the unit's becoming.

Consider the selectivity first in its simpler form, which would be the sifting of the past. Picking up from Diagram III, the further process might look something like this:

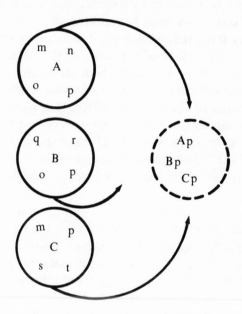

DIAGRAM IV

The quality "p" is sifted from the past, due to its high level of compatibility. In a sense, "p" is almost an appeasement of the demand of the past, for if all three units call for repetition, and "p" is an element of all three, then "p," selected for reenactment in the new occasion, is a way to harmonize the demands of A, B, and C.

However, it is not quite so simple, for the quality "p" in the becoming occasion cannot be quite the same as its occurrence in either of the three past units. Imagine the reasons for this by thinking of the color red existing in a group that includes orange and yellow. Take the same color red and put it now in a group including only red, blue, and violet. While the individual color red may be precisely the same shade in both groups, its effect is changed by its companions. If red be combined with orange, yellow, green, blue, and violet, the effect is yet again different. The selfsame red is different, depending upon its setting. Even so, the quality "p" must be somewhat different in A than in B and C. It will be yet again different in the new occasion. Selectivity, even in terms of harmonization, involves a movement into difference, into novelty.

The dynamics of relational existence will therefore always include novelty, or a movement beyond the sheer past. The past can never be simply repeated. This is seen not only in the fact that the context qualifies the repeated elements of the past, but in the fact that the very process of harmonization eliminates portions of the past. A is repeated in the new occasion insofar as the quality "p" is repeated, but what of the other qualities? They are negated in the very process of sifting out the past in terms of compatibility. These *negative prehensions,* as Whitehead calls them, are not without effect. Part of the effect which takes place in the reenactment of "p" without m-n-o is the loss of a former milieu, the death of a former unit.

Perhaps the effects of negation are more easily understood on the human level. An element in one's past is felt to be incompatible with one's present well-being. If one chooses to deal with that element by negating it, by pretending it does not exist, this negation has a very powerful effect on present reality. "Negative prehensions bear the scars of their birth," says Whitehead, and perhaps the truth of this is seen most acutely in human repressive behavior.

Prehensions in our model must be understood as selective, and the selectivity involves positive and negative feelings of the past. In positive feelings, a component of the past is selected for repetition; negative feelings relegate the rest of the occasion to nonbeing relative to the present.

Again, an analogy may be drawn through human history: those elements which a historian lifts into the thread of human consciousness are woven into the total story of a segment of humanity. But there is more to what happened than those elements of emphasis noted by the historian. History writing involves a selection from the past, not a sheer repetition of the past. Those things that never enter the historians' works are, in effect, lost in the limbo of untold tales. Only insofar as their effects are given some emphasis in the present are they recoverable to any degree. Thus, selection is involved in the movement of the story from past to present. The present must always be purchased at the price of vast portions of the past. "Perpetual perishing" is the tale of a moving, relational existence.

If perpetual perishing describes reality, so does immortality. If it is true that much of the units A, B, and C are consigned to the lost past, it is also true that a portion of each lives on in the present. This vectoral factor of existence is termed *objective immortality* by Whitehead. It is immortality, since it is the real living on in the new occasion of a quality earlier felt as part of A, B, and C. It is objective, because the subjectivity of A lay in the unique copresence of "p" with m-n-o. When that unity is broken, so is the holistic reality of A. In unbroken unity, A is a subject for itself; in selectivity, A is an object for the new subjectivity of the present. While A offers its subjectivity to the world, the necessity of selection is such that A's subjectivity is objectified by the new present. There is only objective immortality in the finite world.

We mentioned that unification of the past may take place through the introduction of a totally new quality which has the merit of rendering many components of the past compatible. The metaphor of color might convey some of the sense of this. An artist, looking in dissatisfaction at her painting, feels a sense of disharmony, missing the result she strove to produce. Suddenly she reaches for a new oil, and adds it precisely so to the canvas. The effect of the new shade is to give a different center of harmony, a different tonality, to every other portion of the canvas. The added element has created the harmony that the previous elements alone could not achieve. Similarly, the components selected from the past may achieve their unique mode of harmony in the new unit of existence by the introduction of a harmonizing factor never before combined with this particular past. In such a case, the novelty created in the present becomes a qualitative leap into that which was beyond the power of the past in and of itself. Yet continuity is nevertheless achieved, since the new quality is used in conjunction with the objectively immortal retention of the past.

The process of becoming thus far described is a model which begins with a physical pole, or feelings of the past, proceeding by a movement called *concrescence* by Whitehead. Concrescence is simply the harmonious unification of feelings. It is the "making concrete" of the actual occasion. Notice, however, that another dimension to existence is being implied in this process of concrescence. That from which the occasion derives its initial power is the actuality of the past, but there is another power at work. If the physical pole accounts for the effect of the past, there must be another pole accounting for the effect of the future. Since that future is not yet in existence, it is not actual, but simply possible. Something that is only possible is ideational, existing simply as idea. Ordinarily, we associate ideas with mentality: one grasps ideas through thought. But if every actual occasion is involved in the dynamics of possibility, then every occasion whatsoever must have some form of that capacity we call mentality. Not thought, not consciousness, but something much more rudimentary must exist throughout reality: the power to grasp a sense of what one might become through unification of the past. What one might become then becomes directive, governing the selection from the past, so that unification is achieved. The physical pole must be complemented by a *mental pole* in order for existence to be unified.

The mental pole is understood as the grasp of possibility, as the feeling for what might be the case. This feeling then affects the way in which the unit of experience sifts the feelings of the past. This feeling for what might be is the aim toward individual becoming; Whitehead calls it the *subjective aim,* the unifying, creative force toward one thing. Through this aim toward self-becoming, the occasion of existence moves toward its own actuality; through the force of this aim, the components of the past are relegated to their respective places. Harmony is achieved with the completion of the process.

Whitehead refers to this final harmony as the *satisfaction* of the process, the completion of its creative moment. The energy which is this creativity now enters the universe as one more impulse of creativity, calling for repetition of the process. The many have become one—but in doing so, the many have been increased by one; a new multiplicity exists, calling for creative unification into a new one. And so the universal dance continues, with the rhythm passing from the many to the one to the many again. In the process, relational existence continually comes into being.

The model now becomes far more difficult to diagram, for the motion of becoming is hard to portray in the static limitation of lines. Imagination now suggests not a circle, but a spiral, formed through many converging lines. These lines are like the physical pole, drawing closer together in the process of contrasting as the mental pole does its unifying work. All lines converge in the vortex of the center, whereupon the spiral is a complete unity, one thing, unified through all its parts. With this internal creativity completed, the spiral bursts into external effectiveness. It forces a new future into existence, for which it itself is now the given past. And the rhythm of the universe is in the mystery of the dance between past, present, and future.

3

THE MODEL AND SIN

IT should be a wonderful universe, then, shouldn't it? If the process model we have sketched is true, and all the world's a dance, then the many contribute to the one and the one, enriched, gives back to the many. The old intuition that justice and harmony are the foundations of the universe would be right, and the world should be idyllic. Sometimes, when we hear descriptions like that, we wince. We look around us and, if we dare to admit it, within us, and it seems the dance has gone awry. Perhaps some invisible violinist is out of tune, or the drummer is deaf, giving an off-beat. Or perhaps we simply haven't learned the steps of the dance too well.

How is it, in a world so good, that we do not enrich each other? How is there room for sin in the process model? Because the model describes relational existence, it offers a peculiar clarity with regard to the dynamics of sin. The interrelatedness of existence provides the structure whereby enrichment occurs: the many are for the one, and the one for the many. But this is also precisely the structure whereby sin occurs: the inescapability of relationships means that the avenues of enrichment may become avenues of destruction. The effects of relationships are internal, and therefore we are peculiarly vulnerable to each other. The world as described by process thought may indeed be beautiful, but it is also dangerous.

The traditional Christian understanding of sin has had a dual focus, the one personal and the other impersonal. Sin as personal indicates a violation of relationships, resulting in a state of alienation from God, nature, one another, and the self. The condition of alienation, however, is one into which we have been born. If there is a sense in which sin precedes us, then obviously there is an impersonal element in sin. This has been described both as original sin and the demonic. Both have been variously interpreted throughout Christian tradition, but a basic connotation is that powers of destruction originate prior to our being, and that these powers can and do overwhelm us, involving us in the condition of alienation which is manifested in personal sin.

In a process world, the past can be understood as the conveyer of original sin and the demonic. This can be illustrated through the story of a high-schooler whose family has always lived in one of the poorest sections of the city. The high crime rate of the area is evidenced by the condition of the school. Windows, once clear, are now either boarded up or barred to prevent breakage; lockers are useless for storage since they are always forced open in theft; "rest rooms" are a macabre misnomer since, in fact, they are dangerous places inviting attack. Teaching is poor, for few teachers survive the unruly classroom atmosphere; faculty turnover is high. Students have organized themselves into ethnic power groups, each of which gains in prestige as it weilds power to terrorize non-members.

The school is not this student's only reality. Unlike some of his friends, he has a close-knit family life; there is humor at the evening meal, and a sense of solidarity as he and his family spend evenings before the television set. Two modes of life are frequently communicated through the stories: there is a portrayal of the rough reality already known, albeit in an adult fashion. The tough investigator/policeman/lawyer enters into a world as harsh as the school, tracking and punishing the enemy. The tactics of the hunter are as violent as those of the hunted, and the scenes bear too much resemblance to the hunters and hunted of the school experience to present any alternative mode of life. The "alternative" is seen on the situation comedies that portray a saccharine reality so far removed from experience that there is no means of differentiating the television fantasy from fantasies of life as it might be in better neighborhoods.

When the boy first began high school, he was frightened by the power groups, and attempted through passivity to avoid the terror they presented. If he could only be invisible! In fact, of course, he discovered that he could be: conformity was a way of becoming invisible. If he was just like everyone else, then he would not endure any special violence, or at least no more than average. Conformity, however, suggested a still more powerful way to cope with the problem. Why not conform to the hunters? If one joins the powers of destruction, surely one is safe from the powers of destruction. So at sixteen, the boy became a leader in one of the terrorizing power groups, exercising his power over the frightened incoming youngsters of the freshman class.

Has this youngster escaped destruction? His life has become as split as the two worlds of television. His harsh "real" world is the world where violence and violation dictate the nature of relationships. His family life is a less affluent and less consistent version of the fantasy world, exercising an increasingly limited power of influence over his life outside the home. His ability to develop a richness of humanity wherein his relationships are avenues of well-being is stunted: poverty of spirit is his deepest poverty.

If original sin and the power of the demonic refer to that which precedes the individual and is greater than the individual, have we not, then, given names to the reality just described? The boy was not responsible for the violence of the school when he first entered it, nor for the poverty and crime in his section of the city: long before he was born, the conditions were forming. These conditions are transpersonal in that they are not the result of any single person of influence; rather, they are a confluence of many powers, some remote and some near, all of which create an environment that will pressure toward destruction.

As the society most immediately affecting one becomes increasingly incorporated into the personal past, it is woven into the continuing formation of the self. The past, which was originally an objective reality into which one was thrown without one's consent, enters into one's subjective reality. When that past works against positive relationships that enrich the person, then that past can be named demonic, and the incorporation of that past into the self can be named an instance of demonic possession. The person so affected becomes a bearer of the demonic toward others.

Sin is involved in assent to the demonic. True, the power is greater than the individual, since it comes with all the weight of a past that cannot be avoided. But insofar as there is assent to that past, there is responsibility for perpetuating that past. The sin is toward the self and toward others: toward the self, since every future moment of existence must reckon, not simply with a societal structure of evil but with a personal history of assent to that evil. In the assent, the evil is made subjective, woven into one's life. With each instant of assent, the evil is strengthened to the level of habit, becoming more difficult to resist.

Sin toward others takes place in two ways. In a process uni-

THE MODEL AND SIN 25

verse, that which one is in oneself becomes an effect upon others. To assent to evil in the self is to become an influence toward evil for others, thus increasing the power of the demonic. As the oppressive power of evil in the immediate environment is increased, resistance to that power is made much more difficult for others as well as for the self. In addition to this inward effect of one's choices for evil on others, there is also the external effect which accrues when one's destructive actions bring about physical or psychic harm to others. Regardless of whether the sin toward others is internal, external, or both, it is obvious in a process universe that sin with regard to oneself can never be limited to the self alone: always, that which one is in the self has an effect upon others. Sin toward the self has a rebounding effect on those in relation to the self.

Sin imprisons. The sin of the demonic imprisons one in a particular form of the past. By choosing to become a bearer of the demonic, one allows that past, which was originally felt as oppressive, to become the determiner of one's reality. For example, in the illustration of the high-schooler, we began with two major influences: home and school. The demonic power of the social environment, which was at first only one structure from a past that still allowed other alternatives, was granted the power to overwhelm the alternatives. The demonic consumes the past and denies any future but its own perpetuation, under the illusion that the future must be only more of the same. The lie in the demonic is in the fact that the family influence was also real, and in the fact that no past can be simply repeated. By denying the multiplicity of past influences and the novelty in the immediate future, one becomes imprisoned in the particularity of a past which is allowed to swallow up all other forms of existence.

The power of the demonic can be seen in any situation in which the cumulative weight of the past denies a richness of well-being to anyone. Structures of society that contribute to racism, sexism, poverty, or oppression of any type can be experienced as demonic, shaping one's present toward an impoverishment of spirit held in bondage to the past. The structure of the demonic power is overwhelming, making the individual feel helpless, to the point that the only "reasonable" alternative would seem to be to join that power. Does the society say that blacks are servile? Perhaps the best way for a black to survive in such a society *is* to be servile, and the demonic power is reinforced. Does society say women are inferior to men, not capable of bearing the "burdens" of full equality? Then perhaps a woman will find that her best mode of survival is to develop modes of dependence that capitalize upon her supposed helplessness. The demonic power will be reinforced.

The process model stresses the fact that relationships are internal; through relationships we become what we are. We, in turn, affect the becoming of others: others must internalize our effects. In Whiteheadian terms, there is a transmission of feelings from the entire past. Obviously, in such a model, the strength of the past is enormous. How one deals with the past is open, but that one *must* deal with the past is not. Since the dealings are through transmission of feeling, there is an inheritance in the present of that which each element in the past was in itself. Was an element of the past destructive? Then the present will inherit the feelings of that destructiveness. That which was there is now here. Conformal feelings bring about a transference, so that the past lives in the present.

The whole Christian doctrine of original sin attempts to describe just such a situation. That which was done in the past has an internal effect upon the present, adding a determining power to the present. That power is a call for repetition. It is not as if the temptation to sin were simply an external matter; the situation is far more dire. The temptation is internal, brought about by the inevitability of conformal feelings transmitting the reality of one occasion to another. The process model indicates that this basic sense of original sin is the foundation for the further power of the demonic. We must internalize the past. Obviously there is strength in numbers in such a situation. This is why societal evil is so powerful: a particular form of behavior is reinforced by innumerable instances of its repetition. When all of these instances must be felt, then the influence toward conformity will be particularly strong. The situation of original sin is then given a specific societal shape.

Our experience of sin takes more forms than that of the demonic. There is also the imprisoning power of sin that comes, not from being overly bound by the past but through fear of the future as death. Death itself is not sin, any more than the past is sin. But just as the past, when experienced as a threatening and overwhelming power, can become the occasion of sin, even so death can be experienced as a threatening and overwhelming power, leading us to sin.

Death is as complex as life. We find our physical life through bodily stability, which in turn is sustained through the surrounding environment. Our emotional life comes about through the rich food of love in relationships. There is a deep interdependence between these two facets of our living: our physical condition affects our ability to participate in emotional relationships, and these in turn affect the health of the body. To add to the complexity, there is what we might call spiritual existence, or the sense in which we integrate our total living in terms of purposes and meanings that go beyond ourselves. Death can come to us through all three facets of our lives: physical death, of course, threatens our total existence. But emotional death and the death of meaning are also severe threats to our well-being. Part of the pain of these latter two forms of death is the paradox that while we are experiencing those deaths, we continue to live: our bodies are still sustained by the environment. Hence against the living death of emotional/spiritual loss, we sometimes see the finality of physical death as preferable.

Death does not wait for the future: it invades the present. Most obviously, it becomes part of present experience through anxiety. The knowledge or fear of death can be a foreboding which colors the present, so that the present is no longer experienced in its modes of richness. Instead, these are dwarfed by that which is yet to come—and yet which is already present through anxiety.

For example, consider the case of a particular woman as she faces her own imminent death. She has been accustomed to walk in the park each noon after lunch. The enjoyment takes on a keenness throughout the seasons, and she particularly enjoys the changing modes of play seen in the children who come to the park. But on the day when she confirms her growing fear that the discomforting symptoms are indeed the first stages of an illness that will soon end her life, her perceptions of the world around her change radically. The trees are lightly tinged with green, preparing for their burst into springtime splendor; children run and play tag: how can the world so ignore her pain and fear? How dare the trees bloom against her death, or children squander in ignorance their wealth of time? Yesterday she saw similar sights with pleasure; the difference between yesterday and today is death. Knowledge brings the death of the future into the present, annihilating the beauty of the present with the fear of that which is not yet.

Death also enters the present through the loss of relationships in the process of our living. Sometimes death parts us long before death happens: there is a death which can come to emotional relationships apart from the death of our bodies. Nourishment comes to us through relationships; when important relationships fade or are broken, then that nourishment ceases, and we experience a form of death. Here the problem is frequently compounded by self-recrimination: had I done thus and so, had I been thus and so, would this have happened? Would not love and life-as-it-was have continued? The bewildering continuity of physical life against the reality of an emotional death only intensifies the pain. With the loss of a relationship, there is a loss of ourselves, for we are formed in the mutuality of relation.

We also experience forms of death in the present through threats to the meaning of our existence. Is there a crisis of faith? Then there is a crisis in which we are threatened by a form of death, for when we have so constituted ourselves that a way of seeing God and the world is essential to our self-identity, loss of that way of seeing is like a loss of ourselves. Our world can appear to be in shambles, crumbled around the shaken foundations of faith, and where are we in the rubble? Death comes in many forms, invading the present.

Yet none of these forms of death is sinful. It belongs to the nature of finite existence that we know a "perpetual perishing." As we saw through looking at Catherine, we are continuously moving beyond a past and into a future, and therefore we are continuously in a process of change. It is possible in such a universe to move beyond past forms of relationships, and we shall surely move toward death. And since our perspectives are so limited, we must expect that our viewpoints can hardly be mirrors of absolute meaning, whereupon, of course, our private constructions of the world will be challenged. All three forms of death belong naturally to our condition, and while each can be experienced as evil, not one is evil in and of itself. But because the forms of death are a threat to our existence, death can be an occasion of sin just as invidious as that which we found in the structure of the past experienced as demonic.

Neither fear nor anxiety with regard to death is sin. These are appropriate responses, and are in fact expressive of the vitality of life. Through fear and anxiety, we can take measures for the protection of life. Sin enters the picture when our response to death is to close ourselves off against a future that is still possible for us.

Perhaps this can be seen most clearly in a response to the death of relationships. The paradox that physical life continues despite the demolition of the emotional life occasions a strange form of imprisonment, for one can take refuge in physical life as if it were in fact the only form of existence. One is thereby locked away from the danger of death entailed in the emotional life. The trauma of divorce can illustrate the principle. A relationship is over, and the reality of existence is the throbbing ache of the loss of one's self. The depth of the pain is searing, but physical existence continues, and the sharpness of the emotional pain turns to an ache and finally a numbness. Meanwhile, one continues to live in a world where there are relationships. But how can one dare to risk such pain again? What if there is a deep undesireableness about the self which is hidden in the superficial dailiness of contacts, but that would be dreadfully revealed in a relationship that moved beyond the surface of life? How could one risk exposure of such an awful truth—isn't it better to hide it? And so one can draw deeply inside, allowing only the "safe" forms of relationship to continue. While this behavior might be appropriate in the early stages of healing, there comes a time when the behavior turns to sin. The turning point is when the refusal to go beyond the surface is not for the sake of healing but for the sake of protecting the present against a future that is too threatening. Complications multiply, for of course the very healing process required is only completed through reaching beyond the surface of relations into the depth of giving and receiving from the places where one really dwells. Thus continuation in a place of hiding becomes a sin against the self.

Once the behavior turns to sin, the initially protective wall starts growing. Always, in sin, we build a prison for ourselves. The refusal to live toward others from the depths of who one is then acts as a way of filling those depths with stones, until finally they have been reduced to shallowness, and there are no longer any depths to give. One becomes imprisoned within the self against the risk of relationality; the future is denied because of its threat of death. But the chosen mode of life is a deeper form of death than that which would be experienced in another failing relationship. Sometimes we escape death by choosing death, but the death we choose is worse than the death we escape. In such choices, there is sin.

We can also respond in sin to the threat of physical death. The natural process of living toward a known death involves stages, each of which allows us to integrate the approach of death. This integration involves strong negative emotions—anger, hostility, denial—but these are appropriate to the process, and in no sense are they sin. The movement into sin is at that point where one refuses to move into the integration process, where one refuses death its appropriate form. A deeper mode of this sin is not in the exigencies of a known and relatively immediate death, but when we constitute our living almost entirely as a protection against death. What happens here is that one allows the death that is in the future to pervade that future so that the future is seen solely as a form of death. Protecting oneself against death then requires that one ward off the future. One then builds one's present into a prison, but of course death is not the prisoner; the self is.

There is also temptation to sin in the threat against our spiritual meaning. Sometimes a person can hold a form of Christian faith that is not only considered orthodox but that seems to rule out any alternative mode of belief. This position can be equated with the entirety of Christian history. Differences can be accounted for by granting that there have always been heretics, just as there are today, but of course this is only in accordance with scripture. Tares grow with the wheat, and there will always be unbelievers in order that the true believers may shine forth. What would happen if such a person began a study of Christian history? At first there might be no problem, given the ability to read all stories as reflections or repetitions of one's own. But if the study continued, gradually the reality of history's tales would impose itself, entering the crack of newness presented in every moment. Realization would follow that the Christian faith has taken many diverse forms; no single mode of faith—not even one's own—has been held un-changingly for two thousand years. Further, with eyes to see it, one could discover the sorrow of much evil in Christianity's his-tory, often justified in the name of "right belief." The center of life's meaning could be challenged: what are the options? There is the possibility of dismissing the histories as if written by heretics or cynics. If this happens, then the continued maintenance of faith will become impoverished, imprisoned against the past. The former security of faith will turn to that afforded by a maximum security prison. Alternatively, the former faith could be totally denounced as false: perhaps all faith is but an illusion, deceiving one into meaning; perhaps a bitter cynicism is the best option. Again, however, one builds a prison, this time against one's own past, for in fact faith was experienced redemptively. Both responses are a denial of the past, imprisoning one in the present. Richness is relinquished in the death of meaning.

In a process universe, every moment inherits from the past, but it cannot simply repeat the past. The richness of the present is the degree to which it incorporates its past in a positive movement into the future. Each form of faith inherited from the past was in its own day a response to its contemporary conditions, for good or for ill. To remain true to that inheritance, one must be willing to receive faith creatively. The spirit of faith is in the dynamic movement whereby it can dare to incorporate all data, moving constantly into a creative future. That which appears to be death can, through faith, be a gateway to resurrection.

Sin cannot be considered only through the past and the future. There is also the mode of sin that affects experience of the present. This sin is the violation of relationships, whether those that contribute to us or those to which we contribute. Strictly speaking in a process universe, we are still referring to a past (the relationships that affect us) and a future (our effect upon others). But in the dailiness of our lives, the immediacy of this past and future flows into our sense of the present. And here, too, one can give way to sin.

In process terminology, the many become one and are increased by one. Existence is a movement, a dance, of mutual enrichment: the many contribute the wealth of their experience to the becoming one, who in turn contributes to all successors. As we saw through Catherine, if it were not for the value she received from many sources, she could not have achieved her objectives in terms of becoming a teaching historian. Suppose that Catherine recognizes this dependence but sees it not as an enriching process that calls forth her own responsibility, but simply as her due. Conceivably, she could assume that since she has been helped by others, she ought to be helped by others, and that her basic right in life is to receive such help. Her own ego would then be the determiner of the value of others: insofar as they contribute to her well-being, they are valued; insofar as they do not directly impinge upon her welfare, they are inconsequential. There is little attempt to understand from another point of view, save as it becomes helpful to her own cause. She has become a receiver of the good, and gives to others only to foster the sense in which others will continue to give to her. In effect, others have become as objects to be valued in terms of usefulness.

This egotism is sin, for it is a distortion of existence. Catherine makes her own self the terminal point of all relationships, when in fact she is not. In a process universe, every actuality is a center, in which case no actuality can become an absolute center; we are in a universe of "centerless centering." Every actuality is a receiver and a giver; the giving is for the purpose of receiving, and the receiving is for the purpose of giving. When Catherine violates this reality in her life, she sins against herself and others. She attempts to imprison herself in the present by making her own well-being the end of existence; it is as if she builds a wall against her giving for the well-being of others. Their own well-being is of little concern to her, save as she perceives it affecting her own. In fact, since others are the source of her richness through relation, their full well-being should be of concern to her. Her failure to give back is a failure to enrich. To the extent that she in fact impoverishes others, she impoverishes herself.

In a reverse situation, Catherine's emphasis would not be on what she receives, but on what she gives. Her self-understanding is "it is more blessed to give than to receive" with a vengeance, for she sees herself totally at the disposal of others. She attempts to respond to all demands upon her, negating herself for the sake of others. When she is tired and weak she consoles herself by considering it the cross she deserves, and if someone attempts to compliment her or give to her in return, she becomes profusely embarrassed. "No, no," she says, and immediately attempts to deny the compliment or to turn it back; if she must receive the gift, she quickly gives it to someone else.

Her refusal to receive from others is a distortion of reality, for in fact she is as dependent upon others as she would like to think they are dependent upon her. If Catherine in the first instance absolutized herself by making herself the subject of all others, Catherine in the second instance absolutizes herself by making herself the object for all others. In neither case does Catherine enter into the full meaning of her own subjectivity, which is that of a receiver/giver. Her life is in both cases built upon a lie, denying the full richness of a self.

Absolutizing the self is the denial of relational existence. Extreme forms of the sin move by degrees to modes of degradation and/or violation of others or of self. Regardless of degree, the sin becomes once more an imprisonment against the true nature of reality. Habituation in the sin builds the walls of the prison stronger. Release must come by renewed strength in the weakened pole of reality—self or others. But in the imprisoning nature of sin, that other pole lies beyond the walls that have been built. How, then, is the other pole to be regained?

Throughout all the forms of sin considered there runs a single thread: sin is based upon and requires a distortion of the nature of existence. Assent to the demonic requires that the demonic be given a determinative power, as if the demonic conditions encountered are the only conditions possible. But to reduce the past to a single power is to deny the full complexity of that which really does precede us. To distort the past into a single influence is also to deny the inherent ability to transcend that influence.

Distortion takes place again when the power of the future as death becomes the occasion for sin in the present. To consign the future solely to death is to deny the reality of life. Even though the forms of death are inevitable in our finite condition, and even though perpetual perishing marks all existence, it is not so that only death pervades the future. Perpetual perishing is also perpetual birth, and every death allows the possibility of resurrection life. To see the future only in terms of death and to act accordingly is to distort the fullness of promise in the future.

Distortion is perhaps most obvious in absolutization of the self with its denial of interdependence between the one and the many. To live as if either the one or the many were a terminus point in existence is a distortion of the process world. Because distortion is fundamental to each form of sin, one might say that the most basic description of sin is "The Lie." Sin is the pretense that reality is what it is not; action in accordance with this distortion then involves us in modes of existence that go against the grain of things. To maintain the distortion requires a continuous denial of the fullness of reality, and the energy required to maintain "The Lie" drains us of our vitality.

By distorting reality and living against the grain of relational existence, we cut ourselves off from the full resources of existence. We lock ourselves away from our true well-being through sin. The paradox is that while we ourselves built the prison, we built it with our own existence. Therefore we do not have the strength to break the prison down, and we are trapped by and in sin. Release must come from beyond ourselves in a counterforce to sin. We require a force in the past strong enough to counter the demonic, a force in the future that is stronger than death, and a force in the present that can enable us to live in the full interchange of relational existence.

4

THE MODEL AND GOD

THE discussion up to this point has dwelt primarily on an understanding of experience. The dynamics of relational existence can yield not only the richness in our situation but also the experience of sin. If the power of sin is its imprisoning nature, then the experience of release from sin can lead to a doctrine of God. What may not have been so obvious in our presentation of the model in chapter 2 is that the model of relational existence also pushes toward development of a doctrine of God. This should not be surprising, for if experience tends toward a doctrine of God then a model based upon experience should also move in this direction.

The model as given thus far is incomplete. It is not simply that Whitehead goes on to discuss the sense in which relationality turns into the togetherness of things so evident to us in our world, nor even that Whitehead describes the rise of consciousness through complexity and intensity. These things belong to an application of the model in the world. What is further needed is an explanation of the power of the future.

What is the future? In terms of the model, the future must be understood in an immediate sense: it is that which an occasion might become. The distant future is not lost to view, for given the relationality of existence every occasion has some sense of its effectiveness beyond itself. The immediate future is more critical, however, since it deals with the occasion's own becoming. The future is that possibility that is grasped by the mental pole, influencing the formation of the subjective aim by which the occasion becomes itself.

Consider the power of the future in relation to Catherine. She decides to become a professor of history, and therefore she chooses to go to graduate school. This decision can be explained in part by her past: her successful completion of college, her resources, her interests, the encouragement of family and friends.

However, the major factor in her decision and subsequent action is not the past at all; it is the future. She desires to be that which she is not. This desire toward the future powerfully affects her present, causing her to order her world in such a way that this possibility of teaching history might become an actuality. "The future enters into us in order to transform itself in us long before it happens," said the poet Rilke, and his enigmatic intuition seems highy appropriate as we consider the effect of possibility upon the present.

Whitehead would make the claim that possibilities are not effective simply once or twice within a lifetime, but that what is seen at that particular point in Catherine's history is in fact part of experience in every single act of concrescence. The mental pole of every actual occasion is a grasp of a possibility that comes to it not simply from the past, but from the future. There is real novelty in the world; the future has power.

The difficulty comes at the point of Whitehead's major principle that where there is power, there is actuality. Power does not materialize out of nothingness—if it does, incoherence is introduced into an otherwise carefully developed model. Power rests in actuality. The future, however, "exists" as possibility, and possibilities by very definition are not actual. How, then, can that which is not actual have such power? The problem is further complicated by the infinity of possibilities that affect actual occasions. If Whitehead wishes to find a source in actuality for the power of the future, he must find a source not simply for one future, nor even for the future that materializes in each instant of becoming, but for all possible futures whatsoever. Whitehead needs a source for possibilities per se. Only an existing entity, an *actual entity*,* can provide such a source.

Actual entities, however, have been so defined that each must eliminate possibilities in the process of becoming its determinant self. The welter of data received through the physical pole is simplified and unified through an aim toward a single possible form of existence. If the very process of becoming involves elimination of possibilities, how can an actual entity *ground* possibilities?

---

* Whitehead used two terms to describe actuality: "actual occasion" and "actual entity." However, whereas "actual entity" could apply both to God and to finite reality, "actual occasion" was always used only in reference to finite reality. The dynamics of existence for God and finitude are seen to be the same, but there is a necessary distinction in *how* they apply. In order to preserve this distinction, Whitehead never used the term "actual occasion" for God. We will follow his usage here.

Furthermore, the possibilities associated with each actual entity are limited to that occasion's standpoint: how can a single actual entity ground possibilities for all reality? The dilemma, then, is this:

Possibilities exert power in affecting the actions of actualities.
But all power must be located in actuality.
If possibilities exert power, they must do so through the agency of an actuality which is their origin.
But no finite actual entity thus far described can perform this function.

The problem rests in the finite nature of the actual occasions and in their movement from the multiplicity of the physical pole to the integration of existence through the mental pole. What if the order of concrescence were reversed? Would the same limitations hold? The mental pole per se is not limited in terms of possibilities; to the contrary, a mental pole not bound by the prior restrictions of the physical pole could conceivably be infinite in possibilities. If a unique entity "began" in the mental pole and was "completed" by the physical pole, perhaps a source for possibilities could be named. This entity, of course, would have to conform to the characteristics of existence if the metaphysics is to retain its coherence: relationality must occur through feelings of others and effects upon others within the dynamics of a physical pole, mental pole, subjective aim, concrescence, and satisfaction. But the entity would be a mirror image of all the others in order to account for the power of possibilities.

The situation is somewhat analogous to putting a puzzle together, having it almost done, and then finding the last piece missing. The place is ready, the outlines of the final piece clearly shown. However, that final piece which will complete the puzzle must be the reverse of those surrounding pieces in the puzzle. Where the puzzle loops in, the last piece must loop out, otherwise it will not fit, and the puzzle will remain incomplete. Completion of the puzzle depends upon an exact reversal of the shape. Such a reversal does not render the puzzle incoherent; it completes it, fully in keeping with the principles of puzzle-making. Even so, the reversal of the dynamics of reality for one actuality in order to account for the power of possibility does not violate the model, it completes it.

How would it work, this reversal of dynamics? An actuality beginning in the physical pole moves toward unity; an actuality beginning in the mental pole moves from unity. But note that an actuality that begins in the mental pole cannot properly "begin" at all. If an entity contains all possibility, then that entity can no more begin than possibilities begin. Possibilities are time-related only in reference to actuality; in their own nature, they are nontemporal. Relationality to time takes place purely in the context of the successiveness of actualities. If possibilities are nontemporal, existing eternally, then an entity containing all possibilities must likewise be eternal. When Whitehead says, then, that God "begins" in the mental pole, he is not talking about a time when God did not exist. Quite the contrary, he is talking about the sense in which God's eternal nature is the basis for all the divine activity. This activity proceeds from the mental pole. To keep this eternal quality of the mental pole in view, Whitehead always refers to it in God as the *primordial nature*.

What does it mean for God to "begin" primordially through the mental pole? It must mean, in terms of the model, that God's primordial beginning is a "satisfaction" in which all possibilities are everlastingly unified in terms of value. There is much meaning condensed into that statement; it should be unpacked first by noting the sense in which possibilities are given value.

Possibilities in and of themselves are vague with regard to value. For instance, someone might have suggested to Catherine that she become a medical technician. Is that a good possibility or a bad possibility? "To become a medical technician" is neither a good nor bad possibility in and of itself. In order to value it, we need some reference to actuality. We would ask whether Catherine's inclinations, talents, and background were conducive to such a possibility, and then value it—but even here, we would only value it with regard to her. Knowing that her real abilities take her in another area, we would be inclined to judge it negatively. But perhaps another's situation would make such work ideal—in that case we would judge the possibility positively. Always, actuality is required for definiteness of value with regard to possibilities.

What does it mean, then, that God unifies all possibilities, giving them value? It means more than that one or another possibility is assigned a value by God; it must mean that God is the actuality in reference to which the possibilities receive value. Because God unifies the possibilities, they achieve the value of concrete unity; because God holds all of the possibilities together within the unity of the divine nature, they are harmonized; because possibilities are harmonized within the divine nature, they are given beauty. If God is the locus of all possibilities, the very fact that it is a single reality which gives a home to possibilities means that the possibilities are clothed in the value of unity, harmony, and beauty. God *is* the valuation of all possibilities. This is the primordial satisfaction of God.

In the reversal of the dynamics of existence, satisfaction must issue into the subjective aim of God. For finite reality, the subjective aim is first for itself (toward the achievement of harmony), and secondly for others (toward affecting the world beyond itself). Every finite reality, becoming itself, hurls its effects upon the newly becoming world, calling for repetition of its own achievement. God, "beginning" with eternal satisfaction, must reverse the dynamics of the subjective aim: first God's aim is for others, which can now only be all finite reality, and secondly God's aim serves to direct the divine concrescence through the physical pole. Both concrescence and the physical pole must be as applicable to God as satisfaction and the mental pole if the model is to hold.

If God "begins" in the primordial nature, then the physical pole will be consequent upon that primordial "beginning." For this reason, Whitehead calls the physical pole in God the *consequent nature*. What must this physical pole, or consequent nature, be like? Remember that a physical pole is simply the feeling of realities other than the subject. Hence in this definition, to consider God as having a physical pole does not at all contradict the spirituality of God; on the contrary, the physical pole might give us the most adequate understanding of God as spirit. We ordinarily term persons spiritual when their concerns go beyond themselves, when their sensitivities relate them to a range wider than ordinarily accomplished. Such spirituality is in part a wide attunement to the physical pole; hence to associate a physical pole with God is by no means to deny God's spiritual nature; it is in fact a way to define God's nature as pure spirit. That is, finite spirituality is always partial, given the selectivity involved in our feelings of others. Further, few of the relations affecting us are raised to the level of conscious relationality; most, by far, remain at subliminal levels of awareness. But God's physical pole is unlimited by any need for selectivity, given the already achieved unity of all possibilities in the primordial vision. God can feel every actuality in the universe in its entirety. God's physical pole, therefore, unlike ours, is all-encompassing. Consequently, if ordinary usage be followed, God is the most spiritual of all beings; God is pure spirit.

To return now to the matter of divine concrescence, God's eternal satisfaction generates a subjective aim which directs the concrescence of God. In keeping with the dynamics of reversal, the aim moves toward the world, and then through the world to direct the concrescence of God. In the everlasting process, the consequent nature is integrated with the primordial nature in unity.

In moving toward the world, the aim flows from the divine satisfaction. God's aim is that the harmony of possibilities shall issue into a harmony of actualities. How this aim is fitted to the world will soon be suggested; for the present, however, simply note that at this stage the fulfillment of the aim depends upon that which is other than God, the becoming realities of the world. The second stage of God's subjective aim is consequent upon the first, and now depends entirely on God, since it relates to the concrescence of God. The actualities of the world shall be felt by God through the consequent nature, and integrated into the harmony of God, the primordial nature. This is to say that the harmony of possibility within the primordial vision is ever more deeply intensified through God's feeling of reality according to the subjective aim of harmony.

To expand further upon this integration of the consequent and primordial natures, consider that just as a finite occasion feels its physical prehensions of others in terms of its own subjective aim, God also feels the world in terms of the divine aim toward an actualization of harmony. Just as the finite reality unites the physical with the mental, thus achieving harmony, even so God unites the feelings of the world with the primordial vision, intensifying the harmony already achieved in the vision of possibility. What must happen in this divine intensification of harmony is that a merely possible component of harmony becomes actual, through the feeling of the world integrated with the vision. God, as well as finite reality, is a unification, a becoming. Whereas the world's becoming simplifies, God's becoming "complexifies." The divine satisfaction is everlastingly intensifying—if that satisfaction is one of harmony, the harmony moves into deeper and deeper intensities. God's eternal satisfaction, based upon the primordial vision, has an everlasting dimension, based upon God's feelings of the world everlastingly transformed into integration within that satisfaction.

By coming full circle back to the satisfaction, we can now indicate more specifically how this satisfaction affects the world, and how God accounts for the power of possibilities. God integrates the feeling of the world within the context of harmony. The harmony of possibility is one where the relationality is multiple: all things are possible in a realm of sheer possibility. The introduction of the actuality of the world functions to relativize the value: *this* mode of relationality now has greater value than *that* mode of relationality relative to this particular becoming standpoint in the world. God's feeling of the concrete world, integrated with God's vision of harmony, is at the same time an indication of precisely what modes of harmony best suit the realities of the world which will succeed the completed actuality, now integrated into God. Diagram V on the following page illustrates the point.

The feeling of the way God's harmony might be mirrored in the world is found in the newly becoming occasion as its own possibility for its own immediate becoming. Hence the full nature of God, moving according to the reversal of the poles, accounts for the presence of possibility to the world. Insofar as possibilities primarily relate to our future goals and visions, be they immediate or distant, God is the source of our future.

This completes our sketch of a model of reality to be used for theological reflection in the expression of Christian faith; the model is developed far more technically and extensively in Whitehead's *Process and Reality*, particularly Part I as a concise statement of the basic categories of dynamic existence, and Part V as an extension of these categories to consider some of the implications of the reversal of the dynamics as applied to God.

To summarize the model, existence is through and through relational, with every actuality, whether a subatomic particle or God, demonstrating relational dynamics. In turn, relationality constitutes reality as becoming, as change. Relations occur on the finite level as feelings from the past evoke new unifications of that past. The past is unified through a selective comparison of feelings in terms of a single possibility of becoming. This possibility becomes actualized in the unification of the new actuality; upon completion of this process, the creative energy which accomplished this unification is turned to transitional energy, or the relational thrust into the future. Relationality occurs on the divine level through God's feelings of the world, integrated with God's vision of harmonized possibilities. God's vision is the source of possibility for the

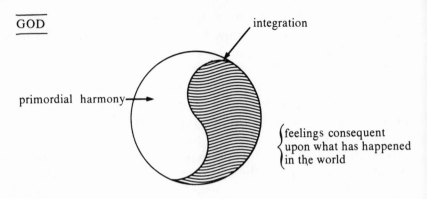

GOD

integration

primordial harmony

feelings consequent upon what has happened in the world

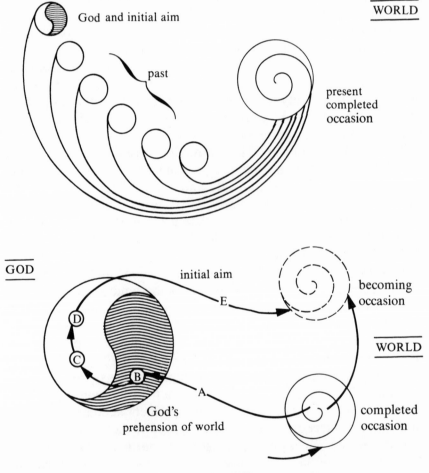

God and initial aim

WORLD

past

present completed occasion

GOD

initial aim

becoming occasion

WORLD

E

D

C

B

A

God's prehension of world

completed occasion

DIAGRAM V

The completed finite actuality is felt internally by God through prehen-
sion, indicated by line "A." (A difficulty with the diagram is that it
suggests distance between God and the world—the lines are drawn simply
to indicate the direction and sequence of prehension, and not to indicate
spatial distance or externality for prehension.) God, feeling the world
("B"), integrates it within the primordial vision ("C"). This integration
with harmonized possibilities has the effect of suggesting a new mode of
harmony ("D") which is now relevant to the becoming world. "E" then
represents both God's superjective nature relative to the world, and the
world's prehension of God. The occasion's prehension of God, as with all
prehensions, is felt internally by the occasion.

world. God's integration of feelings of the world with the primordial vision results in one possibility rather than another becoming
relevant to the world. God's harmony is shaped to the situation of
the world, and made available to the world as a real possibility for
its future.

If the dynamics of God and the world are to be understood as a
mirror image of reversal, the same is not so with regard to divinely
willed harmony. The harmony of God is not begrudged the world.
Rather, the harmony of God holds the world together, fitting the
possibilities for each single occasion into a harmony that blends
with the possibilities for other occasions. The world is to be an
echo, not a reversal, of God. Whether or not these possibilities for
harmony are achieved depends upon the decisions of the world.
Each occasion, in the solitude of its own concrescence, decides its
orientation toward God and the world.

One further theological implication of the model needs to be
drawn out. Notice that in the model, every single occasion in the
world begins its concrescence with physical feelings, and that the
most important of these feelings is the one from God. The aim
received from God orients the occasion toward an optimum mode
of harmonizing the feelings received from the world. *Every* occasion is touched by God. But this touch comes at the very base of an
occasion's beginning; Whitehead calls it in the *initial aim.* Since
this aim is at the foundation of each momentary existence, and
since consciousness is a late phase of each occasion, the touch of
God is necessarily in the preconscious stage of those occasions
that develop consciousness. This means that when we wish to talk
of theology and experience, we must recognize that the experience
of God is not necessarily given to consciousness. There is an

indirectness to knowledge of God drawn from experience; the relationship with God, while constant, is not necessarily apparent. Ordinarily God is hidden in the world.

Because of this hiddenness, the reality of God is inferred from experience rather than known directly from experience. Therefore we are particularly dependent upon criteria of intellectual consistency and coherence in developing formal notions of God. Does God exist? Then what we say of God must be intellectually in keeping with what we understand as existence. Otherwise, there would be an arbitrariness to our concept of God which would undercut the power of the concept, weakening its ability to address the whole of our reality. As we have seen, Whitehead follows this by insisting that the concept of God should not be an exception to existence, but an exemplification of what it means to exist.

There is a strong importance to this reliance upon intellectual criteria when we move from philosophical developments to theology. To speak theologically of God is to speak of the relation of God to human need—God is considered as creator, redeemer, provider, sustainer, judge, king. Do we require a grounding to our existence that is more than ourselves? Why not simply accept the mystery of existence as given; why must we find a ground to existence in the understanding of God? Our need pushes us beyond ourselves, to an ultimacy that can be known both intellectually and emotionally as our source and destiny, and we name God the creator. Through sin does existence seem somehow awry, distorted? Rather than rest content with that as a tragic or absurd given, we dare to say that God is the great redeemer, forgiving and restoring us in order that we might achieve a destiny beyond our failure. Are we dependent, and does our dependency extend beyond our daily needs for physical existence? Do we know a spiritual need for an ultimate sustenance of our deepest being? We name God as that provider and sustainer. Further, we ask that in the all-encompassing governance of our universe there be just that: a governance, some ultimate power of rightness addressing the evils and wrongs—and God is judge. Shouldn't this ultimate rightness be unchallengeable? If it is "right," should it not also be eternal? God must rule in a realm that is stronger than our evil, enduring everlastingly in an established, unshakable order of justice. God: creator, redeemer, provider, sustainer, judge, king—the theological assertions concerning God are so intensely tied in with human need that theology faces the challenge in this post-Feuerbachian, post-

Freudian age that our doctrines are no more than wish-fulfillment, supplementing our finite sense of poverty with an infinite realization of what we know or imagine to be good. In such a situation, the church's responsibility to give a reason for its hope is fulfilled in part through attention to the philosophical context of theology. This does not mean that philosophy becomes the arbiter of faith, and it certainly does not mean that philosophy supplants what we know of God through revelation. It simply means that faith dares to express itself within the widest possible understanding of existence. Whitehead provides this by developing a model of God which is rationally consistent with an understanding of relational existence. The experience of God in relation to human need may then indeed fill in the content of what we know as the nature of God, but the resulting doctrine of God will not be reducible to human need.

The use of a philosophical frame of reference within which to develop theology is therefore increasingly important because of these two considerations: first, because relationships with God are not necessarily directly given to consciousness, and in fact more often are effective at preconscious levels of human experience; second, because theological developments are by nature so integral to human needs that without the wider frame of reference provided by philosophy, theological statements run the risk of being based only on the needs which they address.

Through the process model, we have the basic philosophical outlines of a doctrine of God. How does faith utilize these outlines to express the conviction that God addresses our needs, releasing us from the prison of sin in order to lead us toward the richness of relational existence? The entirety of theology, whether we are discussing a doctrine of God, of Christ, of the church, or of the last things, is an attempt to answer just that question.

Part Two

GOD FOR US
A Process Doctrine of God

5

GOD REVEALED

THE discussion in Part I suggests a dilemma: there are two basic obstacles to knowledge of God. First, there is the problem of God's hiddenness: while the model suggests that God is actually pervasively present in the world, this presence is at the beginning of each actual occasion. The presence is then overlaid by the responsive activity of the world. The world becomes the veil of God, hiding the face of the divine presence.

Second, there is the problem of sin. If sin is basically a distortion of existence, then sin is like a second veil, obscuring still further the true reality of God's presence. In every instance of sin, there is an "as if" quality: one lives "as if" the past blocks all change in the present; one lives "as if" the future were only death; one lives "as if" the self were absolute. The influence of God in the initial aim, however, is always toward an optimum mode of self-creation for us. God's aims open us toward the wider past, toward the possibilities of the future, toward the mutuality of relationships. The denial of these is at the same time the denial of God. How, then, can God be discerned through the veil of sin?

Against this, the whole tradition of Christianity affirms that God is self-revealed in the world. Usually Christian theology speaks of revelation in two senses, and each might be understood to address the two obstacles. General revelation is the witness to the nature of God through the creative mark of God in the world, like footprints not yet erased from the sand. Special revelation is the unfolding of the character of God through the history of Israel and Jesus; this mode of revelation is redemptive, addressing the distortions of sin.

Process theology sees the dynamics to be the same in both general and special revelation. The discussion of how God is revealed through the veil of the world leads toward the intensification of revelation in the incarnation of God in Christ.

In chapter 4 it was suggested that God's aims for the world flow from the primordial harmony of God. Each aim is God's adaptation of the divine harmony toward conditions in the world. Consider the situation through a metaphor of light: the primordial vision is like a beam of light, containing all color within it—but as potential, not actual. God's aim is then like a prism, reflecting the light to the world. However, the colors in the light do not become visible, thus truly revealing light, until they meet with the actuality of the world, be it a drop of moisture in the air or a flower upon the earth. When the light is finally reflected, it reveals not only its source, but that which it touches as well.

If we follow the metaphor, God's light is revealed through the actuality of the world. Just as light reveals the nature of the objects that hold it, even so the actualization of God's initial aims in the world reveals the shape of the world. That means that the revelation of God is never pure; it is always twofold. God and the world are seen through the same light.

We must go beyond the metaphor to speak of a further qualification: what is actually seen as we observe the world is not the initial aim of God, but what has been done with that aim in the world's own dealings with it. Remember the dynamics of process: the actual occasion receives the influences of God and the world; the influence from God is directional, orienting the occasion toward its best mode of being in the world. The occasion deals with this influence in the privacy of its own concrescence, becoming what it will. The initial aim is adapted into the subjective aim. Only upon completion of the process is the occasion itself an object for prehension by others. The practical effect of this for revelation is that we can never see directly what God's aim is for another; we can only see what the other has become.

The stages that result in revelation are therefore reconstructed as follows: each element in the world receives an aim that has been peculiarly fitted to it in light of its particular past. At this stage we refer simply to the initial aim, but it is already reflective of the world as well as God. It represents the real possibility that God can offer to the world, given all of its finite circumstances. Then the aim is adapted by the occasion itself. The world, in its solitariness, decides what it will do with all the data from its past, including the data received from God. True, the divine aim is the most influential, giving a way to deal with all the past. However, that aim is still but possibility, and as possibility it carries implications of alternatives. The occasion has the power of decision within all its alternatives available. Thus the completed occasion is the result of what it has done with the aim from God. Revelation through the world is two stages removed from the fullness of the divine harmony in which it originates. It is the harmony as adapted *to* the world by God, and the harmony as adapted *by* the world in the world's response to God. The revelation is therefore indirect.

A further complication occurs when we attempt to read nature as revelatory of God. We become interpretors of nature, which means we are removed by one more stage from the aim initially given by God to the world. Consider an illustration of this: the heavens present to our vision a remarkable drama of beauty. From our perspective, we see the sun moving across the sky, sometimes in a splendor nonetheless wonderful because we are accustomed to it: the sky, an incredible blue; the clouds, forever in motion, as if they dared the sun to catch them in their race toward the horizon; and then evening comes. It is as if the sky begins to feel itself as color, finally exploding into experiment, testing gold, tinged with pink, becoming rose, a touch of violet, and finally the deepening indigo that will give way to night. And the night sky! The moon to replace the sun, and first a single star, daring its dance beside the moon. One by one, others join in, and when the sky's dusk is fully turned to dark, the sparkling stars reveal their dance in stately silence across the universe. And we watch!

With equal sensitivity, the Psalmist might cry out, "the heavens declare the glory of God, and the firmament his handiwork!" while one like Camus might muse in wonderment, giving quiet deference to "the benign, indifferent universe." Both watch, and see, and wonder, and interpret. Revelation, indirectly given through the medium of the world, is ambiguous, subject to varying interpretations, depending upon the total situation of the interpretor, the interpretor's particular circumstances, and the givenness of the observed world.

Consider a further ambiguity: aims given to occasions in the natural world may mediate order and beauty, and nature may then display a serenity which we interpret as reflective of God. The ocean, sparkling in sunlight as if to recreate on its daytime surface a remembrance of the stars of night, may seem majestic, mysterious, serene, its waves gently tapping the shore. But what of those times when its depths churn up an angry gray, with waves crashing upon the earth in a fury that smashes pavement, floods homes, and wreaks awesome destruction? How do we read the one as reflective of God, and not the other? And does God indeed lead the ocean to crash the boundaries we hoped were so secure? What can we read that reflects divine harmony in the roar of an ocean gone wild? And suddenly, perhaps, it seems we can read what we wish in the world of nature, constructing as many notions of God—or of no God—as the variables of nature will afford. Dim comfort it is that the overall way of things works to the support and intensity of life when the particularities of existence threaten to overwhelm us. A God of harmony and purpose and persuasive love might be revealed in nature, but ambiguously so, and in a way that can only be read if the other factors in our situation are conducive to such a reading. The immediate situation in the world is only ambiguously revelatory of God, although the makings of revelation are there.

Given the constancy of God, the cumulative witness of the world is more revelatory than the immediate witness of the world. Here we speak of the sense in which the world has inexorably moved to greater and greater complexity, greater and greater intensity, greater and greater order. It cannot be argued that the order is only in the eye of the beholder, for the beholders are themselves a part of the world perceived. Order within the observer is therefore order in the world as well; further, order apparently gives rise to its very perception. Consider the perspective provided through a phenomenon such as the Grand Canyon, where to walk through it is to witness the progression of the world of nature toward life. According to the record of the fossils, once life is achieved the progression moves steadily through eons of time into deeper modes of complexity. Each stage of development supports the next, but is transcended by the next, as if the world responds to a call always pulling it beyond one achievement to yet another of increasing complexity. In such records we witness our past, and read our own story of continuity and transcendence, continuity and transcendence, again and again: there in records of stone, now in records of words, flesh, experience. In humanity, the world of nature comes to expression; it wakens to consciousness, looks at itself, wonders, questions, speaks. In such a context, the very question about order depends upon order; the question itself is a witness to that which it asks. But the question, like order itself, takes us beyond ourselves, seeking the future, seeking God.

Why does nature move toward intensity; why does it continually move beyond its past; why does it advance always to a future which leaps beyond the boundaries of the past, yet always in keeping with the preparation of the past? By taking the witness of this movement into account, we can interpret the present, whether beauty or terror, in light of the long history of the earth. Past and present together give plausibility to the interpretation that the world is reflective of a power beyond itself which leads it to deeper modes of complexity, intensity, harmony. Can the source be less than the call? Must not the source of such a call be itself a complex, intense harmony? And does not the movement of the world toward such qualities become revelatory of this? Granted, the revelation is indirect and hidden in ambiguity, but when one takes care to look at the evolutionary evidence of the world, the revelation is there.

To move from consideration of general revelation to special revelation, we must look at the implications of the rise to consciousness in the world. The movement toward complexity is through an increase of contrasts held together in the unity of each actual occasion. In process thought, consciousness follows from an intense form of such contrasting.

Why is consciousness a function of contrast? Perhaps this is best explained through an illustration from our own experience of consciousness as a flickering, more-or-less aspect of our existence. We sleep, and are unconscious until we dream, wherein consciousness emerges in the image world of impressions, intuitions, feelings within the self. In our waking life, consciousness also varies, from the rote consciousness involved in habitual actions to the perked interest aroused by attention to a situation or task. We experience consciousness as an intentionality directed toward the relations between different things, whether in relation to themselves or in relation to our own immediate purposes. When contrasts are heightened, consciousness is increased; when contrasts are muted, consciousness lessens.

Habit becomes an interesting illustration of the loss of contrast, and hence the freeing of consciousness from the habituated activity. Habitual behavior is simply the convenience of repetition of activity. The activity, when first begun, demands a high degree of consciousness. One must master the coordination of effort involved in balancing a bicycle, or shifting gears on a car, or correlating fingers and keys on a typewriter. The consciousness involved is intense, directed toward the contrasts of body and machine in an effort to synchronize them. Practice after practice is required, until finally the contrast between body and machine is lessened—indeed, the bicycle or car or typewriter becomes almost like an extension of the self. Once the activity becomes habit, the contrast effectively decreases, and sometimes we even speak of performing the activity "unconsciously." The actions become a rote-like background against which we can direct ourselves toward other contrasts in the renewed creation of consciousness.

Consider the amount of concentration necessary when making a difficult decision, when studying, or when working. Sometimes we think long and hard, and grow tired with the effort. In a process world, it is no wonder we grow tired, for concentration is not simply a utilization of consciousness, it is the creation of consciousness beyond our accustomed levels. Always, in the creation of consciousness, there is a contrast between the data at hand and possible ways in which the data might be ordered. There is a contrast between what is and what might be, between the past and the future.

If God is truly persuading the world toward depths of harmony that are reflective and therefore revelatory of God, then surely as the world attains consciousness God will utilize consciousness to achieve a fullness of revelation. The aims of God pull the world toward complexity and harmony so that in its own way the world might be reflective of God. The aims of God pull the world toward the image of God. Whereas the nonconscious world gropes blindly toward this image, reflecting it but dimly, the conscious world has the possibility of forming itself clearly in keeping with this guidance toward intensity, complexity, and harmony. For is not the magnetic pull of the future increased as it crystallizes into an image in consciousness?

Consciousness is the crown and completion of any true harmony in our experience, for it allows the knowledge of relationality to intensify the harmony of relationality. If God lures the world to a reflection of divine harmony, and if the world is essentially relational, then the harmony achieved in the intensity of one occasion is given as well to enrich all future occasions. Every occasion becomes a datum for the future, influencing what the future can be: "the many become one and are increased by one." Harmony is individual, but the individual is for the sake of the larger society; likewise, harmony is for the society, but the society is for the sake of the individual. In a process universe, the two statements do not contradict each other, but simply portray the different facets of the rhythm of existence.

Given this situation, it follows that the welfare of all creates the welfare of each, and the welfare of each contributes to the welfare of all; such is the rhythmic movement of harmony. This movement is optimally attained in consciousness, for only in such a state is the harmony embraced and enjoyed for its larger as well as its smaller dimensions. The unconscious occasion but dimly feels the wider world beyond itself, and that primarily as a repetition of itself. In the conscious world, where the weight of the future enters more fully into the present, the vision of the future as societal enters into the enjoyment of the individual. Consciousness is thus the crown and completion of any true harmony. As the world moves toward consciousness, it moves toward deeper possibilities of reflecting the divine image. Given the continuity of the world and the sense in which human consciousness emerges from the natural world and within the natural world, all of creation can be embraced within the harmony actualized through intensely conscious existence.

In such a context, revelation of the nature of God cannot be seen as tangential to the divine nature, but as integral to the divine nature. If the power of initial aims is the sense in which they offer harmony, and if that harmony is an adaptation to the world of the harmony that is God, then the clearer that harmony is made, the more effective it can be. God, seeking to persuade the world toward the intense harmony of the divine image, will do so all the more powerfully as that image becomes clearer to the world. If God's purpose for the world is an intensification of harmony, then God's purpose for the world inexorably entails revelation of the divine nature in and through human consciousness.

Thus far, there is a possibility of general revelation such that the initial aim of God, while given as the first touch of existence for every single occasion, becomes the vehicle for knowledge about God. The knowledge is ambiguous, telling us about the world as well as about God, but the knowledge is possible. Further, just as we can read the presence of God through the evidence of the world around us, it is so that God is at work within us for our good. We, too, are composed of actual occasions, and we, too, are touched in every moment of our existence by the guidance of God. Just as it is possible to see the trace of God in the world of nature, can we also see the trace of God through God's influence upon us? Can we read anything of God through our own consciousness?

The three following chapters will attempt to do this on the premise that general revelation allows or leads to an understanding of God as the one who is pervasively present to the world, the one who is ultimate in wisdom, and the one who is the power of justice. Inevitably, even though there will be no specific dependence upon the special revelation of the biblical sources, the Christian context in which general revelation is even termed revelation will influence the development. There is no such thing as a value-free interpretation of the world. However, since the thesis is that God's creative work in the world can indicate something of God's nature, lifting the veil of hiddenness to some degree, the initial development of the doctrine of God will work primarily with the dynamics of existence. The further development of the doctrine of God through the answer to the distortions of sin must move beyond general revelation, depending explicitly upon the special revelation of the biblical texts. This will follow in Part III through the development of christology.

God is revealed in the world. Sometimes, especially in the spring, we encounter a long series of gray and rainy days. To be sure, there is light, but our spirits long for the brightness of the sun. Finally there comes a day when the clouds seem whiter; then they seem as if they are trying to contain a brightness too much for them; finally and suddenly the sun breaks through. We began this chapter by discussing the hiddenness of God, both through the sense in which God's presence is at preconscious levels of existence, and through the distortions of sin. This hiddenness is no more final than the gray of the springtime skies. General revelation, or the mark of God in the world, is like the light that illumines the world despite the overlying clouds, and special revelation is like the bursting through of the sun.

6

GOD AS PRESENCE

WE exist in creative response to relationships; this means that existence is through and through relational. Despite this immersion in a world of relation, we sometimes experience a sense of isolation, of watching the crowd, of feeling that there is no real mattering of ourselves in relation to others: loneliness. Who can touch us in our loneliness?

The problem is intensified when we consider the importance of relationships in establishing our own individual sense of meaning. In the illustration of Catherine, it was obvious that her daily purpose and fulfillment were associated with the relationships of her life, whether family, studies, church, or profession. Meaning is found in the concrete relationships of our existence, or it is not found at all. Loneliness, then, carries as its bitter corollary a sense of loss of meaning—or worse still, the intimation not simply of daily meaninglessness, but of an ultimate meaninglessness which reduces one's life to triviality and absurdity.

Inevitably, however, we judge loneliness to be out of kilter with the way things should be. Persistently, we measure the hollow places of loneliness by the value of the relationships we wish we had, so that there is a restlessness and discontent with the condition of loneliness. But here is a seeming paradox: when we are lonely, we find we have judged the concrete relationships of our lives as wanting, as transient, and without any ultimacy of meaning. It is as if the condition of loneliness takes us beneath the surface of daily relationships, so that whether momentarily or longer, we are dissatisfied with those relations. Loneliness envelops us, and through its haze we feel both distanced from and dissatisfied with relationships. But we are also dissatisfied with loneliness. Why?

We could almost speak of our experience as if it occurred in layers: the outermost layer of daily existence, and a deeper layer—

the place of loneliness—where it seems that relationships cannot follow, so that the relationships are deemed insufficient for us. This deeper layer of loneliness does not seem to have ultimacy, for it itself is deemed insufficient. It is as if there were yet another depth beyond the place of loneliness, providing a place of judgment upon loneliness, just as loneliness has provided a place of judgment upon daily relationships.

The experience of loneliness thus indicates at least three dimensions to our experience. There is the surface dimension of everydayness, often experienced as sufficient for the requirement of meaning. Lurking beneath such daily relations is the recurring sense of emptiness, futility, loneliness despite relation. This dimension takes us inside ourselves, forcing us away from the surface of our living. The insufficiency of daily relationships is that they do not follow us here, to the inwardness of ourselves; the relationships are therefore found wanting. But neither is there sufficiency in this inwardness: the lonely self exists in an echo chamber, crying against the prison of its own solitariness for a relation that can set it free. Since the surface relationships cannot participate in this inwardness, and are judged as "surface" precisely through the inwardness, those relations cannot suffice for release from loneliness. Nor, in their insufficiency, can those relations provide the source of the judgment that the loneliness is itself a negative state. There is, in the very sense of loneliness as negative, an intimation of yet a deeper dimension to reality that has the power of judgment over loneliness. Loneliness is then like a space between two forms of relation: the daily relationality above, and a depth relationality beneath. The dilemma of the lonely self is its alienation from both forms of relation. The former seems insufficient, and the latter seems inaccessible, or even illusory. Both forms become like the walls of the echo-chamber prison, intensifying the sense of alienation, intensifying loneliness.

If only one could rest content with loneliness! Then loneliness might seem more like a great hall than a narrow prison; one could stay the intensifying power; one could hold back the insufficiencies of daily relation and the judgment of ultimate relation, like a Samson braced between the pillars of the Philistine hall. "Loneliness," one could say, "is but part of our human condition, to be accepted stoically or even nonchalantly in the sophistication of unquestioning endurance." In such a way, one might balance the pillars that hold up the roof of futility and despair, and find protection in the hall of emptiness. But too often we push against the pillars of denied relation, and the chaos of futility, alienation, and meaninglessness engulfs us, and we are lonelier still. The great hall is no less a prison than the narrow echo chamber.

What if the imagery be used in a different way: if loneliness is like a space or a room between two forms of relation—the one superficial, the other of inaccessible depth—may we not consider the condition of loneliness not as a room but as a passageway? That is, if in loneliness we have longings for a form of relation which penetrates more deeply into our being than those relations of everydayness, and if this sense of a deeper relation becomes both the judge against superficial relationships and against loneliness itself, may not loneliness—which gives rise to the sense of such a form of relationality in the first place—become a mode of access to such a reality? If we intuit such a form of relation through loneliness, might we not go still further, and reach such a form of relation precisely through the prior condition of loneliness? Perhaps the human experience of loneliness becomes an entry point for an awareness of relation to a God who is usually hidden in the dailiness of life; perhaps we move through loneliness to its further side, and begin to speak of the nature of the God who is for us as an ultimate presence.

How can this be? And what is the import of a God who is an ultimate relation, an ultimate presence? The process conceptuality comes to our aid in laying bare the dynamics by which loneliness becomes a component of our experience, and the sense in which loneliness can intimate the nature of God.

Diagram IV (p. 17) illustrated the beginning of each occasion of finite existence through physical feelings. Every moment of existence begins in relationality through the transition of energy from the past to the present. The past *is* present to the becoming occasion. Diagram V (p. 42) added the complexity that God is also felt by the becoming occasion, since God is the source of possibility which governs that which the occasion may become.

The physical pole is supplemented by the mental pole. The mental pole is the occasion's grasp of possibility, the utilization of that vision for itself which is felt through God. God proposes a way of being; the becoming occasion disposes of this as it wills. The concrescing occasion is responsible for what it does with what it has received. In its concrescence, it is alone with itself, determining the value of its universe. This concrescent activity can be portrayed as a spiral, wherein the occasion moves from its feelings of the past (including God) into its own integrative activity, intent upon becoming one reality in the midst of its manifold relations. Upon its completion, it bursts into transitional relation again, now hurling its effects upon the future, joining with God and the whole universe in calling that future into being, even as it itself was called into being. In the flashing movement of existence, every momentary concrescence is followed by transitional relation, and every transitional relation is followed by concrescent aloneness. Concrescence is like the breathing space in the sea of relationality, the aloneness through which one becomes a self through integration of the relations which contribute the material through which the self becomes.

Thus far the model is more descriptive of aloneness in the midst of relation than loneliness in the midst of relation. The difference is crucial, for aloneness can be full of meaning, while loneliness involves loss of meaning. One can be alone, and yet intensely aware of relationships which are integral to the self, both constitutively and valuationally. To be lonely, however, is to experience the devaluation of relations, and an isolation despite relation. The fact that each moment of concrescence is an aloneness with itself is the basis for the further experience of loneliness, but it is not identical with loneliness. To push toward an understanding of loneliness, we need the further discussion of consciousness.

Each occasion of existence is both mental and physical, with the mental pole being that capacity for grasping a possibility for becoming in relation to the actuality of the past world. Very few actual occasions appear to have consciousness, which is the awareness of the grasp of possibility in contrast to actuality. Consciousness is a possibility of the mental pole; it is a particular development of the mental pole, but it is not itself reducible to the mental pole. Consciousness comes to actuality through the strength of contrast between what is and what might be. Thus consciousness is a function of the contrasting integration of the mental and physical poles; it is, therefore, produced through concrescence, and is necessarily a late phase of concrescence. Consciousness cannot be produced in the initial stages of concrescence, for the physical pole is the sheer feeling of energy from the past. Only as the many feelings are integrated can consciousness arise, for the activity of integration is the activity of contrasting.

What provides the contrast? There are two sources: first and foremost, a grasp of the "might be" in contrast to the "what is." In order for this type of contrast to obtain, however, the second source must also be present. There must be a wide range of positive prehensions of the past. If most of the past is felt negatively, so that only a narrow sphere of reality is admitted into positive influence during concrescence, then the contrasting activity will be minimal. Consequently, the mental pole will integrate the past with a minimum amount of novelty: repetition will be assured. The vast proportions of occasions in our world are of this variety, with the result that there is a basic stability to the natural world; its rate of change is slow relative to us.

When an occasion is open to a wide range of influences received positively into the concrescent process, then the manyness of influences itself presents a ground for contrast, plus a problem for integration. The more influences allowed, the more novelty is called for. The "might be" comes into play as ways of integrating the many into the unity of concrescence come to the fore. The contrast between the many and the "might be" produces consciousness as itself being a means of integration. Consciousness, then, relies upon the prominence of the mental pole, a prominence that increases through the intensity of contrasts which the occasion can sustain.

In loneliness, as contrasted with aloneness, the relations which are constitutive of the self are valued negatively. Ordinarily, relations are valued in varying degrees: they range from intense importance to one's self-constitution to minimal importance. Further, there is a fluctuation within each relationship, depending upon the immediate purposes of the individual. For instance, a son may be intensely important to a mother, but if the mother is involved in writing, the relationship to the son may well slip to the background of consciousness. When the mother and son are engaged in conversation, however, the values in the immediate experience may reverse: the writing may become background, and the relationship between mother and son becomes foreground. Thus daily existence admits a myriad of relationships, each with its own value, contrasted with the fluctuating purposes of existence. The contrasts of relation are varied. Not so, however, in loneliness. There is a leveling of relation through negativity. There is a painful sameness to all relations in loneliness, wherein the contrasting variability and interest is silenced.

Yet there is consciousness. Where is the contrast that produces the consciousness of loneliness? It can only come from the "might be," but the "might be" in the process vision of reality is located precisely in the initial aim from God.

Earlier, we spoke of loneliness as a prison between two modes of relation: the devalued everyday relationships, and the sense of ultimate relation through which loneliness is judged as askew. We are now in a position to correlate the existential sense with the philosophical model, wherein we can move into the implications for God. Loneliness follows from the devaluation of finite relations. It cannot negate that relationality, for existence is thoroughly relational. But the relationality is devalued, and in the devaluation, all finite relations are leveled to a sameness. One can, in this process of devaluation, live a robot-like existence, moving in a contrastless world with minimal consciousness. Yet given the propensity of human existence for consciousness, the contrast of the "might be" forces itself upon us, demanding that we visualize a relation that could follow us into our inward processes of existence, meeting us with presence and providing us with meaning.

In the model developed and illustrated through Diagram V (p. 42), the "might be" that comes from God is always for an optimum possibility for concrescence, given our situation. God not only begins our existence through the touch that mediates possibility to us, but God also feels us at the conclusion of each momentary existence, integrating that which we have chosen to become into the divine awareness. We are surrounded by God as our source and destiny in every moment. This indicates that the "might be," which comes to us in our devaluation of finite relations, is in and of itself rooted in a unique presence, for there is no other reality in our experience which is both our source and our destiny. There is a uniqueness to the aim we receive from God which goes beyond the content to the uniqueness of its source in relation to ourselves.

This unique source is something that is experienced again and again by each successive moment in our existence. If God is always present in the provision of the initial aim, then there is no contrasting absence whereby God's presence could rise to conscious notice. This would mean that the very constancy of God's presence would paradoxically function to hide God's presence from consciousness. This hiddenness is further emphasized by the fact that the content of the initial aim, as has been repeatedly mentioned, directs each concrescent occasion toward an optimum mode of existence in the world. Thus God's aim directs us toward the world, not necessarily toward God; and again, God is present in a mode of hiddenness.

When, however, the contrasts of the world are leveled as in loneliness, might it not be the case that a new contrast emerges, touching the edges of consciousness with a sense of the divine presence? Whitehead speaks of a peculiar category known as "transmutation," by which he means the identifying of many occasions by a single characteristic which they all hold in common. As the contrasts of relationality are leveled, they are deemed insufficient, and their very variability becomes held as part of that insufficiency. We might speculate that in loneliness, we tend to categorize all relations alike, negatively valuing the variability in them which ordinarily is the source of richness and contrasts. Transmutation occurs, and the many relations are devalued for variability. Is there not then a natural contrast provided between the variable finite relations and the one invariable divine relation? And might not this contrast suffice to begin to lift this divine relation out of hiddenness into awareness?

We have mentioned the invariability of God's presence as one factor that contrasts with finite relationality. There is yet another factor of contrast that follows from strict usage of the process model. Every finite occasion is felt by another in the mode of objective immortality. No occasion is effective for another until it is determinate. Upon its completion of becoming, its concrescent energy becomes transitional energy. Since God concresces conversely from every finite occasion, God's concrescence never ends: God is the only entity we prehend which is still concrescent. This is not a violation of the metaphysics; it simply follows from the reversal of the polar dynamics. The definiteness which is established by all finite occasions after the unification process is established by God through the primordial quality of the mental pole. Finite occasions end in definiteness, thus allowing the transmission of energy; God "begins" in the definiteness of the primordial vision, so that God's transitional creativity is copresent with God's concrescent creativity. For finite occasions, definiteness is the result of subjectivity; for God, definiteness is the presupposition of subjectivity. Hence God, unlike any other actuality, is felt by the finite occasion during the divine concrescent subjectivity, not after—for there is no "after."

If in loneliness the prehension of God shifts from the world-oriented content of the initial aim to the God-derived nature of the aim, would not this peculiar feature, which surely differentiates this aim from all others, play a part in the resulting contrast? And would it not indicate a divine mode of presence to the prehending occasion that would differ markedly from finite modes of presence? Two points of discussion might clarify this: the nature of "objective immortality" in the process model, and the account of mystical experience, which could be seen to illustrate the difference the continuing concrescence of God might make in the sense of the divine presence.

With regard to objective immortality, it is illustrated in Diagram IV (p. 17). The concrescing occasion was there shown as including elements from its three predecessors in its beginning process of concrescence. In the diagram, the three predecessors—A, B, and C—each contained a quality denoted by "p"; the new occasion, taking account of A, B, and C, did so by prehending each of them through the quality of "p." This would mean that A, B, and C function in the new occasion through that quality; this is what Whitehead means by "objective immortality." The past functions in the internal constitution of the present. Since the past continues in the present, there is an immortality to the past: it lives on. But it does not live on in its subjectivity: it is objectively immortal. Its subjectivity is restricted to its own moment of becoming.

There is an analogy to this in our own experience, for frequently we speak of important figures of the past "living on" in the memories of people in the present. We honor past heroes and heroines, building monuments to them and designating certain days in observance of them. This gives a kind of immortality to these figures, for they continue in history long past their time. But the immortality is certainly not subjective; we do not consider that these people from other centuries subjectively participate in our memories. Their influence is such that their existence has an effect upon our values and our actions—but we are the ones who know it and experience it, not they. The subjectivity belongs to us; the subjectivity of those so affecting us has long since concluded.

"Objective immortality" is thus a functioning reality in every prehension—except one. God is the only reality whose concrescence continues in transitional creativity. God's concrescence is not past, as is the case for all other prehensions; God's concrescence is copresent. Might not this uniqueness be conveyed through the initial aim?

Mysticism might give us an illustration where this is so. Mysticism offers a number of parallels to our usage of the phenomenon of loneliness, for the mystic, too, tends to move into areas of inwardness in search of the divine presence. If loneliness is a leveling of finite relationality, constituting all finite relations as variable and/or superficial, there is a parallel sense whereby the mystic at least initially tends to categorize finite relations as insufficient for the soul's needs. The mystic also frequently experiences a place of loneliness, a "dark night of the soul," in the inwardness of experience; the mystic, too, speaks of alienation and isolation. The parallels break down insofar as the person experiencing loneliness tends to do so not purposefully but meaninglessly. The individual does not seek loneliness, but is rather engulfed by loneliness. The mystic, however, usually intends the mystic journey. There is a purposiveness to the mystical experience of loneliness, whereas there is not in the more ordinary modes of existence. The difference is that the mystic seeks the divine presence on the other side of loneliness, and indeed expects it, or at least hopes for it. The lonely individual is more apt to stumble upon the divine presence, or to sense it as an unnamed and haunting possibility at the boundary of loneliness.

The purposiveness of the mystic is an openness to the presence of God. In account after account, mystics will speak of God breaking into the soul in a fullness of presence, so that the consciousness of the mystic becomes entwined with consciousness of God as the copresent one. For the mystic, God's presence is not simply *to* the soul but *in* the soul. Why should this not be, if God's concrescence is everlasting, and thus everlastingly copresent to every prehending occasion?

If the continuing presence of God can be conveyed to and in the soul through the initial aim, then we indeed can account for the sense of ultimacy in the divine presence. The depth dimension to the relation to God is based in the tremendous contrasts provided between God and the world—contrasts which are ordinarily hidden in the invariable presence of God, and in the world-directive content of the aim from God. When these contrasts begin to emerge through the peculiar conditions of loneliness—or, indeed, mysticism—then God as the supremely present one can begin to be revealed.

What is the result of the sense of God's presence? Is the world devalued in contrast to the ultimacy provided by God? Following the process model, it is necessary to say that the sense of God's presence must push one back into the relationality of the everyday world. The understanding of God is of one who feels the world in order to offer redemptive possibilities to the world. To have a sense of God is to have a sense of God's purposes toward the well-being of the world. The more surely one is attuned to the reality of God, the more surely one is conformed to the divine purposes: but if the divine purposes are toward the good of the world, then to be aware of the divine presence is to be directed again toward the good of the world. If one laboriously crosses the empty places of loneliness in order to reach God, then one is flung back across those places into the everyday world of finite relationships. Conforming to God's purposes involves being plunged headlong again into a world wherein meaning is constantly being created through the relationships of existence. The presence of God releases us from loneliness to presence in the world, and in that finite world we find ourselves again involved in the creation of meaning.

What, then, can we say theologically about God, based on this understanding of God as presence? If we push the experience and the model further in conjunction with Christian faith, God as presence leads also to an understanding of the faithfulness and love of God. The process model portrays God as giving us birth in every moment through the touch of the divine will for us. The model further portrays God as our destiny since God feels our reality upon the completion of every concrescing moment of our lives. God surrounds our moments, embracing our lives with the everliving divine presence. There is in this an intense faithfulness to God, for the import is that God continually provides presence, and that even in our deepest loneliness we might become aware of that presence.

Long ago the Psalmist cried out in awareness of God's surrounding presence, and the Israelites as a people again and again voiced the revelation of God as a guiding presence. Is this not the existential import of the pillar of fire by night and the cloud by day guiding the Hebrew people? And is not the very name of God, revealed as Jahweh, understood in the Hebrew as "I will be there for you"? The prophets witness to the presence of God in our lives, and as Christians we name Christ as an ultimate presence of God in human history, calling Jesus Immanuel, "God with us." The model, working with the dynamics of the experience of loneliness, simply explicates for our own relativity-conscious times what faith has long proclaimed: the nature of God is expressed through presence, and that presence is one of faithfulness and guidance.

God's presence is faithfulness because it is unfailing; existence is impossible apart from the presence of God to us in our beginning and in our ending. God's presence is guiding, because the content of God's touch is directive, making present to us a way of being in the world. In the process model this is necessarily so, for God is the source of our possibility precisely through God's interweaving of the feelings of the consequent nature with the vision of harmony in the primordial nature. That which God offers us is the best that can be for us, given the circumstances with which we have to work. God's presence to us is therefore also God's love, for unfailingly to will the good of the other is assuredly a component of that which we call love. Given this, we can also say that God's presence to us contains judgment, for the initial aim is surely an evaluation of our own past in terms of its possible good, and in terms of the wider good of the world to which we contribute our existence.

To say such things of God goes far beyond the initial experience of loneliness which presses us to say that God is an ultimate presence. However, the sense in which loneliness is judged to be out of kilter with reality lends an existential basis to the statements. The restlessness in loneliness may give us the means to feel the aim of God, but to feel God as the source of the aim will lead to renewed valuation of the content of the aim. And always, the aim of God will push us toward relation, creating value in the finite relations that are given to us, working for an optimum good. When in our loneliness we touch God, we know ourselves as also touched by God, and in the knowing, we are open to the pervasiveness of the divine presence. But it is the nature of divine presence to nudge us back to the world, pushing us toward renewed attention to the content of that touching, guiding, creating aim for our good. The aim inexorably directs us toward our best way of constituting ourselves through and for the world. As the world again becomes for us a place of importance, the contrasting sense of God as presence may dim to memory. The memory, however, finds its echoes in the world of finite relation—not in hollowness now in the prison of an empty self but in the fullness of finite forms of presence. The inward presence of God turns to the outward presence of God, for the God who is present to us is present to others as well;

the God who guides us guides others also; the God who cares for us cares also for others. The whole world is touched by God, and therefore it can mediate God's presence to us. Divine presence pervades finite presence, launching us into the world again, for its good and for ours. Meaninglessness fades, crowded out by presence, and presence—human and divine—insists upon and achieves the meaning of love.

7

GOD AS WISDOM

THE doctrine of God as wisdom relates to needs experienced as a result of our temporality. Temporality involves us in the situation of "perpetual perishing": the passage of time undermines every achievement, challenges every relationship, threatens every good. Ultimately, of course, the many experiences of loss we undergo in our lifetime are like prophecies of the final loss of ourselves through death. Temporality involves us in uncertainty and insecurity, and can evoke in us emotions of anxiety and fear.

We might try to answer the problem of time by dwelling not on the past but on the future. The future, with its lure toward possibility, creates in us a restlessness with present achievement so that the loss of such achievement itself becomes a positive thing, a movement beyond ourselves toward some new goal. Thus the future mode of temporality addresses the problem of temporality; it redeems the past through promises of richness yet to come. We plan a particular future: the possibility of studying this subject, marrying this person, contributing through this profession. With such a future, what difference does the sureness of loss make? Even the loss which is death is but a small price to pay for so rich a treasure! The ticket to life is worth the price of death. In the joy of well-marked possibilities, we make peace with temporality.

To a degree there is an appropriateness in such a resolution: life *is* worth the encounters with death it entails. And surely both past and future offer compensations for the peculiar loss each offers. Against a dim future, there is a savoring of the past through its present power in memory. When, on the contrary, that past holds too much pain, it can be transcended by an emphasis on a new future. But neither the past nor the future can be erased; both impinge upon our presentness in an ambiguous mixture of loss and hope.

So long as the present is experienced as fulfillment, the ambiguity of loss and hope can be interpreted positively. The very edges of the present in past and future sharpen the brightness of the moment, giving it the added delight of giftedness. Because the present moment was not, but is; because it is, but will not be, there is an inherent marvel in its presentness at all. The temporal nature of the present, bounded by a past and future which it will be and was, gives intensity and zest and wonder to each moment . . . so long as the content of each moment is not antagonistic to well-being.

It is impossible, in finite existence where value competes for value and each choice is a denial of other choices, for every moment to be experienced as fulfillment. The temporality that gives such delight also holds terrors, and finite existence is plunged into both. Time is both life and death. The transience of the present can as easily evoke anxiety and insecurity as delight and zest.

Traditionally, the doctrine of God's omniscience has been one powerful way in which the ambiguity and terror of time has been answered. The power of divine knowledge is such that the past and the future are eternally present to God. If they are eternally present, then "past" and "future" are but finite experiences that are swallowed up in God, and by attempting to align oneself with the divine viewpoint one can make peace with the terrors of history. A problem with the answer is first that it answers the problems of time by denying time, and second that a consideration of knowledge, human and divine, through a process model cannot allow the type of omniscience which absorbs past and future into present. Divine wisdom, not divine knowledge, must be developed as the process answer to the problems of temporality. Trust, not security, is then the more appropriate response to the challenge of time.

How could divine knowledge be seen as an answer to the contingencies of time? Traditionally, the attribute of divine omniscience has been associated with God's knowledge of all things at all times and all places: God encompasses all times in the single totality of divine knowledge. Past, present, and future are but a finite unfolding of that which has, is, and always will be known to God in a single seeing. Consequently, past, present, and future are finite distinctions, perceptions from the limited perspective available to us. In God, all times are as one, and hence known in an eternal insight wherein past, present, and future are forever known and forever present in one eternal "now."

Notice how easily this doctrine of God's knowledge addresses the problems of temporality. Is the past lost? But the past is not really past, for it is present in the eternality of God. The pastness of things is perspectival, rooted in our finite limitation; the past only *seems* to be lost. Another way of saying it is that while the past may be lost to us, it is not lost to God. Therefore, the past is as present as God.

How does God's knowledge address the future as threat? In the traditional formulation of God's knowledge, there is no room for contingency. If God knows the future, then God knows it infallibly as that which will take place—it is known to God as if it already had taken place, so sure is the divine knowledge. Will it rain in Chicago on July 4, 2179? God knows that it will! Is there any way, then, in which that rainy day is contingent? Is it not as sure as the divine knowledge? Contingency is but the necessary illusion of finitude, describing, not events themselves but our knowing of events. Could we know as God knows, contingency would be eliminated, and with it, the future as future as well. For if we knew infallibly what would happen, precisely as it would occur, is not that "future" present?

Thus the traditional function of God's knowledge in relation to the problems of our finite temporality is fundamentally to deny the reality of time. If God's knowledge is such that the past and the future are continuously present in God, then distinctions are finally not real distinctions, but simply descriptive of our limited knowing. In the denial of temporality, there is neither the perpetual perishing of value nor the threat to the attainment of value. The past is not really lost, and the future will not really replace the present. Nor are the possibilities of the future really shrouded in clouds of contingency, such that the fear of the past is intensified by anxiety over the future. Fear and anxiety should melt away with the comforting knowledge that in God's knowledge, past and future are engulfed in an eternal present.

This interpretation of God's knowledge, phrased in variations of the above by theologians throughout the Christian tradition, creates a tension with our own experience of knowledge that is so integrally related to temporality. Is knowledge without temporality still knowledge in any meaningful sense? If in fact the transience of time is integral to every moment of our experience, can the abstraction of that transience still yield a knowledge of the same thing? For example, a child anticipates the advent of a particular day, so that the days preceding the awaited one take on their meaning in light of their closeness to the longed-for day. Moving toward Christmas, or a birthday, or a summer vacation crowds each day of waiting with an importance of anticipation. The experience of transience is so integral to the child's self-understanding that if the experience is abstracted through a knowledge that reifies the present, then the present is paradoxically lost. Time is so integral to human experience that if human experience is to be known at all, it must be known as temporal.

It will not do to say there is a nontemporal knowing of the temporal. Such a knowing reduces the moments of living to the celluloid frames of a motion picture, creating the illusion of movement through static instances. There is then a capturing of observed time, but the life that made it worth capturing in the first place is not thereby made present. To know the temporal nontemporally would be to distort the temporal, and thus not to know it as fully or as richly as its actual temporality demands. Thus a knowledge of the temporal that denies temporality is not a true knowledge at all. If one looks to such a "knowing" as a security against the terrors of transience, one is caught in the dilemma that the security, and not the transience, is illusory. A divine knowledge that denies temporality is less-than-perfect knowledge, and cannot address the problems of time.

If the above is valid, then it follows that there can be no security against history as such. Not even divine knowledge can protect us from the sureness of loss, for there is no divine viewpoint which obliterates the reality of our temporal condition. Is there no recourse, then? Is the God discovered as presence irrelevant to the peculiar finite problem of time? How ironic if the God who answers our spatial alienations through the uniqueness of divine presence is powerless to answer our temporal anxieties precisely because the perfection of divine knowledge cannot deny that which is real.

If we attempt an understanding of God based upon the dynamics of existence as process, then it will follow that God's knowledge is precise, knowing all reality just as it knows itself. Temporality is introduced into the divine nature. But *because* temporality is introduced into God's nature, there emerges the power not of knowledge but of wisdom. This wisdom offers trust and hope in the midst of our histories.

In the process model, God's knowledge must be considered twofold, according to the twofold distinction between the primordial and consequent aspects of God. God's primordial nature is the vision of all possibilities whatsoever, harmonized in the very process of being known. God's knowledge of possibilities is God's valuation of possibilities, ranking them into harmonies of order, beauty, and goodness. In this knowing valuation, God unifies all possibilities—*all* possibilities. Such a vision calls for symbols and metaphors, for if God's primordial vision is inclusive of all possibilities whatsoever, then this vision goes beyond our imagination. That there are infinite possibilities can be grasped by us, but if we attempt to fill in the content of the possibilities, and then to order them in terms of ultimate complementation and beauty, we stagger at the task. "Infinity" then becomes a symbol for that which is more than we can think. Accordingly, the process model posits an infinite primordial nature in God for the ordering of infinite possibilites into infinite harmony. God's knowledge through the primordial nature is precisely of possibility in infinite modes of suggested existence.

Note, however, the accuracy of this knowledge: it is a knowledge of *that which is possible*. That the possible is ordered into harmony is not a function of the possibilities but a function of God, conveying the actuality of harmony to possibles without annihilating their nature as possibility. The primordial vision is a knowledge of the possible as possible; it is not a knowledge of the possible as actual—and herein lies the reality of the future in its character of genuine possibility.

The consequent nature of God is God's feeling of every occasion that ever existed. It is not God's feeling of that which *will* exist, for until a thing is actual, it is only possible—hence there is a distinction in divine knowledge, if the notion of God as primordial and consequent is an intuition of the reality of God. Through the consequent nature, God knows all actuality whatsoever. It rains in Chicago on a certain day. Does God know it? How? In the process understanding, God knows it by feeling it, both through the reality of the drops of moisture as they fall and through the experience of wetness as the drops touch the earth, be it upon the pavement, or a leaf upon a tree, or the wet cheek of a secretary rushing to reach shelter from the unexpected noontide storm. Every actuality that comes into existence is felt in its entirety, as it felt itself, by God.

Diagram V (p. 42) might clarify the sense in which God knows actuality. The diagram is repeated here with certain variations:

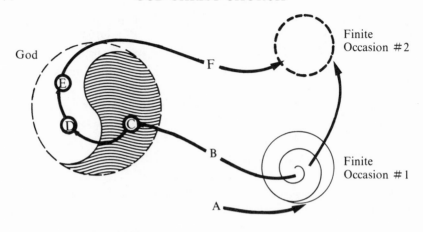

DIAGRAM VI

Finite occasion #1 has received the initial aim (A) from God, plus the energies from its past world. In its spiraling activity of concrescence it has unified those influences in terms of its own decision concerning its purposeful existence. Upon its completion, it contributes its own energy to the universe, both to God (through line B, God's prehension of the occasion) and to the world (here, its effect upon occasion #2). God, feeling the occasion in the consequent nature (C), integrates it into the primordial nature (D). The result of this integration (E) is that a possibility which may previously have been sheerly possible relative to the world now moves into real possibility as an optimum mode of achieving harmony in the world, given the reality of occasion #1. This feeling in God becomes line F, or God's initial aim for the about-to-begin occasion #2.

As noted in chapter 2, successive occasions must feel their predecessors selectively, for there is no way by which the new occasion can repeat the past exactly as it felt itself. Basically, the new occasion must combine factors that were not present in the former entities, and must combine these factors in such a way that simplification occurs: the occasion must reduce the multiplicity of influences to the single complexity that will be itself. Therefore, there can be no sheer repetition of the past in the finite present.

The same necessity, however, does not hold for God. It is not the case that God must simplify the many into a new unity in order to become actual. God, "beginning" in reverse of the finite occasions through the mental pole, is eternally unified in terms of the primordial vision. Since this vision is a harmony of *all* possibilities whatsoever, there is no actuality which cannot fit into that primordial harmony. It will affect that harmony, causing shifts within it, but it cannot de-harmonize God. If *every* possibility has been ordered within God's primordial harmony, then no possibility-become-actuality can reverse that harmony. Therefore, there is no categorical necessity to limit God's prehension of any actuality in the world.

The reverse is rather the case. If God's primordial vision is a harmony of possibilities, and if the actuality of God confers the dynamism of actuality to the vision, then the actuality of God also acts as an impetus to the realization of the vision in terms of its component parts. That is, there is a primordial actuality to the harmony of God by virtue of God's own reality. The reality, however, is imposed upon a universe of possibles—the possibilities themselves do not strive for existence, but the reality of God strives toward their existence, in order that the feelings of harmony in the vision might become more and more intensified by the everlasting actualization of that harmony. How can this actualization take place? Only as the possibilities are realized outside the nature of God, and then received into the nature of God. The fullness of the actuality in the world intensifies the actual reality of the vision of God. Given such a situation, far from requiring selectivity for the divine concrescence, God requires the opposite—a full prehension of the full finite reality.

The effects of this for the knowledge of God are simply that God, and only God, knows every reality, every actuality, precisely as it experienced itself. Was the finite occasion conscious? Then God experiences it so. Was it painful? Then God feels its pain, not from the outside, but from the inside. Was it insentient? Then it remains insentient in God's knowledge of it. God's prehensions of the world feel the world in the entirety of every atomistic bit of the world. God's knowledge of the world, then, is absolute and complete, even to the inclusion of its own experience of temporality.

The possibilities of the primordial nature and the actualities felt in the consequent nature thus constitute the knowledge of God. The wisdom of God is not simply God's knowledge, but God's use of that which is known. God's integration of the consequent nature into the primordial nature is the reality of God's wisdom. And it is God's wisdom. And it is God's wisdom, rather than God's knowledge per se, that saves us.

In the integration of the consequent and primordial natures, God feels the world as it is and as it might be. The world is transformed in God's integration, for it is an integration into divine harmony, into the depths of God's vision of the togetherness of all things in complementarity and love. There is a point in this integration (to be developed more fully in Part V, "The Kingdom of God") where God's wisdom flows in two directions—Godward and world-ward. God feels the world as it felt itself, and integrates it into the divine harmony. In this integration, there are implications for the continuing participation of the occasion in that divine harmony, and also implications for optimum modes of being for the immediately becoming world. The harmony in God has a world-oriented dimension; this is the function of the initial aim, prompting the becoming world toward its own best utilization of its past and its own highest creativity for itself and the future. In this sense, the integrative wisdom of God continually offers redemption to the world.

The effect of God's wisdom is that no matter what threats and contingencies we may experience, God is faithful to lead us into a creative mode of dealing with these problems. This follows from the fact that God's wisdom is not a cold calculation of bits and pieces of knowledge, as if God were some gigantic computer knowing all things and feeding information to the world. Rather, God's wisdom follows from the divine feeling, wherein God feels the world and thus knows the world in a coexperience. This feeling knowledge, integrated within the depths of the divine resources in the primordial nature, becomes a redemptive wisdom for the world, a creative wisdom, a faithful wisdom, offering modes of being to us as real possibilities which have been deemed so through the depths of God's ordering in absolute knowledge of that which is and that which can be.

In accordance with this, the previous statement of God's knowledge of the future as traditionally formulated must be revised. God knows the range of possible futures which lie before us, given our total situations. In God's knowledge of our possible futures, God must also know the probable future. After all, while it is inaccurate to name God's knowledge as computer-like, it would be absurd to think of God's knowledge as less than that which we can create through our own technology. God, knowing all actuality in its varying patterned responses, safely knows the combinations which predict the probabilities of our futures. But even for God, the element of contingency is real. That which happens finally depends upon those concrescent choices whereby the world, in its solitariness, chooses from among its alternatives that which it will become. And God waits upon the world.

How does this affect our problems with temporality? A process view can align itself with the understanding that the past is made present in God. However, as will be seen in the development of chapter 17, this is more than simple preservation. Rather, it is a living knowledge of every occurrence according to its own self-experience. Because of the absolute accuracy of this knowledge, transformation of the past from its own perspective is possible in God. Thus God's knowledge of the past is a knowledge transforming the past through wisdom. The past is therefore both preserved and yet transformed through the medium of divine knowledge and wisdom. Our own dealings with the past as loss can become positive and creative as we ourselves reflect this process. For us the past is preserved through memory. But the transformation of the past is not in its memory but in ourselves. The finite mirroring of the divine process can lead us into creative ways of dealing with the loss of the past.

What of the fear of the future? The primordial nature is the source of the future, for the primordial nature is the locus of all possibilities. The future is that indefinite complex of possibilities from which we forge each new present; hence the future, as possibility, has its locus in God's primordial nature. Which possibility shall materialize out of the future as a newly made present depends on God and on us. Thus contingency is real, awaiting the outcome of finite decision and divine integration of those decisions with the realm of the possible. Since, however, the availability of possible futures to us does depend upon God as well as upon us, we can have a realistic hope and trust with regard to the future.

This follows from the everlasting integration of the primordial and consequent natures of God into the unity of the divine life. This integration constitutes God as an everlasting presence. Note the distinction: one must say God is an everlasting presence, not an everlasting present. The differentiation is that God is the co-presence of all the world within the unity of the divine nature; this unity encompasses the past in union with God's future; it is a unity of participation, of presence, in and with and through God. But this unity is also God's wisdom in the divine integration of the world into the totality of divine life. God's presence and God's wisdom are the same reality.

From our finite perspective, then, God as presence is God as guidance for our future, or God as wisdom. If God's presence with us is always a guidance relative to our immediate future, then our attitude toward the future can undergo a radical change from that fear and insecurity which was first cited. If we feel the future as fearsome, as a threat to the values we hold dear or the values we hope yet to achieve, the sense that God's wisdom is ever given in guiding aims can allow us to accept the challenges of the future, to dare its risks. No matter what contingencies or wrong choices occur, either inadvertently or willfully, God's guidance is faithfully redemptive. God as wisdom, against the openness and contingency of the future, evokes our trust instead of fear.

Finally, a sense of God's wisdom with regard to our temporality forces us to accept our responsibility for our own future. We can trust God to offer redemptive possibilities, no matter what may transpire—but what it is that will have to be redeemed depends upon the activity of the world. God's redemptive activity conjoins with our own responsively creative activity; it does not obliterate our activity. We become God's coworkers, and the future follows upon the choices of our responsive activity. God invites us into a future that we must create in our response to God. In our awareness of divine wisdom, we replace fear with trust, and move into the contingencies of time. And God waits.

8

GOD AS POWER

DIVINE presence answers the human need of loneliness, and loneliness itself may offer a key to knowing the ultimate presence which is God. Loneliness gives way to love. Divine wisdom answers the problem of insecurity, eliciting trust when the contingencies of time would evoke our fear. Thus God as presence and wisdom answers problems experienced by the individual: loneliness is the alienation of the individual from society, and insecurity falls primarily to individuals facing the problems of the past and the future. What is the importance of God's power for us? What is at issue in our conviction that God is omnipotent?

Whereas divine presence and wisdom answer individual problems, power is related to the societal problem of justice. Justice is the well-being of society: a society has well-being when its members find that the society helps them develop their humanity, through which each member enriches the other. Interdependence and reciprocity are involved, together with a valuation of the diversity of talent and ability in human existence. A dynamism necessarily infuses such a society, for if to receive means also to give, then the society actively seeks to perpetuate itself in the continuous creation of conditions which will foster well-being.

We ordinarily understand justice to refer not only to the maintenance of good in mutual well-being, but also to the redress of evil and the restoration of well-being to those for whom it has been violated or lost. However, if the first brief description given above seemed visionary, then this second qualification means that a full justice can never be achieved. Too often injustice has crushed its victims, making reparation impossible. How is a broken mind repaired, a lost limb returned, a stunted ability to love reshaped, a murder undone?

Often in our histories persons have been outraged at societal injustice, and inflamed to the point of revolution in order to bring about a just society according to a new vision. The power of that vision motivates the struggle for its achievement, but it encounters the power of entrenched ways and means of past and present. Inevitably, the movement toward what-might-be involves loss of present values and/or lives. If that future vision is made a present reality, then perhaps a wider form of well-being is attained—but those who were lost in the process of its attainment do not participate in the new order. And some, whose well-being depended, in fact, upon the old order, will find the new "justice" to be a most unjust factor in their continuing lives. Justice is partial.

The more one begins to consider the problem of justice, the more impossible and visionary any full justice appears to be. Admittedly, the difficulty lies in the perfection of justice visualized, for if one pushes a notion of justice as an inclusiveness of mutual well-being then plainly the notion becomes an impossible dream. Only if the past can somehow be brought into the present, and only if a sufficient flexibility of vision can allow radical diversities to co-exist in well-being, only then can justice in its fullest dimensions be established. Under the circumstances of our finitude, however, such conditions cannot be secured. Is the notion of justice necessarily to be tailored to a smaller scale so that we might find contentment in lesser conditions?

To do so, however, involves three dangers. The first concerns the very nature of justice itself insofar as it concerns itself with relationships of well-being in society. If the field of justice is restricted to any area or group or time, so that some are categorically outside the range of well-being, then justice is contradicted at its core. The contradiction is like a cancer allowed to exist within an otherwise strong body. Unchecked, the cancer infiltrates the so-called healthy cells; the body sickens, dies. When a body of people constitute themselves as a society of justice, actualize conditions of well-being for many within that body, and yet systematically exclude others from participation, then the so-called justice harbors sickness within it that can destroy the health of the whole body of people.

Likewise, when a society of justice turns in upon itself, ignoring conditions of injustice beyond its border, then justice itself is fed by injustice. In a relational world, no entity, be it cell or society, can exist apart from its receiving and giving to others. The society that turns in upon itself denies the extent to which its very existence is dependent upon other societies beyond its borders. It does, in fact, draw from those societies. If it allows injustice to reign unchecked—or if, in fact, its self-concern leads to its fostering conditions of injustice upon other societies, then once again, justice is contradicted. The body is cancerous. Accepted limitations to justice contradict the nature of justice, and hence lead to its decay into injustice.

A second danger lies not with the contradiction to the nature of justice entailed by its limitations in scope or vision but in complacency. If well-being is the foundation of a society, then the society must be dynamic. A new generation succeeds the old; new technologies replace the old; new problems crowd out old answers. In a society where well-being is acceptably restricted to some, justice moves in a closed, contained channel. The definitions that form that closure and rationalize the restrictions cut off the routes of novelty which could infuse the society with the needed dynamism. Instead, the status quo is a valued condition which must be maintained against the disruptions of new perspectives and questions. Insofar as the effort to block out changes of an extensive nature succeeds, then stagnation occurs: dynamism is lost; complacency replaces vision; justice withers.

Finally, unless a vision of justice holds within it the real possibility of its fulfillment, it cannot inspire the hope which is so necessary to effective action. If the vision of justice is acceptably limited, such that there is a complacency in society with regard to those restrictions, and if a full justice is inherently impossible, then the hope for a better society, which inspires efforts to achieve that society, is lost. The loss of hope is the loss of effort; the loss of effort is the reinforcement of complacency, which is the loss of dynamism—justice yields to injustice.

The principle can be illustrated by a simple and all too common experience in the life of any disadvantaged group. Joan desires to be a pharmacist; she is aware that the field is one that has traditionally been restricted to men, but nonetheless she is drawn to the study of pharmacology and longs to make it her profession. In a world where few if any women have ever entered such a field, Joan's pursuit of her goal would be endangered by a sense of futility. Why bother pursuing the appropriate coursework when she might never attain her goal? While she might well begin her studies, the discouragement of being refused intern positions and largely ignored in her classes would begin to cloak her amibition in despair. The despair would affect her work, so that finally her own efforts would wane—"just like a woman," might be the response of her peers, "no perseverance." And Joan might turn to typing.

If, on the other hand, Joan finds a situation in which there is a new openness to women in the field of pharmacology, she would see a reward for her efforts—she would be working for an achievable goal. The sense of possibility translates to a sense of hope: there is a reason for her work; zest marks her studies; she achieves her goal. The difference in the realizable nature of the goal is the difference between hope and despair. Hope is catalytic, giving momentum to efforts which greatly aid achievement of the goal; despair is debilitating, draining one's energy into the negative achievement of failure.

We find ourselves, then, in a strange situation. Justice, to be sought, must be visualized as achievable. An illusory justice cannot inspire the necessary hope. But our finite situation is one where we have never experienced any society of full justice. Even if it could be attained for a present generation, we know that the component of justice which requires redress for past wrongs is simply impossible for us in many cases. And yet it is so that we strive for justice, and sometimes against overwhelming odds. There has never been a time when recorded history shows a full equality for women such as women seek today: how do women dare to think such a society can be created now? Third world countries have "always" been exploited by the nations they help to make rich; how can they hope to enjoy the reciprocity in which their own welfare is also achieved? Societies traditionally form into hierarchical orders, with designated ethnic groups kept in the menial positions of servitude that support the higher levels. Isn't the system so entrenched in human nature that it cannot change? The most that can be hoped for is that one subservient group might climb higher, leaving its slotted position to yet another. The pragmatics of our world mitigate against hope that justice can be achieved for all.

And yet we do work. We dare to dream. We struggle against odds. How is it that we maintain a vision of justice, insist that it can be actualized, and throw our lives into its achievement? The hope cannot be rooted in our finite experience, for all of our experience denies the full condition of justice. How paradoxical, that we nevertheless experience hope—and how thoroughly necessary for the gains that are made and that might still be made.

Process theology suggests that the power of hope against despair is not paradoxical at all, but rests with the nature of God as the power for justice. God is the source of the vision and of the reality; there is a locus for justice in the nature of God. The effect of God upon us is the transmission of vision, along with the conviction of its worth and attainability. God is the source of hope. This is the significance of the doctrine of divine omnipotence for us.

To probe the reasons for this, consider again the dynamics of the actual entity, compared now with a description of the dynamics of justice. In an actual entity, the many become one, giving rise to a new value in the universe. The becoming of the entity involves an integration of the felt values of the past—the one, in freedom, chooses those elements best suited to its own ideal of itself, creating itself as it weaves the manyness of the past into its own new unity. This, which is done in the freedom and privacy of its own becoming, is ultimately given again to the many: the individual creation is offered to the future, in part evoking that future into being. Furthermore, this offering is not restricted to a single succeeding occasion; it cannot be so private an achievement. Rather, it is appropriated by the entire future, entering as it does into many past actual worlds. Just as the many initially made the becoming of the new entity possible, even so the new entity now contributes to the becoming of many others: its own enrichment, made possible by others, is now given for the enrichment of others.

These dynamics are remarkably similar to a dynamic description of justice. In a just society, the one and the many—the individual and the community—would interrelate in a mutually enriching harmony. The conditions of the society would be conducive to the well-being of the individual, making that well-being possible. As the individual freely develops in a richness of existence, that individual contributes value toward the increasing richness of society. Interdependence in relationality is a basic condition of justice: acting for the other's good is at the same time acting for one's own good, and the impoverishment of one is the impoverishment of all. To return to our example, Joan achieves her goal—the society, with its educational system and its extension of freedom of opportunity to women has contributed to her well-being. As a result, Joan is a particularly conscientious community pharmacist, approaching her work with gladness as well as diligence. Through the way she fulfills her own humanity, she contributes to the well-being of the community.

Note the two forms of power involved. There is the power of

84 GOD-CHRIST-CHURCH

self-creativity and the power of influencing others. In Whiteheadian terms, there is the concrescent power of the subject for itself
and the transitional power of the subject for others. In both cases,
there are natural limitations to power: in the instance of self-
creativity, one is limited by the possibilities of one's nature and of
society's structure. Joan illustrates this: she cannot choose to be a
bird or a tree, or to leap tall buildings at a single bound—these do
not belong to the possibilities of her existence. These are natural
limitations placed upon her self-creativity, and they are fixed.
Society's structure further defines her possibilities, but in a more
fluid way—societal restrictions are based not upon nature but upon
custom. Therefore, these limitations are subject to question and to
change.

The limitations to power in its transitional, influential mode are
even more marked. No one is the sole influence on others, nor can
anyone fully determine one's effects upon others. Joan may wish
to persuade a friend to enter the field of pharmacy with her. She
brings all her influence to bear: her own delight with the work, her
progress in her studies, the encouragement of her peers. In what
she does and says, Joan becomes an influence upon her friend. But
he has other friends as well, who are equally enthusiastic about
their own choices of profession. Joan's influence is balanced by
theirs. Ultimately, of course, it is the friend who determines how
influential Joan can be in light of his other influences and interests.
Joan's power of influence is therefore limited by the fact that she
can never be the sole influence, and by the fact that her friend must
decide for himself. Hence transitional power is limited both
through its context of manyness, and through the self-creativity of
the influenced individual.

How do these two forms of power apply to God, and how can
such an application give us confidence that there is indeed a realm
of pure justice? In process theology, God is described in terms of
the dynamics of an actual entity, with the single difference that in
God the dynamics move from the mental pole to the physical pole
rather than from the physical to the mental. This reversal of the
poles becomes particularly important when considered in relation
to the extent of God's self-creative power.

Self-creative power is the ability to integrate all influences upon
one's becoming in terms of a decision concerning the nature of
one's own character. This decision is limited only by the possibilities that define the parameters of reality. What are the possibilities

that define the limit of deity? Where do we look to find these parameters? In the case of Joan, we look to the givenness of what it is to be human in the many instances of human beings, and in the shared physical characteristics variously manifested in the genetic make-up of human beings. Joan's possibilities for her own development will be within the range allowed by her humanity in its specific setting. But if God is one, then obviously a source for limiting the divine power through reference to a kind is simply absent. The parameters of deity are found within the self-contained possibilities of the single reality which is God. However, when we consider these possibilities according to the primordial nature, it appears that *all* possibilities have their locus in God. The only limitation upon actualization of particular kinds of possibilities would appear to be the constructive limitation of existence itself— for if God is to exist, the possibilities must be unifed. Unification is order and valuation in terms of harmony—the terms are almost synonyms with one another in this instance. The implication is that for God to exist—for the infinite possibilities to be localized at all—God must be good. God, by self-definition, must be good, for if God were not a unification, a harmonization, of all possibilities, God simply would not be. Yet it is a self-definition, for how this harmonization takes place requires a divine ordering of all possibilities. The very ordering is free in that it is God self-determining the divine existence both in terms of the *that* and in terms of the *how*.

Is there a question then of the beginning of God—of a time when God was not, when there existed simply the sheer chaos of possibility, out of which a singular divine entity becomes self-created? But how could this be? It finally comes down to the paradoxical situation that possibilities simply do not "exist" unless there is a "something" for which they are possible. If there is no actuality, then there is no possibility. This means that to talk of possibilities pre-existing God is to talk nonsense, so that we are forced to the conclusion that possibilities *are* because God *is*. We must say that God is the eternally self-created one, created out of the divine concrescent power, self-determined from all possibilities, existing necessarily in goodness. What is God's power relative to the divine existence? Absolute, when considered in relation to the self-decided character of God, and when considered in relation to the primordial nature of God.

Existence in a process universe is concrescent, taking the influences of others through the physical pole into the unification of the self. What is God's power in relation to the unification of the divine feelings of the world? God is not only a mental pole, or a primordial nature, but God is also the physical pole, or the consequent nature—this nature is consequent upon both the primordial ordering that is the self-determined divine character, and the happenings in the world. God's power, relative to the integration of the physical feelings of the world into the divine nature, is again absolute—not in terms of what is integrated (save indirectly) but in terms of how it is integrated. What God feels depends upon what the world has become, and this "whatness" is partially the result of God's influence in the first place but, more determinatively, it is the result of the world's decisive utilization of God's influence in its own self-becoming. This would be the world's transitional influence upon God. But how God deals with those influences is sheerly within the control of the divine power. Is God the harmonization of all possibilities in a valuation solely self-determined? Then God will feel the various occasions of the world in light of the divine will toward harmony. Such evaluative feelings mean that the world is felt comparatively in relation to harmony, both with regard to finite modes of harmony and with regard to the ultimate divine harmony. Judgment is inexorably involved in God's feelings of the world, and in the integration of those feelings within the divine nature. The world, felt through the physical pole, would be pulled into a harmonious unification with the mental pole in the unity of God. God, in concrescent power, exercises full control over what will be done with the world in this divine unification, for God exercises unlimited power in the divine self-definition. In this omnipotence, God is the final and full achievement of justice.

The many for the one and the one for the many: justice involves a rhythmic interdependence; justice involves a mutual enrichment and harmony. In Part V we will develop an argument for the resurrection of the world in God so that the world, felt by God, would be understood to participate subjectively in the divine harmony. Insofar as that interpretation is coherent and consistent with the process frame of reference, then it will build upon the omnipotence of God with respect to the divine concrescence to make the notion of God as justice more concrete. God is heaven, and heaven is God. The many finally enjoy the unity of the one, each contributing what value has been achieved and benefiting from the values of others in the transformation of judgment and harmony. Justice is not an illusory dream; justice is as real as God.

ᵥIf God exercises omnipotent power over the integration of the world within the divine nature, thus everlastingly overcoming evil in justice, what is the power of God for us in relation to the temporal order of things? How, if at all, does this transcendent realm of justice address our finite experience of the mixture of justice and injustice?

In a process universe, everything affects everything else: to be for oneself is also to be for others; to know concrescent power is also to create transitional power; the power of becoming issues into the power of influence. That which one is, one is for the universe. This is no less true for God than for the most insignificant portion of actuality: to be is to have an effect. As God feels the world and pulls the divinely recreated world into divine justice, this actualized reality of justice itself gives rise to God's feeling for optimum modes of justice in the temporal world that is becoming. What God does with the world in the divine nature influences God's own influence on the becoming world. Therefore God's continuous effect on the world is always in terms of specific modes of order for the specific combinations of realities in the world. God always exercises an influence toward an achievable order of justice in the temporal world. Hence God's relative power toward the world is reflective of the divine harmony. God's creative power in the world is always toward justice, and toward an achievable mode of finite justice. That the justice that is possible is *achievable* is due to God; whether or not the justice is *achieved* is due to the world.

The justice that is inherent in God's influence for the world may be controverted. This follows from the very structure of existence. That the many are for the one and the one for the many is simply part of the order of things. How each one participates in this order depends upon the self-creative decision of each entity. Consider the following illustrations of injustice:

A man finds employment in a textile mill; conditions are oriented toward the production of as much material as human labor can produce, with the value placed by management on the product rather than on the human being whose labor produces it. Wages are minimal, work is long and harsh. The man develops brown lung disease.

A chemical factory in the Far East discharges its waste materials into the water, contaminating the drinking supply of the nearby village; children in the village are born with deformities; the cause is traced to the contaminated water. No change is made in the factory disposal procedures.

One people are deprived of their living space by another; the stronger group herds the smaller group onto a piece of land barely suited for agriculture, and then ignores the deterioration and decimation of the people.

An old woman clutches her purse, making her way down the grimy city street toward the store in her area of the ghetto. A young man crashes into her, rips the purse from her hand, leaving her lying on the sidewalk with a broken hip.

A mother, living in a famine area of the African desert, watches in agony as her small child slowly dies of starvation; in the same world, another family throws its extra food away.

The many for the one, and the one for the many: these are the dynamics that allow each instance of injustice, but they are also the dynamics that make redress of the injustice possible. The textile factory managers act as if their own creative power of influence stops with their own material gain, whereas their actual influence feeds back again into the impoverishment of the workers' well-being; the chemical factory is operated as if its responsibility is limited in its effects solely to those who buy the chemicals; in fact, its influence is much wider, as is its responsibility; one people universalize their own needs, as if the perpetuation of but one people is the sole consideration; the young man utilizes the woman as if she existed solely for his own good, and not he for hers; the family with food confines its ability to nourish to its own realm, ignoring its interdependence with a wider world. In each case, injustice is the absolutizing of the self or the self-interest group, with no account of the rhythmic nature of interdependence.

Because of interdependence, injustice is possible: given the denial of responsibility on the part of the one, the many will suffer. However, it is also interdependence that makes justice possible: given the nature of reciprocal existence, and given the requisite of order for a world, this order may manifest harmony of the one and the many in justice. Whether or not it does rests with the responsibility of the world. That it can, in specific modes suited to time and place, rests with the influence of God. God and the world together are responsible for the reality of justice in the world; the power of God makes it possible, and the responsive activity of the world makes it real.

Given the role of God's power in the achievement of justice, and given our increased awareness of our own responsibilities in an interdependent universe, there is a ground to hope in the face of injustice. The dynamics of existence make injustice possible, but only as a perversion of the interdependence which allows the growth of order in the first place. Interdependence, working smoothly as the many for the one for the many, is the divinely created basis of order, and therefore is the foundation of the universe. To work toward justice is to work *with* the dynamics of reality. Divine power assures it. Further, inasmuch as the mode of justice that is seen relative to any situation is a mode that is suited to the world through the creative ordering of God, then that mode of justice is truly achievable. Once achieved, it will then be surpassable, opening up still further modes of justice—this is necessarily the case in a process universe. But that it is achievable is also the case, based upon the reality of a God who orders all possibilities in justice, and fits possibilities to the world in a realistic fashioning of optimum modes of existence. Since modes of justice are thus grounded in reality, and are really achievable, then hope is appropriately a component in all our efforts toward achieving our visions of justice. Hope is catalytic, and ultimately is the most important ingredient in the struggle for justice, insuring the perseverance that brings justice about.

The reality of God's power relative to the world is such that there is ground to hope for the achievement of justice. This hope is due to the concrescent power of God as the locus of full justice in the transformation of the world, and to the faithfulness of God's influential power—God influences the world in keeping with the divine character, and thus leads the world toward modes of justice. If God is for us, who can be against us? And so we address the evils of our existence in the hope that they can be overcome.

Part Three

PRESENCE

God in Christ:
A Process Christology

9

JESUS

GOD of presence; God of wisdom; God of power: a discussion of God based on general revelation can lead to an affirmation of such a God. Yet, particularly in dealing with God's power in relation to injustice, it became increasingly necessary to return to the theme sounded in chapter 3, the problem of sin. If general revelation leads to a knowledge of God as presence, wisdom, and power, special revelation leads to the sense in which this God addresses the needs and distortions and tragedies of sin.

General revelation is suggested simply through the dynamics of existence as we consider the world around us. In no sense does this consideration take place in a value-free context, as if somehow we could release ourselves from Christian conviction in a pure and objective consideration of the world. But it is possible to develop an understanding of God without direct recourse to biblical revelation. This is not so in the instance of special revelation, which depends upon the actions of God in human history as given through the biblical witness.

Special revelation, as indicated in chapter 5, takes place through intensifying the image of God in human consciousness. While this may occur in an ultimate sense in Jesus, revelation begins far before that time in the long history of Israel. How does God create that people, save through a covenant that reveals the divine nature? Whether the covenant is considered through the dim recesses of the past, recorded as a relationship with Adam, Noah, and Abraham, or through the giving of the law through Moses, or through the call and response represented by the prophets, always the covenant is at once revealing and creating. Through the covenant, God's will toward justice in relationships is revealed; through the people's participation in the covenant, justice in relationships is enacted in society. Faithfully, God lures the people into being a people who will reflect the divine character. Insofar as the people become a society of justice, the image of God is created in human society; insofar as they fall away, the image is distorted. Always the constancy of God is like a goad, pricking the people into relationships which exhibit justice, and therefore fulfill the covenant.

The revelation includes divine wrath against injustice, but of course this simply intensifies the revelation of God as love. Justice in the Old Testament is seen in the concrete caring of the people for each other within society; justice involves appropriate relationships toward well-being. When the people act against justice, they act against love: the disadvantaged are cheated and downtrodden still further; the stability of a just society is undermined; all become impoverished in spirit. If God is indifferent to human society, then of course we cannot expect any divine response to such a situation. Instead, the Old Testament reveals the intensity of God's care for human well-being, and the prophets thunder down divine wrath against injustice.

But more often than not, the wrath revealed is human as well as divine. Consider one Old Testament illustration of wrath in the thirteenth chapter of Hosea: "Samaria shall bear her guilt because she has rebelled against her God," writes the prophet, "they shall fall by the sword, their little ones shall be dashed in pieces, and their pregnant women ripped open." The actions are clearly those of warfare. Humanity, not God, devised the atrocities mentioned. Assyrians wield the sword and decimate the towns and villages. How is it divine wrath?

In a process world, God acts with the world as it is, leading it toward what it can be. The aims of God will transcend the given, but must also reflect the given. When injustice is a violation of relationships, not only between neighboring persons but also between neighboring nations, then violence follows as the most concrete form of that violation. What kinds of aims can God give in a context of violation and violence? For the world has determined its course. It may be that the slight avenue of transcendence open is that the cause/effect relationship between violation and violence be seen in such a way that both will be denounced. The effects of injustice can serve to reveal the evil that is the heart of injustice. Thus even though the momentum of violence has built to an irreversible destruction, the very naming of that destruction as "wrath" is the grace that denounces it in favor of a better way.

In Hosea, the "better way" follows immediately upon the above

text: "Return, O Israel, to the Lord your God, for you have
stumbled because of your iniquity . . . I will heal their faithless-
ness; I will love them freely, for my anger has turned from them. I
will be as dew to Israel, he shall blossom as the lily. . . ." In the
midst of these ascriptions to the love of God is a single phrase that
calls attention to the nature of God's love: "In thee the orphan
finds mercy." Justice in relationships so that none are without help
is the way of God; it flashes like a jewel against the contrary ways
of injustice. Divine wrath turns the evil of human injustice into a
call for justice; judgment is the opportunity for salvation. And in
the painful exigencies of the direct human condition, God's nature
is revealed.

The revelation through Jesus builds upon the revelation through
the Old Testament; Christian history builds upon Israelite history.
The richness of Judaism made Christianity possible. The revelation
of the nature of God, seen and still seen through a whole people,
was also given through the one person, Jesus. Through this one,
yet another people are given birth so that they too might reflect the
image of God.

How can such a singular revelation be given? Bear in mind the
dynamics of the initial aim in process thought. The harmony of
God is adapted to the conditions of the world. Continuity and
novelty mark the aim: the preparation of the past makes a particular aim possible so there is continuity; transcendence of the past in
the direction of increasing reflection of the harmony of God makes
the aim novel. The past and the future unite in the initial aim,
leading to the creation of the present.

Through these dynamics, it would be possible for one person so
to reveal both the nature of God and the nature of what we are
called to be as human beings that we could call this person "Immanuel, God with us." Incarnation is coherent in process thought,
given the following historical conditions.

First, the past must be such that there is a readiness for this
revelation. "The fullness of time" is absolutely essential, for all
aims must have some continuity with the past.

Second, the content of the initial aim toward incarnation must be
a full communication of the nature of God. In general revelation, as
noted earlier, there is a hiddenness to God since aims adapted to
the world are generally more reflective of the world than of God.
An aim toward incarnation must overcome this, although in continuity with the preparation for such a revelation. The full purpose of

God which defines the self-created divine nature must be communicated in the initial aim.

Third, the initial aim would have to be adopted fully by the recipient. Usually, the aims from God are adapted by the world. Incarnation would require a full conformity to the aim, for to the degree that the recipient deviated from the aim, to that degree incarnation would fail. This condition means that God's full communication of the divine nature in the initial aim would have to be met by a full acceptance of that nature in the subjective aim of the finite occasion. To use an expression fully developed in several process christologies, the finite occasion would be "co-constituted" by the divine and human aim.*

Fourth, if all of this is to be achieved by a human person incarnation cannot be a once-for-all happening but must be a continuous process. In process thought a person is not one actual occasion but a series of many, many occasions. For incarnation to occur, there would have to be an assent to incarnation in every moment of existence. Incarnation would have to be continuous.

Notice that in no way would such an incarnation do away with the humanity of the one through whom incarnation took place. To the contrary, the humanity of the person would be highlighted. If human nature is perfected in a just society, and if God's aims, flowing from the divine character, are always toward love and justice, then any person in whom full incarnation was a continuous reality would always be living in the perfection of love and justice. The humanity of this person would be brought to perfection.

Furthermore, incarnation in a process world could only take place through the cooperation of the individual. The dynamics of incarnation are no different than the dynamics of any actual entity; the difference is in the content of the aim and the quality of the response. Incarnation would be cooperative, bringing the full freedom of both God and the world to perfection. Therefore, neither through the dynamics of the aim nor through the content of the aim is there any abrogation of the full humanity of the one manifesting the nature of God for us.

Jesus is born in "the fullness of time" in Israelite history. His people have over a thousand years of the covenant behind them,

---

* The unique ability of process categories to illumine christology has long been explored. John B. Cobb, Jr., and David Ray Griffin have developed the topic in *Process Theology: An Introductory Exposition* (Philadelphia: Westminster Press, 1976).

deeply ingraining them with the awareness of God's nature as love and justice. Furthermore, Jesus is born at a time when the people were deeply restless in the bonds of political oppression; expectations were high for a redemption wrought by God. Some expected a single person, a Messiah, to be appointed by God to break the bonds of oppression and bring in the kingdom of God. Many expected this action to be a cataclysmic event, overturning the natural order in a re-creation of the world according to divine love and justice. The resurrection of the dead would signal the advent of this new order.

All of this is in the past of Jesus. But the aims of God transcend the past, and can bring about deeper reflections of the divine harmony than the past alone makes possible. That this happened in the case of Jesus is evidenced by the use the apostle Paul makes of the phrase "much more" in the fifth chapter of Romans. Again and again he turns to this superlative to speak of the abundance of grace received from God through Christ. He writes, of course, from the viewpoint of the resurrection, as do the gospel writers. The resurrection becomes the lens through which the story of Jesus is viewed; through the resurrection, Jesus is seen not only as the expected deliverer from oppression but as the manifestation of God for us.

We, too, look through that lens to know God. In the light of the resurrection, we encounter the life of Jesus in the pages of the gospels. What is revealed? We read of Jesus dining with tax collectors, apparently heedless of his society's disapproval of such people. Exclusion of the oppressor, not consort with the oppressor, was the proper behavior of the day—as, indeed, it appears to be of every day and every people. But Jesus reaches out in acceptance toward those who were shunned for political reasons.

We read of his acceptance of the lame, the blind, the deaf, and his ministry is marked by healing. Scholars of the New Testament period tell us that at the time of Jesus there were many communities established for the purpose of anticipating the kingdom of God; a mark of many of these was a "purity" which excluded all of those with physical handicaps. In contrast to this, the gospels portray Jesus as calling out to those who were lame, blind, deaf. Not exclusion, but an inclusion which frequently included healing was his attitude. Thus his acceptance of others reaches not only toward those shunned politically, but toward those who were shunned for their misfortunes.

Sinners are called by Jesus, and are accepted even prior to repentance. The story of Zaccheus tells us, "He has gone in to be the guest of a man who is a sinner." The result of Jesus' graciousness is that Zaccheus does indeed repent and reform: "and Jesus said to him, 'Today salvation has come to this house, since he also is a son of Abraham. For the son of man came to seek and to save the lost' " (Luke 19:9–10). Jesus accepts the unworthy.

The gospel of John speaks of Jesus' encounter with a woman from Samaria, and here the proscriptions against her would have been on three counts: she was a woman, and therefore not a proper participant in theological dialogue; she was an outcast due to her lifestyle ("you have had five husbands, and he whom you now have is not your husband" from John 4:18); and she was of the despised half-breed people, the Samaritans. Yet Jesus enters into a spirited dialogue with this woman, revealing directly for the first time in this gospel that he is the Messiah who is called Christ. The nature of God and of worship and of salvation form the substance of the dialogue. The disciples, returning from the town, are astounded. Jesus overturns the accepted boundaries of society in his openness toward women.

There is a reciprocity to the love that is given by Jesus. He gives, seemingly unendingly, but he also receives in a way which is so simple that it often escapes our notice. In the gospel of Mark there is an unobtrusive verse in the very first chapter: Simon's mother-in-law was sick, and Jesus was told of her ailment. In verse 31 we read: "And he came and took her by the hand and lifted her up, and the fever left her; and she served them." He gives; he receives. The Samaritan woman gave him water, and he drank; a blind man, healed, followed him to serve and be served; Zaccheus, the sinner, shared his food with him; the disciples gave as well as received friendship. In such simple modes of daily interdependence, Jesus gives and receives, receives and gives, in the reciprocity of love.

There is also an important note of judgment in the love of Jesus. We can see this by focusing in on one particular gospel story, the account in the seventh chapter of Luke. Jesus is at dinner in the home of Simon the Pharisee. During the meal, "a woman of the city who was a sinner" enters, and begins to minister to Jesus in a strange way: she "began to wet his feet with her tears, and wiped them with the hair of her head, and kissed his feet, and anointed them with the ointment." The host is indignant: in the text, he is portrayed as despising both the woman and Jesus—the woman because she was "a sinner," and Jesus for not having the discernment to cast her aside. Evidently this indignation was not voiced—that would violate Simon's dignity as host. Despite his reserved silence, the text goes on to say that Jesus answers him.

The answer is both a judgment and a response to Simon's needs. Just as in the Old Testament judgment is an opportunity for salvation, even so Jesus' judgment holds the possibility of a richer mode of existence for Simon. The judgment begins with a parable of two debtors, one owing a large amount, and the other a small amount. The creditor remits the debts of both, whereupon Jesus asks Simon which of the debtors will love the creditor more. The answer, of course, is the one who was forgiven the larger debt. His gratitude will be correspondingly great. The woman, with her fullness of gratitude and love, is a woman who is acting in the knowledge of forgiveness; Simon, with his small love, is unaware of his own need for forgiveness.

Consider Simon's plight. If he excludes the woman from his home and the presence of Jesus, he will preserve his well-ordered world. The woman's presence challenges the way he orders his world. She ought not to be there. But she is, and Simon's own guest receives her attentions. Doesn't this mean that his own exclusiveness is not appropriate? Isn't his own self, along with his valuation of the world, brought into question? His felt need is to condemn both the woman for her way of life and Jesus for accepting her; this would re-establish his prioritized world, and reaffirm his own self-constructed worth.

In a world of full love and justice, the welfare of one affects the welfare of all. To despise the welfare of another is to lessen the welfare of oneself. To lessen the welfare of oneself, in turn, impoverishes the whole. Inexorably, a society of true justice is a society of true love, requiring an extension of well-being throughout the society. By excluding the well-being of the woman from his concern, Simon was impoverishing himself in two ways. On the one hand, he had so drawn the lines of his self-concern that he was in fact a small self—defined by small loving. This diminution of himself was an impoverishment to society: the woman would be ignored or excluded by him, not enriched. On the other hand, Simon's self-limitation was such that he had foreclosed the avenues of his own growth: his exclusion of the other was the reinforcement of the smallness of himself. Had Jesus answered the man at the level of his felt need, and played the part of the gracious guest who conforms to the host's expectations even though those expectations are not shared, then the man would have been left in his smallness. He would have been gratified, no doubt, by the confirmation of his exclusive world, and he would have felt a pleasant affirmation of himself, but he would never have noticed how restricted and impoverished that self was. Nor would he have seen that those restrictions involved him in guilt that placed him as well as the woman in deep need of forgiveness.

Jesus responds judgmentally, revealing Simon's true need. Through the brief parable and through direct confrontation ("you gave me no water for my feet, . . . you gave me no kiss . . . you did not anoint my head with oil . . .") Jesus reproves the man. This very act of judgment against him is witness to Jesus' love, for by awakening Simon to his true need, Jesus provides the catalyst for change. Suddenly Simon has the opportunity to see his smallness, and to break out of his exclusive prison to an inclusiveness of being which can reach out to others, enriching and being enriched in the realization of justice.

Jesus calls the woman and the Pharisee to a new mode of life. If Simon responds to Jesus' judgment, then he must let go of his preestablished values. Letting go one world, he must participate in the creation of another. But if his security is built up out of the very predictability of a world, if his strength is based upon the absoluteness of order and value, how can he let go? How could we? Likewise, Jesus calls upon the woman to "go and sin no more." The implication of the text is that she is a prostitute. Her very livelihood depends upon one mode of life; if she gives it up, where will her next meal come from? How can she live in a world that allows her no other route to physical sustenance? How can she dare to let go? How could we?

The Pharisee requires his preestablished world for the sake of what he perceives to be his psychic survival; the woman requires her preestablished world for the sake of her physical survival. Jesus confronts them both with the demand for a new order; he dares them both to enter a new future. He turns their worlds upside down, and the overturning is fearsome and dangerous, calling for the terror of sacrificed security. It is as if he asks them both to walk upon water, for all surety and balance and safety are gone when the foundations become fluid. How can they dare such a thing?

The foundations of the new world to which he calls them are

simply the foundations of the interdependence of love. If love always looks to the real needs of the other, then love cannot predetermine what those needs will be and how those needs will be met. Love must always take its boundaries from that-which-is and that-which-can-be; there is an openness of vision in an interdependent society of love and justice that cannot be restricted by past situations, even though those situations might have been valid responses to love in their own time.

Ideally, such openness and risk may all be very well; in the real world, how can we dare this? In the gospel account, the daring seems to follow simply from the presence of Jesus. Jesus, embodying that kind of love, becomes the new foundation. It is as if the active presence of Jesus is a reassurance offered against the terror of an insecure future, as if the old foundations of the ordered world can only give way because of the dynamic reality of this person. Part of the terror of a new future is the fear that it may not be a *possible* future: what if we let go of the past only to find out that the future we dared cannot be? Where are we then in terms of security? Will not our last condition be worse than our first? And so we imprison ourselves in the past against the terror of a new order. Jesus calls the Pharisee and the woman alike to a new order, but his very call to them is from his embodiment of that order. Jesus *is* living in love; Jesus *is* openness to the other; Jesus *is* the judgment calling us to our true mode of being. Jesus, extending a call to a new order, is himself that order, and therefore a true witness to its real possibility. Therefore he becomes the ground of our daring to attempt such a future ourselves. Jesus becomes the firmness in the water, and we, too, can walk.

No matter which gospel text we take to consider the life of Jesus, we are confronted with one who consistently manifests the love to which he calls others. He breaks down all partitions that divide humans from each other; he embodies a love that is just, and a love that therefore variously exhibits judgment, affirmation, service, or sharing, depending upon the context of love. But this is the life which reveals the nature of God for us; this is the life which offers a concrete vision of the reality to which God calls us; this is the revelation of God to us for the sake of conforming us to that divine image. If we see in Jesus a revelation of God for us, then the way Jesus loves is the way God loves.

To see the life of Jesus as God with us, incarnate in him, is to lift all that we see in that revelation to ultimacy. Consider the implications of this by looking again at the story of the Pharisee and the woman. The reality of Jesus, living the love to which he calls the others, enables the others to trust the viability of that kind of living and to dare to create such a world. But Jesus is the incarnation of God: does this not imply that such openness in love and justice describes the very foundations of reality? If *God* is this kind of love for us, what is there left to fear? God relates to all reality, calling each element in the world toward reflection of a divine image which is love and justice in relationships. Since it is God who so calls us, and since God, in keeping with the divine nature, exerts this lure throughout existence, then our actions in accordance with love and justice are in conformity with the direction of the universe. To act in love is to act *with* creation; to act against love is to act *against* creation. If God is the love we see in Jesus, then all God's actions are in accordance with love. Insofar as the future to which we are called is one lived in love, the future receives its ground in God. All finite forms of security to which we cling against the uncertainties of love are revealed as false securities through the power of the revelation of God in Jesus. When through Jesus we see God as love, then the confidence Jesus could inspire in the woman and the Pharisee is shown to be a confidence grounded in the nature of God—and thus a confidence that is appropriate to every person in every situation calling for ever-new forms of particular love.

Jesus reveals the nature of God as love, and the nature of God's love. Theologically, how do we translate this revelation of God into an understanding of God as God? There are two considerations involved: first, we must see that the fullness of the love revealed in Jesus is attributed to the nature of God; but second, we must be careful to preserve the "Godness" of God. The fullness of the love that Jesus reveals includes an openness to others which crosses the boundaries we define to divide us, a judgment which opens us to the richness of forgiveness and growth, inviting us to togetherness in giving and receiving. How is this love God's love? Jesus, as a human being, manifests this love; therefore, the love is not alien to our humanity—difficult and challenging, yes, but certainly a possible mode of beng human. When we translate the qualities to our understanding of God, do we then make God human too? Do we fall into the problem of anthropomorphism, of describing God in human terms so that what we are saying of God is essentially no more than we can say about humanity? Does the "Godness" of God disappear?

Process theology contributes to resolution of the dilemma with the understanding of "actual entity" as a model for reality. Human beings are constituted by many actual entities, as are all the other things we see in our environment. The description of the actual entity is more basic than the description of the human being. Furthermore, the dynamics of the entity are the route whereby differences can be expressed. While the dynamics are the same for all entities, the content selected and unified in each entity accounts for the differences of things. The same dynamics will enter into the description of entities in a human being and entities in a puff of smoke—or the singular entity which is God, as was noted in chapter 4. The import of this for theology struggling with the problem of anthropomorphism is that now we have a model that is more basic than the human being for a discussion of the reality of God.

The clearest example of the way in which the model helps in overcoming anthropomorphism is in the problem of the sexuality of God. Naturally the biblical texts must speak of God in masculine or feminine terms—human language has no other way of expressing personality. Given cultural understandings of the role and rule of males in the ancient Hebrew world, of course the pronoun chosen was male. Yet again and again the texts of the Old Testament portray God as beyond sexuality. And while masculine pronouns and imagery are generally used to describe God, feminine imagery is also used—God is like a mother in many an Old Testament text. Despite the qualifiers, however, the tendency has been to reduce God to maleness, such that theologies are not only anthropomorphic in this area, but andromorphic as well. When the model for understanding God is humanity, then the features of humanity are projected into deity even when those features are clearly inappropriate to deity. Process thought can avoid this since it portrays such things as sexuality as belonging to composites of entities, whether animal or human, and not to the actual entity per se. Therefore, by discussing God in terms of an actual entity rather than as a series of entities such as are required to constitute human beings, we can utilize the dynamics of the model to express the nature of God in nonanthropomorphic terms. Those features which belong distinctly to humanity—such as the sexuality of Jesus or any other human being—stay clearly within the realm of composite entities, which is the only place where they can occur. It is impossible, in a process metaphysic, to translate strictly human features to deity.

How, then, is the nature of God revealed through God's presence in Jesus? Consider Jesus' openness to others in relation to the sense in which God, through the consequent nature, feels every reality in the universe precisely as that reality feels itself. What is added to the philosophical statement by the biblical revelation is that the openness to all which is stated philosophically is a loving openness. Jesus reveals the character of God as love. In Jesus, openness to the other is in the mode of love; in God, openness to the other which feels the other regardless of place, position, or power is an openness of love. Jesus is open to the other with a will toward the well-being of the other: the openness of God through the consequent nature must therefore be an openness which wants the well-being of the other. Process philosophy requires that every prehension be felt with a certain "subjective form" or qualifying feeling. The revelation of God in Jesus tells us that God's subjective form in feeling the world is love.

Jesus loves in judgment, refusing to affirm actions or desires that cut against the well-being of the self or others. Such love is stern and strong: stern in its determined will toward true well-being, and strong enough to withstand the anger, ill will, or defensiveness called up against such judgments. How is God like that on a process model? Jesus loves with a mutuality which invites giving and receiving; how is God like that?

The fullness of the revelation of God does not stop with the life of Jesus, but continues through the crucifixion and resurrection. In order to answer the questions of the preceding paragraph and to discuss the fullness of God's answer to sin, it is necessary to go on to this further discussion.

10

CRUCIFIED

THERE is a temptation to exempt the crucifixion from the fullness of the revelation of God in Jesus. Did not Jesus himself say, "My God, my God, why hast thou forsaken me?" while on that cross? Theologically, this sentence has lent itself to the interpretation that God is not in Jesus on the cross: the revelation of God would then be limited to the life and resurrection of Jesus, while the cross simply reveals God's wrath against sin. We cannot, however, adequately account for the judging and transforming power of the love manifested in Jesus without looking at the cross as a revelation of the nature of God.

Consider first the sense in which the crucifixion is the crowning manifestation of love in the life of Jesus. One could deeply admire the love that Jesus manifests prior to the cross, for Jesus loves consistently. He encounters moments of fear, such as in Nazareth when he was nearly stoned; he experiences weariness and thirst, such as at the Samaritan well; he knows hunger, for he sent the disciples to buy food. Such weakness does not prevent his loving, but after all, such weakness is common to humanity and can be endured by strong people. And Jesus surely knows the presence of God in him, since he is the revelation of God—perhaps love is easier for Jesus! The cross disallows this mitigation, precisely because love continues not only in the pain of death, but in the pain of the sense of Godforsakenness.

The four evangelists give a composite recollection of the last words of Jesus on the cross. There are academic complexities of interpretation involved, but if we look at the words in their simple givenness, they give a startling witness to the love of Jesus. The earliest evangelist, Mark, sounds the theme with the terrible words, "My God, my God, why hast thou forsaken me?" Matthew repeats the sentence—and it is the only sentence recorded by two evangelists. Pain crowds out the sense of God's presence as hunger, thirst, and weariness did not; surely a pain which penetrates to the depths of Jesus' spirit will be sufficient to kill even so strong a love as he has shown.

With this background, it is a shock to read the words ascribed to Jesus by Luke and John. John begins his account of Jesus on the cross with the words, "Woman, behold your son," and then to the disciple, "behold your mother!" Jesus on the cross still pours forth love in the care of his mother. If we try to assimilate such a text with the qualification that one can care for one's family even in the midst of pain and death, how do we understand the first sentence told us by Luke? "Father, forgive them, they know not what they do." On the cross, in the midst of Godforsakenness, Jesus still loves with the strength and insight to perceive the needs of those around him. That love embraces not only a mother and disciple but the very ones who are killing him. How is there room in Jesus to respond to the needs of others when his own needs scream out his death?

Yet again Luke records another word, this time of comfort to the thief, and we might well feel undone at the depth and inexhaustibility of the love of Jesus. Neither spiritual nor physical Godforsakenness weakens the strength of his loving. On that cross we see supremely the power of love which is revealed by Jesus to be the nature of God. The seeds of resurrection are sown on the cross as love refuses to succumb to distortion or annihilation; Jesus continues to love, through deepest pain.

Does God love so strongly, even in the midst of pain? How can this intensity of the manifestation of love be exempted from the revelation of the nature of God? Through the cross we see not only that God's love is stronger than death, but that God in love endures the pain of death, and that God's love is unconquered by death.

The dynamics of the process model force a strict application of the revelation on the cross to the nature of God. This can be explained by digressing, returning to an illustration of evil given in chapter 8. A young man knocked down an old woman in order to steal her purse. As she fell she broke her hip. On the basis of the revelation of God in Jesus, God is open toward us; God feels us with love. This love is or can be a judgment that wills our well-being, and the crucifixion of Jesus is involved in the revelation of this. How is this applied to the young man and the woman? How is it applied to God?

In a process universe, God launches every occasion of existence with an aim toward its good. This aim is one that is shaped to the particularities of the occasion. The earlier discussion of revelation suggested that the aim reflects not only God, but the conditions of the world. In relation to that young man, God feels his whole past world, and fashions an aim for him which gives him the best possible way for going beyond that world. To say the phrase "best possible" describes the limitations of the aim, for clearly that which is absolutely best—say, for instance, that the young man shall suddenly become a model of industry and virtue—is not immediately possible. Were God to give such an aim to the man, the man would have no hope at all, for there would be no realistic way beyond the power of his past. Despair would increase the evil of his lot.

Assume that the man has not experienced much human love, that he is exposed to violence, that he has not had practice in trusting others, let alone in empathizing with them. In short, while his life is necessarily relational in an ontological sense, it is nonrelational in an emotional sense. The man lives as if he were an island in the universe, with all relationships appearing as the sea that isolates him. Violation and violence have become his pattern of existence, reinforcing his isolation.

Is he responsible for this situation? To a degree he is, and to a degree he isn't. While he did not create the situation into which he was born, he perpetuates it every time he resists the possibility, however slight, to begin to transform and transcend his world. Given the enormity of his situation, the possibilities for transcendence will likely be small—sometimes the best in a particular situation is bad from any other standpoint. If that best is actualized, however, the next "best" will be better, leading further into transformation. The man is responsible, as we all are, for actualizing or modifying the best that is given in each moment.

Responsibility is a matter of degree due to the relational role of the past. Determinism and freedom intertwine in a relational universe; as noted in chapter 3, we are not responsible for a past we did not create, and we cannot avoid that past. Inexorably, we feel its weight. Our responsibility lies in what we do with the past. If the press of society is such that what the man in our illustration can do is little, then his responsibility is correspondingly lessened. When his alternatives to change that past are wide, then his responsibility increases. However, every response he gives is in itself a force that he adds to the past, and that will affect his next moment of response. Responsibility is therefore made more complex, for he is not only responsible for what he does in the present, but he is also responsible to some degree for what *can* be done in the present. One might say that responsibility increases with age, for our own dealings with the past as we created that past add to the width or narrowness of our possibilities in the present.

The man's habituated acceptance of violence is his own responsibility, albeit shared with a society which was conducive to that mode of being. The man is bent on robbing the woman, regardless of its effect upon the woman. God's faithfulness would be manifested in the given alternative to regard the woman; if the character of the man is such that he is, at that moment, incapable of seeing her as a person with her own needs, deserving respect and care, then the aim of God will be toward a step that might eventually lead toward such a capacity. The aim, fitted to the occasion, may simply be to do that which is within the young man's possibilities, which is to refrain from this violation. And the young man ignores the possibility, contradicting the aim and nature of God and relational existence. He violates the woman.

God feels the young man precisely as the young man feels himself; this is entailed in God's openness to the world through the consequent nature. But God not only feels the man in his own self-constitution, God feels him in light of what could have been possible had the man actualized the initial aim. God feels the actuality and the might-have-been, together. This means that God feels the man with more pain than the man feels himself, for God feels the disparity in a way which the man himself has rejected. And God is crucified.

Consider the content given to God through God's openness to the woman. The woman, too, responds to a past; her past includes the effects upon her life of poverty. Her fixed income barely extends to cover the rent for her room, let alone the luxury of food. Relationships are impoverished, for her husband is long since dead, and her children are grown, too involved in fighting their own battles with poverty to give much assistance to the old woman who is, after all, irritable and quarrelsome much of the time. God feels the pain of her existence, both in the way she experiences it and in relation to the might-have-been that has marked her personal and social alternatives along the way.

The young man dashes toward her, and the woman experiences

the shock first of fear and then of pain as she crashes to the ground. Oddly enough, her thoughts circle in a frenzy about the loss of food—how can she buy supper now, with her money gone? But her situation is far more dire, for her bones are brittle, and break in the fall.

To write about such things and read about such things in a book on theology may seem strange, but no theology can afford to ignore the concrete reality of such facts, for they happen, and they happen daily in all their ugliness, in all their pitiableness, in all their pain. God feels the world. If God feels the world, God feels *this* world, not as an abstraction but as a reality. God feels *this* woman's pain, both in the impoverishment of her body and of her spirit through the past and in the sharp terror and agony of the present. And God is crucified.

Notice the severe implication that follows from the fact that God feels the effects of the society upon both the young man and the woman. Society is always felt by God directly as personal, and only indirectly as impersonal. For instance, we might hear of the above crime, feel a monentary pang, and then dismiss it from our personal lives—it becomes another impersonal fact in the cold cruel world. We impersonalize the society. Impersonalization need not be dehumanization, for impersonalization may be one of the ways of coping with societal evil. The society, bearing the weight of the past, has a force greater than any individual within that society; when society perpetuates evils, one can bear with it on the grounds that society is impersonal, and therefore less culpable, and therefore perhaps more bearable. Since God feels the society through every individual within the society, God feels the effects and the perpetuation of the conditions conducive to such effects. God therefore feels the society personally, through each individual within it. The mitigation wherewith we suffer or allow societal evils to continue unaddressed can be no mitigation in the feeling of God. God feels the effects directly, both as given and as received; God can only feel the society as impersonal insofar as God feels our own impersonalization of it. Thus for God impersonalization is indirect; personalization, direct. This means that the sins of society are directly sins against God. And God is crucified.

If God is in Jesus, then God reveals through him that every sin is a sin felt by God and is therefore a sin against God; every pain is felt by God, and is therefore God's pain. The dreadful truth revealed in the crucifixion of Jesus Christ is that the world crucifies God. We crucify God. Each pain we feel and each pain we inflict enters into the reality of the God who is for us.

Process theology gives expression to this revelation through the consequent nature of God. In God's supreme openness to the world, God feels each actuality, and in the feeling re-enacts the actuality of the world within the divine nature. My pain, in being my pain, is also God's pain.

The incredible reality revealed on the cross is that God's love does not cease in pain, not even the pain of death. We easily assert that God continues to love us in *our* pain, but what the theology of the cross expressed in process terms requires us to acknowledge is that God continues to love in *God's* pain. The theology pushes us even further to illumine why this pain is the price of our redemption.

The answer is deceptively simple. God fashions possibilities for us that will lead us toward reflection of the divine image. These possibilities must be real for us; they must be ways in which we can actually go, given the reality of who and where we are. God must know us and our situations in order to know what possibilities will be truly *our* possibilities. How well must God know us in order to give us the appropriate possibilities? Will an objective knowledge do? But what of those hidden realities within us, indiscernible to the most penetrating objective eye—what of those aspects of ourselves that are hidden even to us? God knows us well enough to give us the possibilities which can lead to our transformation because God knows us from the inside out, as well as from the outside in. God feels us as we feel ourselves, even including those depths which we do not allow into conscious feeling. God's full openness to who we are involves God in the pain of who we are, but this unsurpassable truth of God's knowledge is the means whereby God knows precisely what possibilities will be redemptive for us in the next moment of our existence. Through God's crucifixion, God provides us with a resurrection.

11

RISEN

THE edges of God are tragedy; the depths of God are joy, beauty, resurrection, life. Resurrection answers crucifixion; life answers death. If Jesus reveals the nature of God in his life and crucifixion, he most surely also reveals God through resurrection.

A curious aspect in speaking of resurrection is that the New Testament speaks about the results of resurrection, but not about resurrection itself. If we wish to talk of the way Jesus reveals God in his life, we can point to nearly any text in the gospels to see the content of that revelation. Likewise, to speak of God revealed in the crucifixion draws us to the long passion narratives that form the crux of each gospel. But when we wish to understand the glory of the resurrection, we are turned back. Not a single gospel account describes the details of the resurrection. There is no privileged discussion about the exact event. We must look instead to the results of resurrection, whether in the resurrection appearances or in the faith and zeal of the apostles as they proclaim the dawn of the new age heralded by the resurrection of Jesus. The resurrection itself is hidden from our view.

If the immediacy of the resurrection is hidden, the results are not. In fact, the resurrection might be considered through the metaphor of the sun. We cannot look directly at the sun, for the brightness would blind us—our eyes are not suited to that strength of light. Yet the sun, which we cannot see directly, illumines all else, and in its light we make our way in the world. We cannot look directly at the resurrection because it is not given for us to see. Nevertheless, it illumines the entire landscape of the New Testament: the resurrection is the confirmation of that which Jesus revealed in his life and death, and it is the catalyst that transforms the disciples, releasing the power that led to the foundation of the church.

Confirmation and transformation are thus both involved as results of the resurrection. There is an apparent tension between the two words, for confirmation appears to be an affirmation of that which has come to be, while transformation is a movement beyond. Both elements are clearly in the resurrection, and the resurrection, like the life and crucifixion of Jesus, must be taken as revelatory of the divine nature.

By focusing upon the story of the resurrection appearance to Thomas, we might understand these two facets as they apply to an understanding of God for us. In the gospel of John, Thomas plays the role of the misunderstanding disciple, first with regard to the raising of Lazarus, and second with regard to the resurrected Jesus. In both cases, Jesus' answer to Thomas underscores the purposes of God. In the Second account, Jesus has appeared to ten of the disciples, Thomas being absent. Upon being told of the appearance, Thomas scoffs, claiming that he will not believe until he sees the marks of the crucifixion on the one the others claim is Jesus. Accordingly, Jesus appears again and invites. Thomas to touch the scars; Thomas' response is to exclaim "My Lord and my God," recognizing at last the presence of God in Jesus.

In the account, the scars of the crucifixion mediate the truth of the resurrection. But the scars belong to the preresurrection existence; the scars are the result of pain and death, yet they are present as well in the resurrection. The transformation of Jesus that occurred in resurrection is no *creatio ex nihilo,* no absolute new beginning. Rather, the transformation is fashioned through the experience of the crucifixion. Transformation bears the marks of the process leading to the very need for transformation; there is a continuity with the pain of the past in the resurrection life, for the pain of the past adds its shape to the transformation.

If the resurrection is both a confirmation and a transformation, the crucifixion appears to be a central link holding the two elements together. The resurrection power of God does not annihilate the past, it transforms the past. That which was, is affirmed, but given a new dimension, a new context, a new direction.

The dynamics of process thought can help us to express this. Remember the way in which the model describes God's feeling of any occasion in the world, and the unification of that feeling with the primordial vision:

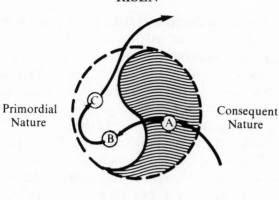

Primordial
Nature

Consequent
Nature

DIAGRAM VII

God's feeling of the world ("A") is through the consequent nature. As explained in the previous chapter, God feels the world precisely as it occurs, with the result that God's feeling can aptly be described as a crucifixion: our pain is ultimately God's pain as well; the edges of God are tragedy. To continue with our illustration of the injured woman, God feels her in that moment of pain as she feels herself; her suffering is God's suffering as well. But this moment at the edge of God is but the beginning of God's feeling of the world. In the process dynamic, every feeling must be integrated with all other feelings in terms of what the experiencer, the subject, chooses to be. With God, that choice of being is primordial, occurring eternally through the valuation of all possibilities in harmony. God does not decide the divine character on the basis of the consequent nature, but God *is* what God is through the primordial nature. The feelings of the world must be integrated into God's character. This means that "A"—the woman in pain—must be integrated into God's character. This means that "A"—the woman in pain—must be integrated with God's vision of harmony. In the process, resurrection *must* occur, for God *is* resurrection through the power of the primordial nature.

The woman is felt in relation to all other feelings in God— feelings of the young man, feelings of the woman's past, feelings of all the world—and primarily, the woman is felt in relation to the eternal harmony of God. This integration moves God's feeling of the woman through the everlasting concrescence of God into the primordial harmony, the infinite resources of God ordered in goodness. This movement is represented by "B" on the diagram, and represents God's own inner redemption of that woman's pain. This redemptive process is resurrection in the sense that there has been a transformation of the woman from her finite context to her infinite context in God—the divine resources are brought to bear, integrating the feelings of that woman into divine harmony.

This integration is hidden in God, but the results of it are given to the world through what is marked on the diagram as "C." God feels a transformation for this woman in two respects: first with regard to her presence in God, but also with regard to the possibilities for her finite existence as her life continues in the world. "C" will be marked *both* by the reality of the woman's context—her age, her place in society, her past creation of herself in her personality and character—*and* by possibilities for her transformation; that is to say, those elements deeply within the resources of God which can apply to a finite form of transformation, mirroring in a finite way the divine transformation. God feels the resurrection of the woman both as actual within the divine nature and as possible for the world. The one will be perfect, the other will be an adaptation of that perfection to particularities of finite existence. There is a "best" for the woman, even in her harsh circumstances, and this "best" will bear the marks of both the world and God, leading her toward transformation.

The marks of pain cannot be abstracted in resurrection. Imagine the possible modes of resurrection which might be given to the woman: perhaps the most immediate would be the simple expedient of unconsciousness, blocking out the immediacy of pain. As we try to imagine further transformations open to the woman, we must be guided by the resurrection nature of God, which according to the revelation of Jesus is a depth and strength of love. It is possible that the woman might be taken to a hospital to receive care, and in that context encounter others who also need care. It is possible that because of her own pain, she might empathize with another in his or her pain; receiving care, she might give care. We might further speculate along the path of the reality of love to consider the possibility that upon release from the hospital, her attitude and actions with her family might be different.

The possibility of such paths would be finite reflections of the redemptive power of God, leading the woman toward a finite mode of resurrection living and loving. If the woman actualizes such possibilities, she will experience a transformation of her pain that is nevertheless purchased through pain. The shape of her sensitivities will be direct inheritors of the scars she has received, and will bear the imprint of pain transcended. Whether or not this happens would depend upon a complexity of circumstances, primarily the response of the woman to the opportunity. Her habituated responses might hinder her movement into transformation, or keep her transformation to a low level—but insofar as it occurs, she will be living in the power of the resurrection, made available to her through the character of God. That God *is* this power is revealed by Jesus in the reality of his resurrection.

The revelation of God that takes place through Jesus' life, crucifixion, and resurrection is one that takes us to increasing depths of the divine nature. That is, in the life of Jesus we see a manifestation of God's love—openness transcending boundaries, judgment making possible forgiveness and salvation, mutuality in giving and receiving. The quality of God's love is given expression in Jesus. In the crucifixion, we encounter the raw power of this love: its source is beyond all finite means of sustenance, for neither physical nor spiritual pain can destroy this love. God's love is self-generated in God's own self-definition. God's love endures through pain and death, inexorably reaching toward the well-being of the other. In resurrection, the resources of love are revealed, but the resources are not separate from God's love, as if God surveyed the resources, and brought them to bear as so many bandaids for the world's ills. Rather, God *is* the resource of love. In process terms, the primordial nature of God—God's own valuation of all things in a togetherness which is beauty and well-being—provides the great resource whereby God is the power of resurrection. But of course God *is* the primordial nature; the vision is not outside of God, but is the very self-creation of God. Therefore the final revelation of God in Jesus is to reveal the nature of God's love as transformative, which is to say the nature of God as transformative. God is not only the power of resurrection, God *is* resurrection. Resurrection depends upon the reality of God, not simply as that which God can do, but as that which God is.

To see this resurrection nature in terms of love and on the basis of the gospel is to say that the fullness of God in Jesus is seen in Jesus' expression of the nature of God. Life, crucifixion, and resurrection take the revelation deeper and deeper, until finally we are led, not simply to a description of God but to the mystery of God as God. And that mystery is an inexhaustible love, manifested in a power that both confirms and transforms the world.

In concluding the section on the life of Jesus, questions were raised which could not be addressed until after a consideration of crucifixion and resurrection. Jesus' love toward others involved components of openness, judgment, and mutuality. How do these qualities translate to God without reducing God to humanity? More specifically, since the element of openness was dealt with at the time, how do judgment and mutuality apply to the love of God for us? And finally, there is still the question of the problem of sin as defined in chapter 3. How does the revelation of God in Jesus answer the problem of sin?

The love of God is such that God desires our well-being. The transformation process whereby the world is integrated into God is a judgment against that which separates any reality from well-being, and a transformation into the depths of God's love. This will be developed more fully in chapter 17, but what can be said at this point is that just as the gospel allows us to understand the consequent nature in terms of love, it also allows us to understand the concrescence of God as a judgment according to love. The result of this transforming judgment is the final reconciliation of all things in the depths of God. The world, transformed through divine judgment, is made a participant in the divine nature. If the actualized primordial vision of God can be understood to be a harmonious togetherness of all things, then the mutuality that we see in the life of Jesus is no less than a revelation of this divinely achieved togetherness in love. God is love. What the model tells us in abstract terms, the gospel tells us concretely through Jesus. The model gives the dynamics, and the gospel clothes the dynamics with the shape of love. The profound nature of this love is revealed by Jesus. The model simply aids us in understanding it, not simply as embodied in humanity but as qualifying the reality of a God who holds all things together.

How does this revelation bring about salvation, answering the problems of sin? The problem of original sin and the demonic originates in the power of the past over the present. When we experience elements in our past as overwhelming us, cutting off all alternatives, we easily succumb to those elements, incorporating them into our lives. We conform ourselves to the image of that which ensnares us. How does God in Christ answer this problem, delivering us from this form of sin?

There is a threefold answer. First, the actuality of Jesus in history places Jesus in our past. If there are demonic powers threatening to overwhelm us, there is also Jesus. Jesus is a counterforce to the demonic through the simple power of his presence in our past. Jesus is the alternative the demonic denies. Secondly, the power of the crucifixion shouts a witness against the power of the demonic. In revelation through the crucifixion, we encounter the reality that God's love endures all pain, without being conquered or overwhelmed by it. This revelation, when we experience it, defies the ultimacy of the powers threatening us. God, too, experiences those powers—the crucifixion says so. God, too, experiences our terror at the threat—the crucifixion reveals it. But God, experiencing with us, endures the threat unconquered, transforming it in the divine nature into resurrection possibilities for us. Because God endures the threat with us, and because God is stronger than all threats, we, too, can endure and look for the form of resurrection fashioned for our immediate moments.

The third way in which Jesus offers salvation from the demonic is basic to these other two. This is the way of proclamation. In the example of the high school student, the boy succumbed to the powers in his environment and perpetuated them. How is the power of Jesus in the past efficacious for him? How is he to take hold of the nature of God revealed in the crucifixion, deriving from this revelation the courage and power to endure and conquer? His very problem is that the negative past, dictating violation as a way of survival, obliterates all other alternatives, blotting out the reality of the revelation of God. How is Jesus a saving reality in the immediacy of his life?

The answer, of course, is that there is no apparent way in which he experiences Jesus as salvific. But God gives initial aims in every moment, and God knows the alternatives created by grace in the incarnation. God knows the necessity for a finite hearing, a finite seeing; this, after all, is the whole burden of incarnation. In God's care for the whole world, there must be an interrelationship of aims—God will lead the church to proclaim the power of God in our histories. The proclamation, if it is faithful to the incarnation, will be not simply words, but will be through the vibrancy of word and act in unity. The church will be led by God to be an extension of the incarnation, revealing God through the proclamation of Jesus in our society, making that alternative known. God has accomplished the incarnation in history, creating that counterforce in our past. As the church proclaims it with its life, then the power of the incarnation will be mediated in society. Proclamation makes salvation a present reality.

There is also sin in response to the threat of the future as death. Death is threefold, striking at our physical existence, our emotional existence, and our spiritual existence. Our lives, our relationships, our meanings, are all subject to the cancellation of death. How does Jesus save us from the imprisoning walls we build against these threats?

Jesus reveals God as the power of resurrection. The future contains forms of death that frighten us, but the future is not obliterated by death. Rather, the future is resurrection as well. To know this through Jesus is to live into the future, looking for the forms of resurrection God gives us. God is stronger than all our deaths, and this strength is imparted to us so that we can live and die our many deaths. Through resurrection, Jesus is in our future and therefore opens us up to our futures.

Again, this power must be mediated to us through the force of living proclamation. The salvation accomplished through God in Christ takes place in history, and must be mediated to us through our own histories. This must happen through the faithfulness of the church in proclaiming its witness to the resurrection. As the proclamation is heard, that word enters into the immediate past of the hearer, demanding a response. God can then weave that proclamation into the rest of the hearer's past, adapting a relevant initial aim which will lead to transformation. The touch of God which begins every moment of existence can increase the resurrection power for each individual's future. As resurrection becomes applied to one's own personal future, the wall against the future will crack; the distortion will face its own denial, and transformation can begin. Jesus, by revealing the nature of God as resurrection, is the means of salvation from the forms of death. Proclamation makes that salvation a present reality.

There is also the problem of sin in the absolutized self. Whether this takes place through viewing all others as objects for the self, or through viewing the self as the object for all others, absolutizing takes place. In the first instance, the absolute subject, there is a distortion of the reciprocity of interdependent existence in a

process world. In the second instance, the absolute object, there is
again a denial of the way things really are. Both forms of behavior
are imprisoning, cutting one off from the resources of relational
existence. How is there deliverance from this form of sin?

We could look to the crucifixion as giving a salvific revelation
against the power of the demonic; resurrection gives a saving
revelation of God against the power of death. We look to the life of
Jesus for the primary answer to the sin of the absolutized self. This
occurs not simply in seeing Jesus as he interrelated with others in
the pages of the gospel. The answer must be more direct, such that
Jesus is seen in interrelationship with the self. It is as if the Jesus
who looks at Simon or at the weeping woman turns from the page
to look into the eyes of the reader.

How can this happen? Proclamation re-presents the life of Jesus.
But the life of Jesus reveals the nature of God as the one who is for
us in love. The God who encounters us through the pages of a
gospel encounters us still in the faithfulness of the everlasting
divine presence. As the church proclaims the gospel, God is un-
veiled. The living God encounters us in love.

Judgment and salvation are simultaneously present in the encounter. The clarity of love in the gospel is a judgment against
every failure to embody love—and the failure is equally great in
both forms of the absolutized self, whether as subject or object.
But the very process of receiving this judgment is relational: this
means that the judgment has simultaneously broken down the
absolutization of the self. Further, since according to the gospel
the judgment is given through love, the encountered relation is one
of acceptance of the self which nevertheless demands the well-
being of the self. The encounter burns through the false absolutization, opening a way for further relation. Brought into the circle of
relation, one finds the prison of the absolute self already broken.
Judgment is salvation.

One further dimension to the salvation received through the
revelation of God in Christ needs to be noted. When we realize that
Jesus reveals the nature of God, and when we see that this revelation bespeaks God's purposes for the world in pulling that world
toward reflection of the divine image, then our approach to the
world is radically altered in the direction of hope and love and
trust. For instance, consider a vision of reality that sees the world
as a place of blind chance, where forces beyond our control are
always buffeting us, where every plan of reason is as a tiny grain of

sand attempting to be as a full dike holding back the sea of chaos. What hope is there in such a vision, how can it move us toward actions of love? How can it lead to the creation of meaning? Or consider a vision of reality wherein not blind fate, but stern determinism governs the unfolding of human life. As it has been, so shall it be; every cause inexorably produces its effects, and if we but knew all the causes adequately, we would see that the world is precisely as it should be, precisely as it must be. How is there, in such a vision, any catalytic motivation to deep forms of human justice? Would it not be the case that one should simply accept the inevitable, drifting along with the ruthless tides of determinism? Consider again a vision of reality which sees isolated, self-sufficient existence as the supreme value; would not such a vision lead to self-aggrandizement, to a utilization of others in the service of the self? In such a vision, would there not tend to be strict hierarchies of valuation, wherein human beings were valued only insofar as they were deemed self-sufficient—with the richest, of course, then being the most human, and the disadvantaged being excluded from humane consideration?

How one considers the nature of reality profoundly affects one's actions with respect to the self and with respect to society. Jesus reveals the nature of God, and this revelation is of a relational reality—of openness, a judgment toward justice, mutuality: love. What happens matters, and the deepest form of human existence is in the responsibility of relationality oriented toward love. The well-being of each enters into the well-being of all. If this is indeed the way of God with the world, then action in accordance with this revelation is not only reasonable, it is required. As we respond to God in trust, then we dare to hope that love can be enacted in our lives and in society. We will move upon the strength of this trust, hope, and love to contribute our own efforts to building our lives and society in consonance with the vision.

To say this in a process understanding is to speak of the internal effect of our visions of reality. How we think about reality is internal to who we are, not external. Our visions of reality are incorporated into how we are, who we are, what we do. Hence when Jesus gives us a vision of reality that changes the world for us, giving it and us an importance of mattering, then that vision is internalized, changing our entire orientation toward life. The vision of reality given us through Jesus is salvific, changing our self-constitution, catalyzing our actions in and for the world.

Finally, the revelation of God in the world is the presence of God in the world. In process terms, God is revealed through initial aims. As was noted in the discussion, in the usual course of events the aims are cloaked in ambiguity. In Jesus God's aim comes to full expression, and the life of Jesus is such that we see Jesus embodying the full character of God. In Jesus, God is present to us. Because of Jesus, we know that God is always present to us. The singular power of this revelation of God's presence is perhaps best expressed by turning again to the gospels and looking at the disciples.

The disciples experienced the presence of Jesus directly, but their overwhelming response was not one in which there was any apparent primacy to faith. Rather, the disciples seemed forever to misinterpret Jesus—in his death they fled from him, and in his resurrection they were dubious. Nor was their response one of glowing hope, for they frequently misplaced their hopes, looking for self-aggrandizement in illusioned places of esteem and honor. Finally, of course, they fell into despair at the trial and crucifixion of Jesus. The one unfailing response that appears throughout the gospels is the response of love. The deepest power of the revelation of God in Christ is the generating power whereby love calls forth love. This love is the basis of the resurrection and the firstfruit of the resurrection, becoming the ground for trust and hope. The presence of God in Jesus is ultimately the creative power of love, giving birth to love which, in turn, gives birth to love yet again. This response of love called forth by the presence of God is the birth of the church. Like the disciples, the church through the ages frequently fumbles in its trust, falters in its hope; but insofar as the church senses the revelation of God for us as an ultimate presence, an ultimate love, the church, too, answers with its echoing form of love. In love is the renewal of trust and hope.

Part Four

WISDOM

*Christ in God:
A Process Ecclesiology*

12

IDENTITY THROUGH FAITH

IN the cathedral of Notre-Dame de Paris, the light glows golden upon the old walls, so that the ancient stone seems strangely soft. The light leads the eye upward, beyond the stone, to a burst of spiraling light, magnificent color: the great windows of Notre Dame. In a splendor striving to foretell the glory of the heavenly Jerusalem, where "the walls are enhanced with all manner of precious jewels," this earthly Jerusalem tells the story of the church within the drama of creation, fall, incarnation, ascension, and judgment. In stone and glass the tale is told, and the deep tones of the organ fill the cathedral with sound, that the medium of music shall join in the magnificent telling.

In the midst of this, there is a strange incompletion. Not all of the windows participate in the telling of the story; some have only the bare outlines of color in a slim border, with the inner portions of the window but a faint translucent green. They await their transformation into history, when they too shall spring into the vibrancy of color through which to tell their portion of the story which is the church.

In this incompletion, a profound note is sounded. By speaking of incarnation, of the sense in which God is in Christ, christology begins. In speaking of ascension, of the sense in which Christ is in God, christology is completed through its very incompletion. The fullness of christology waits upon the church, as God mediates the benefits of Christ to the world. This appropriation of Christ is the ongoing completion of christology; it is also, of course, the doctrine of the church which is ecclesiology.

Part III presented the dynamics whereby God was present in Christ revealed to us. In a process universe, however, God not only affects the world, but the world affects God. God is present to the world, and the world is present to God. That return dynamic must now become the focus of discussion in order to develop a doctrine of the church.

Recapitulating the model, God fashions initial aims for the world by integrating the actuality of the world within the divine nature. God's aim toward harmony will inexorably enter into the initial aims given to the world, but each particular aim is conditioned by what has happened in the world. Otherwise, there would be no relevance to the aim, and no real persuasive power. God works with the world as it is, luring it toward what it can become. The reality of the world conditions the relevance of the possibilities God can make available for the world. We have diagramed the dynamics of this action as follows:

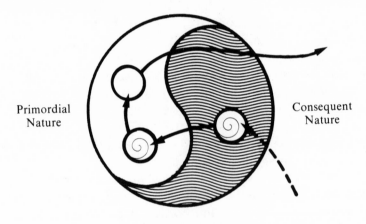

Primordial Nature

Consequent Nature

DIAGRAM VIII

The dotted line represents God's prehension of the world through the consequent nature, where the finite actuality is reenacted. The subjective aim of God toward harmony then pulls that actuality into the whole nature of God, integrating it with the primordial vision. Its integration in the vision actualizes a particular mode of divine harmony, which then becomes suggestive of a finite mode suitable for the successor actuality in the becoming world. This becomes the initial aim given to the world.

The divine movement from the actual harmony in God to the possible harmony for the world can be illustrated through examples drawn from sound and from sight. In listening to a piece of music, be it a symphony or a song, one hears not only the single note but the pattern which the whole is forming. Each note, in relation to those that have preceded it, is affected by the pattern that has been created; in turn, it joins in creation of the pattern. This participation in the pattern is both a realization of beauty and an anticipation of beauty. If the music suddenly stopped, the listener attuned to the harmony could nevertheless feel the possibilities for continuation of the harmony. The more deeply one knows the actual harmony, the more sensitive one becomes to the possible harmony. God, creating the actual harmony, is supremely attuned to this pattern of divine creation; God is also supremely attuned, through the feelings of the consequent nature, to the reality of the world. In wisdom, God transforms the world into the divine harmony; in wisdom, God feels ways in which the becoming world might benefit from and participate in its own reflection of divine harmony. God fashions initial aims for the world.

Consider the harmony from the different perspective of sight, and see the sense in which the integration of the world affects the divine harmony. God, in the primordial nature, contains all possibilities; these possibilities take on the vibrancy of actualization through God's feelings of the world. The configuration which that divine actualization manifests depends upon God's wisdom. The illustration is drawn from the night sky. Stars, like possibilities, are "contained" in the daytime sky; the fact that they are not visible to us does not annihilate their reality. In the day, the stars, from our perspective, are but potentially visible, not actually visible; the blazing light of the sun overwhelms them.

When evening comes, a contrasting darkness replaces the brightness of the daylight sky, and in the twilight a single star appears. When the moon is also apparent in the sky, a pattern forms. The star is seen in relation to the moon, and each adds to the other's beauty, creating in the process the beauty of the whole as well. The contrasting darkness deepens, and other stars appear; each one, leaping into light, changes the pattern of the whole night sky. Five stars may be visible in a particular pattern; another star appears, and the entire pattern changes, bringing a constellation into view. The addition of the new star suggests different patterns of relationality for all the others. As each star contributes the actuality of its light, the pattern of the whole changes.

Consider the illustration in relation to actual beauty and in relation to possible beauty. In the darkness of midnight, the whole night sky might be a panorama of light, still moving in a dynamic pattern that continually shifts the beauty of the whole: a constella-

tion that had been low on the horizon now appears higher in the
sky, and the beauty of midnight differs from that of an hour before.
Which pattern presents beauty? Or is the brightness of the evening
star, shining in harmony with the moon, less beautiful than the
star-strewn universe of midnight? Is it not rather that star differs
from star in glory, not in competition but in creation of manifold
variations of the single theme of beauty, harmony? Further, is it
not so that the changing state of beauty is in fact an essential part of
beauty? Actual beauty includes movement, change. Because it
does, actual beauty suggests new forms of possible beauty.

Even so, apply the metaphor to the process model of divine
wisdom. In the primordial nature, God contains all possibilities in
the harmony of a divine ordering; through the divine nature possibilities are ordered into beauty. This beauty, however, is ever
being manifested anew as the contrasting actualities of the world
bring now one possible combination, now another, to the actuality
of divine realization. The actuality of the world through the consequent nature provides the contrast whereby the primordial vision
comes to light. Harmony, not in vying patterns but in complement-
ing patterns of infinite beauty, inexhaustible, mark the reality of
God in the unity of the consequent and primordial natures.

Insofar as the world is concerned, the way in which this marvelous harmony can be reflected to the world is intensely dependent upon what the world has done. If the actualities of the world
distort the harmony offered by God, then God's integration must
overcome this distortion. The kind of aim which can then be given
the succeeding world is limited to a corrective harmony; it is as if
the edges rather than the depths of God's harmony are then able to
be reflected to the world through initial aims.

The corrective movement of transformation of the world in the
harmony of God will be discussed fully in chapter 17. For now, it is
important to see the relation between the actual divine harmony
and the ways it may be offered to the world as possibilities for the
world. There are two considerations: the relation of the actual
world to the harmony of God in terms of distance or correspondence; and the accessibility of harmony to the world, again in
terms of distance or correspondence.

In the illustration previously used of a young man who steals
from an old woman and injures her, the distance from divine
harmony is obvious. If God holds the many together in comple-

menting, enriching beauty, the young man violates that beauty in his violent disregard for the woman. God feels that action, transforming it in judgment through divine wisdom. That reality is integrated and transformed within the primordial vision, moving through successive stages from disharmony to harmony. However, the distance of the man from harmony in his finite circumstances deeply affects the mode of transformation which can be given him by God. Divine wisdom must fit the edges, not the depths, of harmony to him. Thus the initial aims given him persistently offer the first steps toward redemption. The aims must match the man's readiness and resources. The man will not receive an aim from God that he suddenly become a great philanthropist; that aim is not a real possibility for him. But he very well may receive an aim from God that might lead him to open himself to another's welfare, even in a slight way. Remorse at the sight of the woman's pain, or even awareness that the woman's pain matters—these steps toward transformation are slight, and but dimly reflective of the divine harmony; distance makes them so. Again and again, such aims may be fitted to the man until, in his own moment of choice, he actualizes such an aim. The next step offered will then go slightly beyond the first. In these two steps, the second will be more reflective of divine harmony than the first, for the first is akin to those movements within God wherein the evil is felt in its starkness, and transformation begins, whereas the second step is reflective of a further stage in the divine transcendence of evil. Thus what God can offer to the man depends upon the man's realities in their relation to the harmony of God, and upon the man's responsiveness toward God's guiding aims for transformation.

Consider now the same dynamics in the opposite case of not only a consonance with the divine harmony, but of the actual manifestation of that harmony in history. Consider Jesus. Jesus received the divine aim to manifest God's nature for us; he actualized this aim, conforming himself to it, thus becoming the incarnation of God's will toward the good for us. What must be the effect of this in God, both in relation to the actualization of divine harmony and in relation to the possibilities now made relevant to the world? Jesus manifested the divine nature in our history. In him the harmony of God is mirrored in the world, not dimly but in all its wonder for us. The depths of God, the intensity of divine beauty, the vortex of divine harmony, all receive expression in Jesus, making him the Christ, anointed with God's presence, manifesting God's presence in, to, and for the world.

Sometimes, as we look at the night sky, a single bright star will appear. In its brightness it transforms the night; every star in the sky is changed in relation to this new appearance. It is as if this one star, in unparalleled beauty, crowns the entire beauty of the night. Christ in God is like that bright star, illumining the actuality of the primordial nature through the beauty of his manifestation of that nature in our history. Through Christ the depths of God are touched for the world; new possibilities for reflecting divine harmony in human history shine out for us. The church is born.

How is this wonder appropriated in the continuing history of humanity? What is the concrete nature of the church, born and guided through the wisdom of God? What is the function of the church? Traditionally, the church has been defined through such qualities as unity, apostolicity, holiness, and universality; what do these terms mean if we understand the church in relation to Christ in God? Particularly problematic is the notion of universality, for we are intensely aware of the integrity and value of religions other than Christianity; does the sense in which we understand Christ in God do justice to other modes of achieving harmony? These are the questions to be addressed in developing a doctrine of the church.

In the process model the individual presupposes the community. Imagine one individual, a young man named John, who hears the church's proclamation of the gospel and is moved toward a response.

By responding positively to the gospel, John changes the pattern of his personal past. He may well have had a knowledge of the gospel simply through its effects upon the culture, but that knowledge had not been of determinative importance in John's self-understanding. Now, the gospel realigns the meaning of John's past; it enters his past through his present response. If the gospel is felt as a judgment of that past, John's positive response to the gospel may be felt as an overwhelming repentance. Alternatively, the gospel may be felt as suddenly giving meaning to a past which hitherto defied meaning, and the response may be in feelings of joy. If John's past has been shadowed by encounters with death, the gospel may speak life, and John's response may be one of comfort and triumph together. John hears the gospel, responds to it in light of his own particular needs and his own particular perspective, and in the process changes his past.

Remember that God fashions aims for us in continuity with our past, such that the transformation offered is relevant in light of that past. As John adds Christ to his past, Christ enters into the relevance of the transformative aims which can be offered to John. The resources of Christ in God are, in the wisdom of God, fitted to John's particular situation. Speculate as to the dynamics by which this takes place; slow down the rapid succession of events that constitute John, and cast those events into a detailed analysis of the process whereby they come into being.

John feels his past in a new light; his understanding of Jesus changes the pattern by which he evaluates existence. Jesus is now part of John's personal past, through the power of proclamation. God prehends John, feels him in his responsiveness to the proclamation, and re-enacts him within the consequent nature. Since Christ is now in John's relevant past, the integration of John in God can take place in such a way that John moves into that constellation within the depths of divine harmony made actual by Christ; John's reality participates in Christ in God. This integration of God's feelings—feelings of John in union with Christ—results in a new possibility being given to John for his next moment of finite existence. The possibility that is fashioned for him is made possible through Christ in adaptation and application to John's finite situation. Thus a Christly repentance, a Christly joy, or a Christly comfort and triumph may be the immediate possibilities for reflecting the divine harmony which are given to John.

Consider, however, that whichever one of those possibilities is given to John comes to him in the form of an initial aim, which he then may actualize. In the minuteness of process analysis, many successive entities are involved in John's person, and not simply one. Each entity is the re-creation of John, ever newly responding to an ever newly enlarged past in light of an ever newly given possibility for the immediate future. Who John is, in each instant, is a function of his future and his past, integrated in the unity of the present. this means that when John's immediate possibility for the future is made available to him in and through Christ in God, then John's actualization of that aim is his reception of Christ for him. Through the aim, Christ enters into John's identity. If our future is a part of our present identity, and if that future has been uniquely provided through Christ, then Christ is a part of our present identity. The medium by which this happens, of course, is divine wisdom: through God's subjective aim toward harmony, unifying John with the harmony made actual by Christ, God feels a further mode of harmony for John. We might attempt a diagram of the situation:

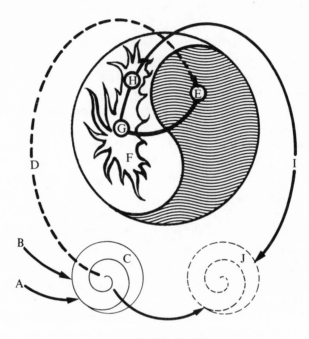

DIAGRAM IX

A = proclamation of Christ in John's past

B = God's initial aim to respond positively to the proclamation

C = John's constitution of himself in a positive response

D = God's prehension of John

E = God's re-enaction of John in the consequent nature

F = Christ in God

G = God's integration of John with Christ

H = the Christly possibility now made relevant to John in his next moment

I = John's reception of this possibility as the initial aim

J = his new constitution of himself

Notice the intense importance of faith in this process. God does not force the world to reflect the divine nature; God waits upon the world, giving it those possibilities for which it is ready. Faith provides the readiness which makes Christ's benefits accessible to John. Apart from John's openness to the proclamation of Christ, there is no feasible way in which John's integration in God can be aligned with Christly possibilities; faith is therefore necessary.

Faith, however, does not appear in a vacuum; faith presupposes grace in this model. That is, the proclamation of the gospel and God's aims to respond to that proclamation through faith precede John's response of faith, and in fact make that response possible. Since John is responsible neither for the proclamation he hears nor the aim God gives him, these elements, both of which make faith possible for him, are entirely gracious in character. John's positive response in faith depends upon this prior grace, and is inexplicable without it. Nevertheless, John's response *is* his response. This means that insofar as he responds positively to grace, he constitutes himself through faith; insofar as he responds negatively, he is responsible for refusing grace. The decision is ultimately his own. In this model, faith is a response-ability, and therefore a responsibility. It takes place within the encompassing reality of grace, which makes faith possible. By grace and through faith, John participates in the benefits of Christ. In so doing, his identity is formed through Christ.

However, John is not the only individual to respond to Christ in faith, and so to be formed through him. Mary, Antonio, Michel, Joan, Freidrich, Krister, Tuyet, Kwasi, Ti-Fam—throughout the centuries and throughout the earth there are those who have responded to Christ in faith; each one, like John, has been united with Christ in God; each one, like John, has received a Christly possibility for the immediate future, formed in conjunction with her or his personal past situated in time and culture, and with the union with Christ; each one, like John, has an identity formed through faith in Christ. The church is the community of all those whose identities have been so formed through faith.

13

ONE, HOLY,
APOSTOLIC CHURCH

J OHN, Tuyet, Kwasi, Ti-Fam, Marguerite—these and count-
less others share in an identity formed through Christ in faith; each
is brother or sister to all others in the family of God which is called
the church. The church, however, is more than the contemporary
members—it extends into the long past; it will extend into the
future. What is the nature of its existence throughout time since its
foundation in Jesus Christ? An answer is suggested by looking at
the traditional dimensions by which the church has been described
for two thousand years: unity, holiness, apostolicity, and universality.

Apostolicity is the sense in which the church is continuously
affected by and responsible to its past, beginning with the testimony of the apostles to the life, death, and resurrection of Jesus.
Unity comes to the church from its future, because of the dynamics
of identity in Christ. Holiness is the present result as the church
exists in faithfulness to both its past and its future. How can
this be?

Apostolicity has been interpreted in various ways throughout the
history of the church, but a central element in any interpretation is
the continual testimony to the resurrection. The first apostles were
identified as those who were witnesses to the resurrection, and
who had been with Jesus in his teaching ministry. Also involved in
their apostleship was the mission to proclaim the resurrection in
order that its benefits might be made available to many. The proclamation was foundational for the church, which was understood as
the community of proclamation.

Proclamation of the resurrection, however, was never simply
verbal. Just as in the ministry of Jesus, so in the ministry of the
early church there was an essential component of service. Healing

and preaching go hand-in-hand in the preaching of the apostles as described in the book of Acts. There is ample evidence not only in Acts but also in the epistles that the proclamation of the word within the community was also in a context of love: edification of the church in body and spirit was essential. People were clothed, fed, and cared for in mutual ministries that embraced total well-being. The church was a giving and receiving community of proclamation.

How could it be otherwise? The ultimate Word is not a paragraph, but a person. If Jesus is the Word of God incarnate, then the heart of proclamation is personal and relational, not propositional. In order to be true witnesses to God's fullness of action for us in Christ, we too must be living words, embodied proclamations, living that which we speak. If the telling of the gospel is simply the recitation of words, then we risk losing the gospel.

This implies that there is both a constant and a relative pole to proclamation. Insofar as both are present, the church is apostolic. The constant pole is the unchanging referent for the church in the life, death, and resurrection of Jesus Christ. God is for us: this is the wonder of the gospel. But to preach such a message is to be gripped by the message, formed by the message. This brings out the relative pole of proclamation, or the sense in which its effect in us leads us to the living testimony written in actions of love and justice.

Consider the necessity of keeping this pole of proclamation fluid, conformable to the specific needs of a time. Suppose that a small group of believers decides that the demands of love and justice require that they form a community to minister to the poor of a certain neighborhood. They research the specific needs of the area, and assign certain tasks to individuals. In the process of carrying out these activities, they find that there are internal needs of the group which also require attention: some of these needs are directly related to the planned activities, but others are rooted in problems stemming from the group's past, whether as individuals or as a whole. So the group develops specific internal ways of ministering to each other, as well as external ways of ministering through word and action to the poor around them. The worshiping component of the community is certainly not forgotten in all of this; in fact, it remains central. However, the way of worshiping soon begins to reflect the depth of concern the individuals feel for the society around them. Intercession mingles with praise; in the renewal of the specific forms of worship that evolve, the people feel themselves energized for the full proclamation of the word to the society in word and in deeds of love.

Their ministry is so successful that they decide to make sure it is preserved. They decide the way to do this is to draw up a careful and precise record of the way they do things. This record includes detailed instructions as to the organizational format, the worship activities, the kinds of ministries and how to do them, and an analysis of the internal needs and how they are addressed. This descriptive account could be read as a formula for success, for in fact it was a record of a success. Surely success achieved once could be achieved again, if the same format were followed precisely! But of course the living word—that which in essence must flow from the responsiveness to needs and situations that surround us—would become a lifeless word in its translation to marks on paper. Description would become rule, and the reality of love and justice extended to real people in real societies by a specific grouping of individuals would be endangered. No subsequent society could exactly duplicate the conditions of the first society in which ministry took place; hence no society could be truly ministered to in precisely the same way.

Try to imagine what would happen if the description of that ministry were in fact turned into a rule for imposition on another community. Imagine that the same group which began the ministry was suddenly transferred to a totally different area. All of the members are whisked away, magically reassembled in a suburban community of middle-to-upper class people, many of whom work in the various professions. If the group utilizes the same forms and methods they developed before, will they still enact love and justice? If a mode of worship totally integrated into the kind of ministry they were living is copied verbatim in the new situation, will not their worship become increasingly separated from their living? Obviously, the ways in which they minister in the second location will be most like the ways they developed in their first location, not by a mere copying of the first experience but by responding as freshly and lovingly in the second instance as they did in the first. The record of the past incorporated into their documents will be useful as a history of who they have been, but they must transcend that record if they are to be faithful to their call to minister. Ministry in the second location must be tailored to the specific needs encountered there. Likewise, the new work will uncover different kinds of needs internal to the group; it might well require a different organizational structure. The new ministry will surely affect the content of prayer and worship if the group retains its faithfulness to the proclamation. Faithfulness to the proclamation of God's love toward us will require that the group be responsive to change, willing to let go of former ways in order to develop ways that are appropriate to the changed circumstances.

Apostolicity, therefore, is a continuity with the past which nevertheless has an essential openness to it. In every generation and in every Christian there must be a faithfulness to the content of the gospel: our words must point to the Word who is a person, living, crucified, and risen. Therefore, our words must also take the form of ever new interpretations of ways in which we can enact love and justice. Word and deed together constitute the church's faithfulness to its apostolic tradition; constancy and openness form the dynamism whereby the apostolic church witnesses to the world.

If apostolicity requires an openness to new ways of acting in love and justice, then apostolicity requires that we be sensitive to the needs of the immediate future. Actions impelled by continuity with the apostolic past will lead us into the newness of how we may minister today. Through faithfulness to the past, we will be open to the future. It is just at this point that we must look to see the basis for the unity of the church. In process thought, apostolicity involves the church's relationship to its past, but in a way that is continually open to newness, to the future. This openness provides the basis for the church's unity in the following way.

Remember the description of the initial aim of God. It comes to each one of us as a real possibility for our immediate future. When we gave the example of John coming to faith in Jesus, we outlined the dynamics whereby his whole identity is changed by that faith. Christly possibilities are available to him. The kinds of aims God can give John are radically changed by his faith in Christ, and we can truly say that John's identity is formed by Christ. Christ is mediated to him through the initial aim.

The initial aim shows us our immediate possibilities for the future. This means that John actually experiences the benefits of Christ coming to him as his future. Insofar as John conforms himself to those aims, he incorporates Christ into his personality. John becomes an extension of Christ's incarnation in the world.

The very notion of identity indicates why this must be so. Who we are depends upon our past and upon our future possibilities. If

John should decide to go to seminary and prepare to become a minister of the gospel, John's whole identity in seminary is not only a function of his life experiences to that date, but even more importantly, his identity is informed by his hopes and plans for the future. Ordination to the ministry—something that, for John, is still three years in his future—is the most dominant influence upon his identity. John talks about his entrance into ministry as a response to a call, as if he were forming his identity in obedience to a future responsibility. Is not the genuineness of that call rooted in the initial aim of God, coming to John as a possibility for his future? And isn't that aim informed by the Christly possibilities made relevant to John through faith? John goes to seminary, and in time he becomes a minister. But all the while, his identity has been forming in obedience to the future, in obedience to God's call in Christ. This illustration of John's identity formed in response to the call to ministry is but one instance of what takes place in every moment of our lives. In every moment John is responding to the call of God, forming his identity in response to that call. John and each one of us are who we are precisely in the way we combine our past and our future in the present. When that future is made possible through Christ, then our identities are formed through Christ. But this formation always comes to us as the future.

Consider the unity that is created if many people share in an identity formed through faith in Christ. The unity we see in a family group stems from its past: brothers and sisters, by sharing the same parents, share the same family identity. Their common past, whether by birth or adoption, defines them as family. For the family that is the Christian church, unity comes primarily from a shared future. Just as the sharing of a past creates a real kinship, even so the sharing of a future creates a real kinship. If John's identity is formed through Christ, and if Kwasi's identity is formed through Christ, and if Ti-Fam's identity is formed through Christ, then all three share in the same identity and become brothers and sisters to one another even though they live so widely scattered in the world. Christ, as the source of their identity, is also the ground of their unity, creating in them a bond as real and as close as family, creating them as the community of church. This unity and community comes to each from the future, through the initial aim. The future, mediated by God through Christ, is therefore the basis of the church's unity.

Focus now upon the content of the initial aim in order to see more clearly how the unity of the church can be realized. A Christly possibility is one that conforms to the nature of God, revealed so clearly in Jesus as an accepting and transforming love, willing and accomplishing our good. Just as the love of Jesus was intensely responsive to the needs of those around him, even so the content of Christly aims will reflect a loving responsiveness to the well-being of the world of which we are a part. The aims from God will be toward well-being. This is to say that God's aims always push us toward care for the world. This push toward well-being stems from the character of God; it must therefore be an unfailing component of every Christly initial aim.

Suppose that John meets another Christian, and they wish to experience their common bond, their unity as members of the one body of Christ. How shall they discover this unity? Shall they begin an exhaustive analysis of the past? If our unity comes to us through our shared kinship in Christ, mediated to us as future, then the way to discover the common bond of unity is to look to the leading of God with regard to the immediacies of the world around us. In an orientation toward service, unity will become apparent, almost as a byproduct of responsiveness to the one God, leading us in ways of well-being. The future, not the past, clarifies the unity of the church.

There are many implications in this with regard to the many different types of churches in the world. We not only see Protestant, Roman Catholic, and Eastern Orthodox, but each of these bodies subdivides into various ways of being Christian. Our usual response is to bewail our diversity, decrying the scandal of so many people who disagree with our own way of seeing things. But has anyone ever joined a church which she or he believed to be false? Has not every member in each congregation chosen, to some extent, to join or remain in that congregation because it seemed to be God's leading, however bright or dim? How, then, can looking to the past alone show us our unity? While the past will indeed reveal the constancy of our apostolic proclamation—we all preach Jesus, crucified and risen—the past will also reveal the many ways in which we have been called to live out that proclamation. Who shall we blame for responding to a specific mode of ministry? The past, with the diversity of the relative pole of proclamation, will obscure rather than reveal the unity which we all share in Christ. Only as we look to the future, and discern the way in which God calls us to further enactments of love and justice in the world will we begin to know the rejoicing which follows when we find a sister or brother in the ever-enlarging family of God. The unity of the church flows from the future by the grace of God, who mediates the benefits of Christ to us.

Notice, however, that this unity is essentially experienced through the relative pole of proclamation. Unity comes through the future aspect of apostolicity. As we are open to the call of ministry, to that living proclamation of the gospel, we are also open to our unity, our bond of kinship in Christ. The union with Christ creates the unity of the church, from which the church moves to ministry, or to that relative pole of apostolicity. This apostolic witness, in turn, is the basis of the message whereby persons may respond to Christ in faith, thus realizing Christly possibilities and creating anew the conditions of church unity. Apostolicity and unity are interrelated aspects of the church, a moving rhythm between the past and the future, wherein the church in the present is ever and ever formed anew.

To speak thus about the unity and apostolicity of the church raises the question of the church's holiness. In the description thus far we have outlined the conditions for goodness, beauty, holiness. Is the church in its concrete reality indeed holy? Is the holiness of Christ in God communicated to the church? Is the church "without spot or blemish," as the apostle claims?

Just as we discussed God in Christ and Christ in God, even so the church must be discussed in both a temporal and everlasting dimension, in the world and in God. Only so can full consideration be given to the question of the holiness of the church. If the church be considered in God, it therefore participates in the nature of God, and hence in holiness. God transforms the individuals who compose the community of the church in the integration of the consequent and primordial natures, and in that divine process God welds the church into the truth of holiness. In God, the church is purified and transformed. A full discussion of this must await the chapter on "The Kingdom in God," but it is important to indicate here that this holiness which qualifies the transformed church in God is not tangential to the kinds of holiness that the church creates on earth.

Thus far, every diagram we have drawn to illustrate the dynamics between God and the world has represented an enormous simplification of the process. We portray one occasion, with but a single line indicating the wealth of its past, and then portray God's prehension of that occasion and integration of the occasion with

Christ in the depths of divine harmony. The process, it must be realized, happens again and again and again; not one occasion, and not simply one series of occasions, but every occasion whatsoever is felt by God and integrated according to divine wisdom into the primordial harmony. Everything affects everything else in this process universe: God adapts aims to the world in light of this intensity of complex interrelationship. Therefore, what the church accomplishes is prehended by God and dealt with by God in transforming wisdom; God blends the whole church everlastingly with that constellation we call Christ in the primordial nature of God. The church is made without spot or blemish by God in God, and there is an effect of this action continuously presented to the world. The effect is in the multiplicity of aims given to the individuals of the church, each aim being given in light of all the others. Thus the very aims of God, reflecting the divine holiness of the church, tend toward a communal form of that holiness on earth.

Insofar as the church manifests holiness, therefore, it must do so in its communal structure. The holiness of the church exists in the communal nature of the church. Again, to use the metaphor of the light and the prism, that single holiness which is the church in God is reflected through the prism of God's purpose for the world, breaking into the many rays of holiness made possible for the world. The rays, however, complement each other, since they all spring from the same source, which is the church unified with Christ in God. Further, the rays complete each other, for only in togetherness do they truly demonstrate the unity of their source. Just as the harmony of colors in a rainbow bespeaks their initial unity in the single ray of light, even so the communal actualization of God's purposes in the world bespeaks the initial unity of that purpose in God's divine integration of the church with Christ in God.

For instance, John, identified with Christ, feels the call to love and justice relative to the plight of poverty-stricken old persons in his town. Fixed incomes in an inflationary age, no opportunities for employment, isolation and loneliness, and the apathy that accompanies the sense of not being valued, of being tangential to a society—all of these problems seem to afflict these aged people, complicated by the fact of frequent physical problems. Yet the people elicit John's love, and he earnestly desires to see more just conditions for them. However, while some of the problems may be met on a personal level, others, such as poverty itself, are societal problems; how can John viably address them? His openness toward the people, his invitation to mutuality with them, and his active love toward them may be great, but John alone cannot create conditions of justice for these people. His single individuality encounters the weight of society, and while his lone voice has some effect, it must be reinforced by other voices if the necessary political and social changes are to be enacted. John may work personal wonders with the people, but the counterweight of the force of habitual ways of doing things works against him.

Joan is also identified with Christ, as are Catherine and others in John's church. They, too, receive aims for love and justice in concrete forms. As John shares his vision for the people with his sisters and brothers in Christ, the vision gains in power. The communal force of the larger society can be countered by the communal force of the church, seeking love and justice for those aged people. Furthermore, within the church itself the communal identity in Christ will create ways of addressing the needs of the aged within the church. These people will be invited to participate in the openness and mutuality of the community in Christ. In community, the holiness of existence in love and justice becomes real; the common identity in Christ requires this. Insofar as the church lives from its identity in Christ, it becomes a holy community.

By so defining holiness, the interrelationship between apostolicity, unity, and holiness becomes apparent. If apostolicity relates to the church's continuity with the past, and unity relates to the church's creation from the future, then holiness is the effect of apostolicity and unity held together in the present. In holiness, the many are as one; in holiness, apostolicity receives new expression; in holiness, and only in holiness, does the actualization of the community of Christ occur.

To make such a statement obviously creates a problem, for is our local church community really holy? The problem is associated with our usage of the word holiness. We are accustomed to think of holiness as a rarity, assigning the quality to individuals in the past of particularly saintly character and deeds. Alternatively, we make holiness an ideal somehow associated only with the future, such as applies to the church with Christ in God. However, to dissociate holiness from the church in the present is a dangerous thing, for it tends to allow justice to be an abstract quality, and love to be a sentimental devotion to the past or the future. If holiness is associated primarily with a few individuals in the past, or if holiness is assigned only to a realm of the future, then the church is relinquishing its identity in the present. The church's unity can only be expressed through holiness; the church's apostolicity depends upon incarnate holiness; holiness is thus the actuality of both unity and apostolicity. Without such holiness in some degree, there can be no church.

The church is called, by its identity in Christ, to *be* love and justice, to *be* openness and mutuality, and in the living dynamism of these qualities, continually to move into deeper forms which concretely manifest these qualities. Always the forms of love and justice are relative to the actual conditions in the world, working transformation. This is the identity of the church, and the holiness of the church; hence holiness must be a present quality, or the church loses hold on its very identity.

Holiness will be appropriated by degrees. In the process model, the initial aim is adapted by the occasion into the subjective aim; this constitutes the freedom and self-creativity of the occasion. The adaptation of the aim is not necessarily in either/or terms; rather, it can be accomplished through modifications that are closer or further from the aim given by God. This means that the community called church will continually be actualizing its identity in a more-or-less reality, that the church in and of itself is fluid, not fixed. It will be more or less holy, and thus more or less itself, according to the ways in which it subjectifies the aims it receives from God. God is faithful in leading the church toward ever deeper forms of love and justice, and waits upon the church to actualize the specificities of love and justice, to be holy. By the grace and power of God, the church is without spot or blemish in God; by the exercise of its own finite responsibility, the church may mirror this holiness in the world, brightly or dimly, according to its choice. In its choice is the measure of its holiness, and the measure of its identity with Christ as community, as church.

Holiness is relative to the circumstances of the present. Since holiness is a present quality, it must be concrete; if it is concrete, it is relative to the particularities of circumstances. This relativization of holiness becomes a guard against both pride and judgmental intolerance. In fact, this relativization of holiness becomes a basis for the diversity and ecumenicity of the church. Consider the situation: the call to the church is to manifest its unity and apostolicity in holiness, which is to say the church is called to the enactment of love and justice, openness and mutuality. Given the relative nature of these enactments, no one concrete achievement can be normative for the others. In fact, to do so would be to work against the continuous achievement of still further realizations of these qualities. This means that no single achievement can exhaust love and justice, and that every single achievement contains within itself a dynamism that leads beyond itself. Pride would be the tendency to take one's own achievement as an end in itself; judgmental intolerance involves the further step of using one's own achievement as a way to measure others. Since holiness requires many forms, true holiness negates pride, and with it, judgmental intolerance. Further, the communal nature of holiness reinforces the interdependence of the many and the one for the achievement of love and justice; gratitude for such interdependence, and for the God whose aims reinforce it, crowds pride from the space of holiness.

Holiness is very much a "here and now" matter, but there are many "here's," and many "now's," which means there must be many ways to manifest holiness. No one shape is exhaustive or determinative. This means that if there is no diversity in the church, no variety of ministries, no incorporation of those varieties into forms of worship, then holiness is lacking. Without holiness, the identity of the church is to some degree in question. Thus the very diversity of the church can express its holiness in faithfulness to its unity in Christ. Uniformity, on the contrary, is against the nature of holiness, and therefore a denial of the church's unity in Christ. The church's unity, coming to the church through the future, must be expressed through diverse actualizations of holiness. Given the togetherness of unity and apostolicity in holiness, this means that true apostolicity is being re-created in many ways. Apostolicity multiplies itself in diversity, and denies itself in sheer uniformity.

This means that the churches recognize their unity in Jesus Christ, and in the proclamation of his life, death, and resurrection. This proclamation has a dual focus: it is word and deed. The incarnation of God in Christ must be completed by the incarnation of Christ in the church, through the means of Christ in God. This incarnation, if it is faithful to the proclamation, will be in the many forms of holiness, each form pushing beyond itself. The unity in Christ calls for a diversity of forms, and the diversity of forms bespeaks the unity in Christ.

14

THE SACRAMENTS

I F the church is to have a diversity of forms, what of the role of the sacraments in the church? Do not the sacraments argue against that diversity of forms? Are not the sacraments uniform in nature, transcending the relativity of time and space, thus requiring but one interpretation, one mode of administration?

In the view here developed, the uniformity of the sacraments no more mitigates against the diversity-in-unity of the church than does the uniformity of the life, death, and resurrection of Jesus Christ. There are many interpretations of Jesus Christ, but only one person of Jesus Christ; further, the one person necessarily gives rise to many interpretations, since the one person is experienced in the relativity of encounter.

Consider an illustration of this through the phenomenon that there are three different gospel recountings of the way in which Jesus healed the blind. In Luke 18, Jesus simply speaks, and through the speaking, sight is restored. But in Matthew 20, two blind men receive the touch of Jesus on their eyes; immediately they regain their sight. Yet one more instance, this time in Mark 8, tells of a man healed as Jesus spits on his eyes and lays his hands on him. In two of the accounts, sight is received instantly; in the last account, sight is received gradually. To the three apparently similar maladies, there are three quite different responses, each of which is effective. The integrity of the one person yields a variety of responses. If each response is taken as the only valid one, ruling out the others, the very integrity which made that response possible is denied. Jesus, in the integrity of his person, spoke and acted according to the needs and context of each blind man. Thus the one person gave rise to different experiences and interpretations. Those different interpretations can be used either as a source of division, or as a source of community.

Even so, the sacraments are in themselves a mediation of the life, death, and resurrection of Jesus Christ for us. The constancy is in the proclamation; the variety is in the way in which that proclamation is received, experienced, and understood. The ways we interpret the sacraments are reflective of the ways in which we understand our experience of relationship with God and each other through Christ. Again, using the metaphor of the rainbow: the one light passes through the prism, breaking into many rays of color. The rays, because of the unity of their source, are creative of a new unity through their togetherness in diversity: the beauty of the rainbow. The sacraments, like Christ, are one; the sacraments, like Christ, are interpreted in light of the encounter with Christ; the many interpretations can be creative of a temporal unity in the diversity which is community.

The sacraments are essential to the life of the church, both because of the constancy of proclamation they provide, and because of the very means through which the proclamation is made. The Word, which is the revelation of God in Christ, is not a treatise in linguistic phrases; it is the person of Jesus Christ. Our proclamation of this Word faces the danger of becoming the abstractions of linguistic absolutes, for we must say this Word in human words. The sacraments are an ever-present guard against this, for in the sacraments the proclamation is made in the reality of bread, wine, water. We repeat the words telling of the life, death, and resurrection of Jesus Christ as we participate in the sacraments, and the beyond-words power of the Word is conveyed in the wordless Word of bread, wine, and water. God is communicated to us; God is for us.

The reality of this sacramental proclamation is of intense importance given the relativity of existence. Without the proclamation of Christ, there is no basis for the response in faith that unites us with Christ in God, thus mediating redemptive existence to us. However, we hear the proclamation according to our circumstances, our perspective, and our needs. Is there not a danger that in our own continuing proclamation of the gospel we have heard, we will communicate instead the conditions in and through which we heard the proclamation, and leave little of the proclamation in the communication? Or in a more positive vein, consider the fact that the holiness that is made possible for us through the proclamation has within itself a dynamism which forever pushes beyond itself to new forms of love and justice. Given the relativity of our life in Christ in holiness, is there not again the danger that the proclamation that is its foundation will be lost in the transformations? The life, death, and resurrection of Jesus Christ, proclaimed and communicated in and through the sacraments, is the foundational life of the church. Through the sacraments, there is constancy to the proclamation within the very relativity of our history. That the sacraments are interpreted variously is to be expected; that the sacraments invariably proclaim the life, death, and resurrection of Christ is essential.

As we have seen, there are two poles to apostolicity, and both poles must be preserved in proclamation. There must be the constancy of the presentation of the life, death, and resurrection of Christ, and there must also be the ever-new manifestations of love and justice. There is therefore a constant and a relative pole to apostolicity. Since the relative gains its catalytic power from the constancy of Christ's person, the relative cannot be cut off from that power through loss of that aspect of proclamation.

The sacraments, in their apostolicity, are also word and deed, but in such a way as to preserve the constant element in proclamation, from which the relative gains its power. In the sacraments, there is a physical presentation of the Word that cannot be spoken, and the ritualized spoken words that relate the activity of Christ's life, death, and resurrection to the ones participating in the sacrament. The sacraments thus provide the constant grounding through which the catalytic power of identification in Christ is ever offered anew. The sacraments, through their unique proclamational nature, are thus intensely important to the apostolicity of the church; they point to the church's past, and make it present. They guarantee the constancy of proclamation.

In baptismal waters, one is united with Christ in death to sin and resurrection to new life; hence the proclamation of Christ's death and resurrection in baptism is given in conjunction with appropriation of Christ. The proclamation is strongly and essentially "for us"; without appropriation, there is of course no sacrament. Likewise with the eucharist: the body and blood of Christ are given with the words, "for you." Hence the unity of the individual with Christ is as important an element in the sacrament as the apostolicity of the proclamation. As the sacraments are celebrated, the individuals join themselves with the Christ proclaimed, and in this activity the "for us" factor is not only said, it is done. In the act of the sacrament, the individual is open to Christ and his benefits, and in this openness, receives Christ and his benefits. Thus Christ is present in the sacrament, not only through proclamation but through appropriation. Since the appropriation of Christ is the unity of the church, and since this unity comes from the future through initial aims, the sacraments are a means whereby the future of the church is made present. Thus in the sacraments the unity of the church is created and expressed.

The sacraments, however, are necessarily communal, and therefore related essentially to the holiness of the church. In baptism, the focus is upon entrance to the community; in the Lord's Supper, the focus is upon participation in the community. In both, the interaction between the one and many in community is for the upbuilding of the church in love and justice, openness and mutuality, in a dynamism that continually seeks new expression. In baptism one is raised to newness of life, which is the community; in the Lord's Supper, one is strengthened for service, which is community, and this communal emphasis is not tangential but essential to the sacrament. Community is internal, not external, to the sacrament.

Baptism, as the sacrament of entrance, is not only apostolic proclamation in continuity with the past, nor is it only the openness to Christ and reception of Christ mediated to us through the future. Baptism is also the acceptance by the many of the baptized one in the community of the present. This communal aspect is not extrinsic, but intrinsic to the sacrament; it must be so, since apostolicity and unity identify one with the community. Likewise in the Lord's Supper: the many are one in their mutual participation in the sacrament. Apostolicity is necessarily present in the proclamation of Christ; unity is necessarily present in the appropriation of Christ; community, and therefore holiness, is necessarily present as the many are one in their participation in the sacrament.

The communal nature of the sacraments is multidimensional. First, it is the creation of the present community as outlined above; second, it is related to the full community of the church, past and future; third, it is an impetus to the societal witness of the church in the creation of love and justice. The sacraments generate the power of community with the past and the future through their present creation of apostolicity and unity. Through apostolicity, the sacraments bespeak the community of the past, and of the many who have preceded the individuals of the present in this same act of participating in the sacrament. The very ritualized repetition of the sacrament gives it a power in this process universe, for it strengthens the being-made-present quality of the past through prehension. Each repetition of an act gives it increasing power relative to the present, propelling its influence into the present, whereupon a conformal prehension of that influence re-enacts it, making it present once again. Therefore, the ritualized expression of the sacraments implies an intense power of continuity with the past. In illustration of this, we could simply point to the intensive resistance that is raised in reference to changing aspects of the ritualistic service in the church. The intensity of repetition gives the past much greater power in the present. The positive aspect of this power is that through the sacrament one can sense the community of the past, and thus make it present. Hence the communal aspect of the sacrament increases the community of the present by giving it the dimension of the past as well.

The communal aspect of the sacraments also relates to the church of the future through the dimension of unity. Christ is the source of our unity and community, mediated to us through our future. This openness to Christ is at the same time an openness to the future, but to be open to the future is to anticipate it. Since our community comes to us from the future through Christ, one can appreciate not only the present creation of community but also the many who will succeed us in this creation of community. Furthermore, for those in the future, we will function as the apostolicity of proclamation in the past, and hence we will be made present to them in the sacrament, even as our past is made present to us. Therefore the community of the future is made present through the sacrament, increasing the intensity of the present community.

This communality of the church in the sacrament is holiness. The presence of one to another, whether in relation to past, future, or present, is for the enrichment of each in and through the many. The upbuilding of the church in love is essential to the nature of the sacrament. This holiness is internal to the church, insofar as it is the effective binding together of the many as one in the identity of Christ, and external to the church insofar as it must have an effect on the society of the fuller culture. In a process universe, everything affects everything else.

Insofar as the community extends the identity of Christ, it will be holy within itself in its internal relations. There will be love, justice, openness, and mutuality within the community as the many participate together in Christliness. However, the dynamism of these qualities pushes to new forms. Love and justice contradict themselves if static, and hence cease to be love and justice. If the church is dynamically embodying Christ, the inner holiness of the church must have an outward effect. The church must be a catalyst for love and justice in society. Again we have come full circle, for the holiness of the sacrament in its creation of community pushes that community to ever increasing and intensifying forms of love and justice, which of course is the acting out of the church's unity with Christ, and the creation of the church's apostolicity in proclamation.

15

UNIVERSALITY

THE emphasis upon the church's witness in the larger society raises the question of the fourth dimension of the church, universality. Is the witness of the church to be universal in nature, extending throughout the world? Is this extension of the church's witness to be an enlargement of the church, baptizing all nations into the Christian faith? Our answer must be a qualified yes and no to both questions. The universality of the church is not in geographical extension, but in the nature of God. This marks a shift in the historical understanding of universality, for traditionally it has denoted the extension of the whole church throughout the world. Certain things follow from understanding universality in terms of the church's relation to God rather than to the world, particularly with regard to the question of the Christian relation to other religions.

Consider the nature of God as developed so far, and the nature of the church following from God in Christ and Christ in God. In this process universe there is an interrelationship between God and the world, such that the world receives from God, and God from the world. God provides the world with possibilities for harmony which are reflective of the divine nature. The harmony of God is the unification of all possibilities in a togetherness that is beauty. This harmony of possibles becomes a harmony of actuals as God receives from the world, integrating the world into that divine harmony. Obviously, the harmony of God is one of ever-increasing intensity through this integration of the world. The world matters to God in this vision of reality, for what the world does becomes the actuality that God integrates into the divine harmony. The world determines what God shall deal with in the divine nature; God determines how the world shall be dealt with in terms of the divine character. Insofar as the world actualizes possibilities that reflect the divine harmony, the world contributes positively to the richness of value in God, deepening the divine intensity. Insofar as the world acts in a way destructive of value, God's action must be transformative. The harmony in God is not lessened, but it will be less than it could have been had the world acted differently. God's will toward the world is for the intensification of harmony in it. This intensification in turn leads to intensification in God.

In Christ God's universal aim toward the good for all stands revealed. However, we have emphasized again and again that the universal aim must be relativized in order to be made concrete. The harmony in God is one; the harmony in the world must be many. Since all temporal modes of harmony come from the one divine source, this common source is reflected in the communal nature of temporal harmony. There is a balancing and blending effect, whereby what is good for one is tempered by the good of the other in an intermeshing network of communal good. This becomes important, for in Christ we see not simply an abstract revelation of the nature of God as an absolute good viewed far off—to the contrary, in Christ we see God *for us*. God in goodness bends to our condition, fitting divine harmony to the human situation. In Christ we see the universal made relative. God's universal will toward our good means *this* action in relation to the blind man of Jericho, but *that* action in relation to the blind man in Bethsaida. The one will toward harmony has many effects.

Can we take this revelation still further, applying it beyond the differences that occur simply within the one locale of ancient Judea? Does Jesus reveal that the goodness of God is always adapted to our condition—that God shapes our redemption according to who and where and when we are? This would mean that the source of redemption is always—and therefore universally—God; the shape of redemption varies by the will and boundless grace of God, who bends to our condition, shaping redemption according to the uniqueness of every particular human situation.

There would be commonalities in such a relativized harmony. Insofar as people share a common culture, a common tradition, a common time, the communal nature of harmony would be illustrated in a common faith and a common mode of experiencing redemption. One might even say that although there would be diverse forms within that basic commonality, the marks of "sameness" would be strong. We could imagine that adherents to the faith in that community would be so impressed with the apparently invariable elements that these could be named "universal." In fact, of course, they would be invariable and therefore "universal" only relative to the varieties and forms within the boundaries of the faith. But if one looked beyond the boundaries, then of course the so-called universal elements would begin to show that they, too, were relative to quite finite boundaries of geography and tradition.

This would mean that no finite manifestation of religion could be universal. If it were not universal, then of course it could not be normative for all times and places. Rather, the universal element would apply only to the source of harmony from which all our finite sources spring; only God could be named as the universal source of redemption. To name the finite manifestations "universal" would be to border on assigning a divine quality to a finite condition. To treat the relative as if it were absolute leads to the idolatry of misplaced worship.

How can this be, given the reality of the incarnation? We have already discussed the conviction that God was in Christ, that in Christ God is revealed as with us and for us. Doesn't this make the relative—the finite person of Jesus—absolute? If God is at work for us in Jesus, doesn't this mean that God restricts the divine activity for redemption to that incarnation in Jesus? How can there be any other way whereby God works for the well-being of humanity? And if there is, doesn't this detract from the incarnation—make it less important, somehow, and faith less urgent?

The process understanding of reality provides one way to understand the ability of God to work many means for our good. In analyzing Catherine's existence in chapter 1, three irreducibly important characteristics of her existence emerged: "one," "many," and "creativity." To have understood Catherine simply as "one" would have been insufficient, for that would have obscured the reality that who she is depends upon many circumstances and many others beyond herself. Alternatively, to understand her as a sort of multiplicity would not have been sufficient—she is, after all, but one person. The missing term, whereby this manyness and this oneness take on their proper perspective, is creativity: Catherine's integration of the influences upon her is a creative unification that results in her being herself. Finally, of course, each of the terms—one, many, and creativity—is dependent on the other two for the fullest understanding of its meaning. Each is like an empty shell without the others. "One," "many," and "creativity" are a triad of relational principles, each of which needs the others for its fullest meaning.

From any member of this triad, we can deduce the other two. This follows from the essential implication each has for the others.

"One" implies, as the conditions for its existence, the reality of "many" and "creativity." Likewise, of course, with the others: the "many" makes no sense without "one" and "creativity"; "creativity" is nothing if there is not something to be created, and the very process of creation is the unification of the many into a new one. Basically, there is a balance, a harmony, between the three terms.

Notice, however, that the balance may be approached from three different directions. It may start with the "one" and arrive at the harmony, or with the "many," or "creativity." However, the final harmony will reflect the starting point. To begin with the "one" will lead to seeing "many" and "creativity" primarily in relation to the original term. They could even be viewed as being for the sake of the "one." But of course the same could be done with either manyness or creativity. If "many" is the route to ultimate balance, perhaps the complexity of the harmony will be valued. For instance, to understand Catherine in terms of "many-ness" is to value the richness of diversity in her life. Contrariwise, if the "one" is the basic route for understanding, her unity and uniqueness might be taken as the chief value. But if "creativity" is the entry to understanding her, then we might value her dynamism, that movement of personality that combines the many into her own responsive uniqueness.

To generalize from this small illustration, couldn't it be possible that these three basic terms might be used by God as different routes to lead us into realization of harmony in our own existence? Each route is a valid, even an ultimate way toward harmony—but there would be three different ultimates.* The three ways would not contradict each other—on the contrary, in a profound sense each would imply the other if one looked deeply enough into any of the routes.

What would the world look like if God used three basic modes to lead us toward reflections of the divine harmony? Wouldn't there be religions which, following the way of creativity, would see into the universal flux of things, of the rising, falling, coming-to-being nature of existence? Forms of harmony in such a religion might emphasize communities attuned to relationality, extending

* The notion of more than one ultimate principle was first suggested to me by John B. Cobb, Jr., His own development, presented in "Buddhist Emptiness and the Christian God," *Journal of the American Academy of Religion* 45, no. 1 (1977): 11-25, focused on a metaphysical ultimate and an ethical ultimate.

beyond the human community to the world of nature. "Given that, this arises," might be a maxim of the religion, and adherents would strive to live in harmony with the nature of this creative world of centerless centers, being and becoming, harmonious depths of ceaseless flow. Buddhism is something like that. There are many variations within Buddhism, of course, but a common quality—a universal quality?—is attention to creativity in the processes of existence.

There might be modes of well-being in the world that find an entry to harmony not through creativity per se, but rather through the manifold nature of the world around us. The concrete many-ness of us all in the world might be seen as an ultimate reality, deserving an ultimate loyalty and commitment. For wouldn't it be possible to visualize the harmony of the many in the one world as a goal worthy of one's best faith and efforts? The "one" visualized might be seen as the complex one of a unified world—although of course there could be many interpretations of what would consti-tute the world as one! There are secular modes of living like that— Paul Tillich calls them "quasi-religions," since they place ultimacy not in the infinite God, but in the finite world. But perhaps God could lead people into such a mode of life, through emphasizing for them through the initial aim a route to harmony via "manyness." Perhaps secularism in at least some of its forms is not the great enemy of religion. What if God redemptively leads some people that way?

Christians, of all people, would recognize a route toward our well-being and toward finite modes of harmony through revelation of God as the "One" who is supreme. Judaism and Islam would vie with Christianity in this regard, for both of them also find their well-being in the "One"—in fact, adherents of these religions raise the question to Christians, suggesting that we have fallen from the purity of monotheism with our conviction that God is trinity.

"One," "many," and "creativity"—each of these terms implies the others. However, only as we push past the surface to the depths of the one, or many, or creativity would we begin to see the interdependence of mutual implication. The deeper we go into a religion, the nearer we get to the heart, not only of that religion but to the heart of the others as well. Buddhism, for instance, is a form of religion that emphasizes creativity. But in the history of that religion there have been telling variations on the theme of creativ-ity. There are forms of what is called Pure Land Buddhism in Japan which stress that only by calling on the name of Amida Buddha in faith is there salvation, for the one has accomplished redemption for the many. By no means is this an anomalous introduction of Christian principles into Buddhism; the fundamental insight is thoroughly Buddhist. But is the similarity to Christian insight entirely a coincidence? Could it be that at the heart of creativity, one might discover the pulse beat of the one? Alternatively, there are forms of Buddhism which place an extraordinary emphasis upon the acceptance of the dailiness of things around us, seeing in this the ultimate, and in the ultimate, just this. Haiku poetry frequently reveals this sensitivity. Does the heart of creativity also yield a pulse beat toward manyness?

Christianity profoundly affirms the one: "There is one body and one Spirit, just as you were called to the one hope that belongs to your call, one Lord, one faith, one baptism, one God and Father of us all, who is above all and through all and in all" (Ephesians 4:4-6). But the very stress on creativity which is found not only in process forms of theology, but also in the whole mystical tradition of the church, gives witness to the impulse toward creativity which the route of the one can yield. Also, secularism itself is uniquely a child of Christian sensitivities—a child who frequently embarrasses us, and one we might like to disown or punish for its wayward individuality, but a child nonetheless. Could it be that our love for the world, inspired through our love for God, has generated the child of secularism? It would take a careful historian to answer these questions, but surely the evidence suggests that the depths of the "one" can be plumbed to give rise to the "many" and to "creativity."

How would God bring about these many manifestations of harmony in the world? The dynamics, of course, would be the very same dynamics by which we understand God to be for us through Jesus Christ our Lord. God responds to the needs of the world, feeling the world as it is, transforming that world in the divine nature and feeling modes of harmony that fit the continuing particularities of the world as initial aims for the future. God bends to the condition of the world in order to fit the divine harmony to the world. In keeping with the divine feeling of the world, God can raise up a Moses, or incarnate in Jesus Christ. Can God not also raise up a Buddha? Or a Confucius? Or lead to the acclaim of Wisdom? Just as Christians unite themselves with Christ by faith, thus opening themselves to Christly identities as God mediates the benefits of Christ to them, can't Buddhists likewise adhere to the teachings of the Buddha? And won't God then be able to work peculiarly Buddhist possibilities of well-being for them? Won't the Buddhist be informed and identified through the Buddha by the grace and power of God fully as much as the Christian is informed and identified in Christ by the grace of God?

Christians are apt to disagree vehemently since the dominant sensitivity is to see not God, but the church as universal. Buddhists would perhaps disagree politely, for where a Christian might claim the gracious action of God, the Buddhist simply affirms the nature (or non-nature) of creativity. What of the Christian objection? Do we degrade the importance of the incarnation if God also provides other routes toward well-being and redemption? What of that verse thundering down from Acts 4:12, "And there is salvation in no one else, for there is no other name under heaven given among humanity by which we must be saved"?

Throughout the Christian ages, believers in God through Christ have gasped in wonder at the magnitude of the incarnation. That God would be for us to the extent of taking on our condition, revealing the divine nature in all the lowliness of a poor Galilean— that God's love should reach to this extent makes us exclaim in joy and gratitude and wonder. But surely God would not do such a thing for a few! Only if the act has universal proportions does it make any sense to us—not just for a handful but for the whole race of humanity; indeed, for the whole cosmos! Only in that cosmic context does such love make any sense at all.

Long before we reach the pages of the gospels in our Bibles we can open to the book of Genesis, and see the love God can have, even for a few. Abraham is worried about the destruction of that wicked city, Sodom—as well he might be, for he has relatives there. But in the story of Genesis 18, the Lord is going down into Sodom to see if there be any righteous ones for whose sake the city will be spared. Abraham fidgets. The city is large, and its reputation is bad—but Lot, his cousin, lives in Sodom. What if there are fifty righteous people there, he asks—would you spare the city for just fifty righteous? And the divine answer is Yes. But truth to tell, Abraham is not convinced that the Lord will find the fifty righteous people, and so Abraham begins narrowing the number. Forty-five, forty, thirty, twenty—and then, "Oh let not the Lord be angry, and I will speak again but this once. Suppose ten are found there." And again the divine answer: "For the sake of ten I will not destroy it," and the story moves on to recount the wickedness of Sodom, where there are not even ten righteous people.

Isn't it so that the history of revelation shows divine action not always on a great cosmic scale, but directed to the particularities of people in their histories? Even for ten the Lord will act thus and so—even for ten! The Lord will go into the city and experience its condition to determine its judgment, not because of universal conditions in the cosmos but because of the dire realities in that one city. Likewise, if God goes through incarnation even for the benefit of ten, how does that make incarnation any less a wonder? Isn't it rather a greater wonder, that such a salvation should be wrought for even these few? Jesus reveals the boundless grace of God, but to say that grace is boundless is to say that we do not determine the limits of grace.

Another aspect of claiming that God can save only through incarnation is that we absolutize the mode of God's action, rather than the God who acts. God bends to our condition, yes, but why does that mean that we then must universalize our condition? Further, if God acts in freedom, how can we limit God's freedom by saying what God does once must be the only way that God can act? To the contrary, we seem to deny the message of Jesus if we limit God to one mode of salvation, for Jesus touches people with forgiveness and salvation in ways as various as their needs. Does God do less? Finally, what we know of God's action in the incarnation is what God has done *for us*. We cannot presume to universalize our own needs, binding God to only ourselves. Just as God bends to our condition out of the divine character of love, even so God might well bend to the condition of others in other ways.

But the scripture verse from Acts states that "there is no other name under heaven given among humanity by which we must be saved." Why can't we read that verse with the emphasis upon the "we," in keeping with the whole revelation that God bends to our condition, providing us with the redemptive mode of harmony to which *we* can respond? We in the church know that God has acted for us in Christ; by faith in Christ God's grace has accomplished our salvation. There is no other name for us, and there is no other salvation for us. What God does with others is up to the divine good pleasure in the faithfulness of the divine character. That faithfulness has been manifested to us in the incarnation—which is greater, not less, by virtue of the marvel that God would go to those lengths even for the "ten."

If God is understood to be the properly universal one, and if our own mode of salvation in Christianity is but one manifestation of God's aim toward humanity's well-being, what does this say about missionary activity? How does it affect the stance of Christianity toward other religions?

Even for the ten God would have saved Sodom. Even for us God goes to the extreme of incarnation. Should we do less? Human beings are a peculiar lot, and while groups of us do very well sharing characteristics and sensitivities that mark us as being twentieth-century Americans, or participants in a certain cultural matrix, there are always those who cannot fit the dominant mode. Not all of those in a western culture find Christianity a route to their own well-being; not all those in an Asian country will experience well-being through Buddhism. Missionary experience, whether Christian or Buddhist, has shown that there are always a few in a culture who are not met by the religions of their own environment. Because these are few, should we feel no concern? Is missionary activity dependent upon wonderful magnitudinous numbers and figures? Or is it for the sake of well-being, whether in the form of a different religious faith for the few, or for the sake of expanding the togetherness of diverse faiths in human community for the many?

Missionary activity is hardly abandoned in a church that places the universality of salvation in the nature of God. But it is undertaken in humility and love: humility, because one knows that salvation comes from God in many ways, and we are simply sharing the way that has been manifested to us; love, because while one might consider going into a work that would garner glory as accomplishing a great deed without which all the country would perish, only if one loves deeply will one go to do a small deed—to see to the ten.

What of our relationship to those who find well-being in other religions? Humility and love—the marks, after all, of the incarnation—are also to be the marks of interfaith dialogue. Humility follows from the knowledge that we are only sharing ourselves, and the message from God that has made us ourselves. But if we wish to share ourselves, then we must be receivers as well as sharers, that the others, too, might be sharers. We listen as well as speak. In humility we do not impose our own mode upon all others, but listen for the grace of God in other ways and other harmonies.

Is there a hint of arrogance as we dare to name well-being through the mode of creativity as a response to the divine faithfulness? Do we inwardly smile and rejoice, rather liking the divine anonymity? How marvelous that God does not insist upon a name tag on every gift! How like the God we know in Christ to work so quietly in the depths of people's lives! But if we see a warm smile in the eyes of the other, we must recognize that the other might be nodding in glee to see the universal effectiveness of creativity, or manyness! For both of us, we might next find the startled shock of a deeper recognition. While at first we might translate the other's experience to the categories we ourselves know, we might also find that deeper level, that truer insight, that our own most revered truths are implied near the heart of that once alien religion. One, manyness, and creativity mutually imply each other. If and when that happens, how would interfaith dialogue proceed? Here is where love might move from intention and concern to reality. The other remains the other, and we can affirm that difference, and be pleased by it. But there are links of likeness, routes to understanding from the depths, not just from the surface appearances of things. With this recognition and understanding, love grows.

But if love grows among the religions of the world—among the peoples of the religions of the world—so that we are no longer competitors and strangers and enemies to be feared, then we will be encountering a new possibility for harmony in the world. The many might become one in an entirely novel way. Couldn't we experience a world community of religions as a unity created through diversity and love? Won't love bind us into a gladness at the differences, and at the samenesses that are cradled within those differences? There would be a new mode of harmony in the world, a new mode of community, a new mode of well-being. . . .

If universality is located in God rather than in our own particularities, then there is a basis for such a new community. There is a basis for genuinely hearing the other rather than trying to make the other like us. God's aims are for the well-being of the world; God's aims take that mighty divine harmony and fit it a thousandfold to the situation in the world, so that all our harmonies might reflect that divine harmony till we be brought to the image of God. Love and justice, bursting the boundaries of outworn forms, take on deeper forms, all through the leading of God. In this newly small earth, where we are forced to know one another in love or die, could we be experiencing a new direction from God toward human community through the affirmation of many who remain many and yet are as one? If that were the case, and if we responded, we might know something of the kingdom of God on earth.

Part Five

POWER

The Kingdom of God:
A Process Eschatology

16

THE KINGDOM
AND THE GOSPEL

CHRISTIAN faith proclaims that we have a twofold destiny: to
live deeply and richly in this life through love, and to participate
everlastingly in the life of God. Both destinies are social in nature:
to live in love is to live a societal existence, mindful of the needs of
all, creating communities of justice. To participate in God is to
know judgment and eternity in solidarity with all creation in the
righteousness of God. The biblical texts use a symbol that denotes
both forms of this destiny, the symbol of the kingdom of God.

The naming of the kingdom is most prominent in the teaching of
Jesus. In the book of Matthew, the kingdom is called the kingdom
of Heaven; in Mark and Luke, the kingdom of God. There is an
urgency to Jesus' proclamation, and an anticipation of the immediate coming of the kingdom: it is near, at hand, in the midst of you!
In light of the imminent arrival of the kingdom, Jesus called his
hearers to expectation and preparation. But two thousand years
have passed since the message—was there indeed a coming of the
kingdom? How did his hearers understand Jesus' urgent call?* In
the time of Jesus, language about the kingdom of God was no
unusual thing—there was a long history to the kingdom which was
presupposed and evoked by Jesus. To the Jewish hearer, the
kingdom involved a whole relationship to God as a people. God,
who had created the world upon foundations of justice, had called
forth a people to live that justice in human community. The God of
creation was the God of salvation, and the kingdom was the realization of that salvation. What, then, was the kingdom like?

* For the past century, biblical scholars have devoted much study to understanding the
nature of the kingdom. Norman Perrin summarizes this work in a small book, *Jesus and the
Language of the Kingdom* (Philadelphia: Fortress Press, 1976).

"A wandering Aramean was my father," begins one recounting from Deuteronomy 26, "and he went down into Egypt and sojourned there, few in number; and there he became a nation, great, mighty, and populous. And the Egyptians treated us harshly and afflicted us, and laid upon us hard bondage. Then we cried to the Lord the God of our fathers, and the Lord heard our voice, and saw our affliction, our toil, and our oppression: and the Lord brought us out of Egypt with a mighty hand and an outstretched arm, with great terror, with signs and wonders: and he brought us into this place and gave us this land, a land flowing with milk and honey."

Thus far, the text contains a concise summary of salvation history, through which the people identified with the suffering and deliverance experienced by their forebears in Egypt. While the history recounts the past acts of God, the people's understanding of the unity of the entire nation meant that it was a past in which they, too, participated. Their participation extended into their own continued response to God's call, as is evident in the concluding line of the litany: ". . . and behold, now I bring the first of the fruit of the ground, which thou, O Lord, hast given me." The entire recitation of the salvation history culminates in the offering; through this offering to Yahweh, the people continue in the responsive and responsible creation of the kingdom.

The way the offering was to be used indicates what the kingdom was to be like. The offering was to be distributed among the Levite, the sojourner, the fatherless, and the widow, "that they may eat within your towns and be filled." Participation in salvation history was maintained not only through identification with the past, but through the enactment of justice in the present community. The justice was precisely at the point of the physical and economic needs of the disadvantaged in the community. Cultically, the Levite had not been apportioned any section of the land, and therefore was dependent for physical sustenance upon those who had the land. The sojourner, whether a wayfarer or a non-Hebrew living in the land, depended upon the hospitality of the people for sustenance, and this hospitality was ordained by Yahweh as part of the justice forming the community. The fatherless and the widow were likewise to be embraced in the economy of the community. In Israel, justice and righteousness translated into the well-being of all, so that none would be without food, clothing, or shelter. Salvation history found its continuance not simply through the people's identification with the past, but through their perpetuation of this salvation as they shared their sustenance with each other.

In its earliest form, the shape of the kingdom of God is this concrete form of justice. There are texts within the Old Testament which demonstrate radical forms of such justice. In the book of Leviticus, for instance, there is the remarkable activity of the fiftieth year, called alternatively the Year of the Lord and the Year of Jubilee. In this year, there was to be a release of all who were in economic bondage of any kind: slaves were to be freed, debts were to be remitted, land was to be returned. The tendency of a few to gain most of the wealth was radically undermined in the Year of the Lord, and the justice whereby the needs of each were met was re-established. Studies in the Old Testament indicate that the Year of the Lord was more an ideal than a practice—while full economic justice was ordained by God to be foundational for the people, it was only partially achieved.

In the development of Israel's history, Israel's conformity to justice became seen as the pivotal issue in the welfare of the nation. Insofar as the worship of Yahweh prospered—which is to say, insofar as the justice of Yahweh was exemplified by the community—the nation prospered; insofar as the Israelites neglected Yahweh—and used false measurements in the marketplace, taking advantage of the poor, the sojourner, and the needy—the nation was besieged with political woes. The judgment pronounced by the prophet Amos is typical: "Hear this, you who trample upon the needy, and bring the poor of the land to an end . . . shall not the land tremble on this account?" Violation of the needy is neglect of the worship of Yahweh; Israel is to live in justice.

There were two further components of justice. First, justice should have an effect upon the physical environment. There was the expectation that when the community lived in justice, the justice inherent in the world of nature would also be strengthened. For justice was not a concept limited to humanity; it had its analog in the wider sphere of creation. In the natural environment, justice was the right ordering of things so that all things flourished. In the interrelated network of existence, the flourishing of nature contributed to the food supply of humanity, but this did not exhaust the purpose of nature. Rather, it existed as well for its own sake and for the glory of God. Given the interrelationship between humanity and the environment, justice in the human sphere would intensify justice in the rest of the created order. As a result of this, the full establishment of justice in the human community would result in a renewal of nature, such that Deutero-Isaiah could say, "The wilderness and the dry land shall be glad, the desert shall rejoice and blossom; like the crocus it shall blossom abundantly, and rejoice with joy and singing" (Isaiah 35:1–2). More is involved than the exuberance of metaphor; deep in the roots of the statement is the conviction that justice in the human community has an effect upon the environment. With the coming of justice, there would be a renewal of the earth to a superlative degree.

If the establishment of justice with Israel would have a catalytic effect upon nature, it would have a magnetic effect upon the nations. Again and again, the prophets speak of the attractive power of justice. The nations, frequently following a divine judgment upon both Israel and the nations, are portrayed as streaming to the city of God, seeking the glory of God. Deutero-Isaiah, writing in the sixth century, foresees a rebuilding of the city of God not only for the dwelling of Israel, but for the nations as well. In the forty-second chapter, the Servant of the Lord—an ambiguous figure, seeming to be at once both the nation itself and a second Moses leading the nation to a new beginning—is declared to be "a covenant to the people, a light to the nations, to open the eyes that are blind, to bring out the prisoners from the dungeon, from the prison those who sit in darkness." The actions are those associated with the righteous kingdom, and the extension of that righteousness to the nations. Again, the prophet Zechariah writing later in the same century declares, "Peoples shall yet come, even the inhabitants of many cities; the inhabitants of one city shall go to another, saying 'Let us go at once to entreat the favor of the Lord, and to seek the Lord of hosts; I am going.' Many peoples and strong nations shall come to seek the Lord of hosts in Jerusalem, and to entreat the favor of the Lord" (8:20–22). Similar statements are found in Micah, Habakkuk, Amos, Haggai, Jeremiah, so that one is drawn to the conclusion that the establishment of the kingdom of God would extend the parameters of justice beyond any one nation, to the whole world community.

These descriptions of the kingdom are drawn from a considerably detailed and complex history, spanning centuries; a depth study would involve a careful inquiry as to the development and interrelationship of the theme of economic justice, the renewal of nature, and the inclusion of the nations. Here we are but able to touch upon these themes as highlights of the kingdom that would have been presupposed by the hearers of Jesus as he preached the coming kingdom of God.

There is yet another element of the kingdom drawn from the Old Testament understanding that is related not to the nature of the kingdom but to how that kingdom shall come about. In the earlier texts, the kingdom was expected to come about in history as the people responded in justice to the call of Yahweh. Events in the life of the nation as it reacted to the fortunes of the empires surrounding it were interpreted in terms of God's judgment upon the people for their lack of justice. Increasingly, however, problems arose: Job portrays the problem in the personal realm, and Habakkuk on the societal. If justice is in accordance with the will/rule of Yahweh, and if one prospers or suffers according to how justly one lives in society, how is it that the innocent suffer? How is it that unjust nations triumph? How is it that a just king, like Josiah, nevertheless finds his kingdom slowly being crushed by the growing power of Babylon? And so the kingdom of God came to be seen not simply as a natural event occasioned by Israel's response to God, but as an extraordinary event which could only be brought about by Yahweh. Yahweh's actions would result in a forceful establishment of the kingdom, inbreaking upon the flow of history, creating a new order. There were many ways of expressing this catalytic event, with one of the most extreme represented in the book of Daniel. By the time of Jesus, a prominent expectation concerning the advent of this kingdom of God was the phenomenon of a universal resurrection of the dead. The dead would be raised; judgment upon the nations would follow, and then the kingdom would be established. The age-old justice would finally be a reality; then indeed nature would rejoice, the lion would lie down with the lamb, and all of the nations would stream to the city of God.

When would this happen? When oppression was the darkest, when the evil forces against justice were the strongest, when all other hope had failed: then Yahweh would act to bring about the kingdom. Thus there were portents to be discerned, arousing one to the hope of the kingdom—and it seems that every generation in that darkening history of Israel, moving from Greek to Roman rule, could discern such times. The kingdom, while not yet, was near at hand: God's power would bring the kingdom about, burning up the old order, bringing in the new. In the former days, God had intervened and created Israel as a people when they were in bond-age to Pharaoh; soon God would intervene and create a final kingdom of justice. Thus the kingdom no longer depended upon Israel's response alone; the kingdom was as sure as the power of God.

This, then, is the background against which Jesus preached the kingdom of God. According to Norman Perrin, Jesus' naming of the symbol evoked the whole salvation history of the Israelites together with their anticipations of God's new mighty act. Jesus' proclamation of the kingdom is further accompanied with actions evocative of kingdom expectations: the Sermon on the Mount surely manifests a radical justice in keeping with the kingdom; throughout the gospels there is note of the miraculous, such as the draught of fishes—surely these signs would be understood in terms of the renewal of nature. Finally, there is an added import given to Jesus' relations with the gentile world—he is approached by and/or extends justice to a Samaritan, Sidonian, Roman, Syrophoenician, and others. Justice, renewal of nature, inclusion of the nations: the marks of the kingdom are embodied in the life of the one who proclaims the kingdom, so that the preaching and the person would serve symbolically to evoke the kingdom expectations of the people.

Given this kind of continuity, there is a surprising feature to Jesus' teaching about the kingdom. There was a high anticipation toward the coming of the kingdom, and a long-embedded orienta-tion toward the nature of the kingdom. Why, then, did Jesus always portray the kingdom as coming upon one unexpectedly and in unexpected ways? There is more involved than the common wisdom that since God alone brings about the kingdom, no one could know exactly what moment God would choose for such action. The unexpectedness goes deeper than this. The biblical scholar John Dominic Crossan points out that most of the parables of Jesus express a particular structure involving the surprising advent of the kingdom, which opens up unforeseen possibilities. This advent then becomes the cause of a total revaluation of one's past, such that the past is given up for the sake of the future. For example, Matthew 13:44 recounts, "The kingdom of heaven is like a treasure hidden in a field, which a man found and covered up; then in his joy he goes and sells all that he has and buys that field." The kingdom, found in an unexpected place, caused the finder to sell all that he had—everything he had worked for and saved is given up for the sake of the kingdom. His life undergoes a reversal—the only continuity with the past is that the past has made purchase of the field possible. The value of the new dwarfs the value of the past, so that no sacrifice is too great compared to the wonder of the kingdom. The advent of the kingdom, reversal of the past, and action in accordance with the kingdom: these are the characteristics that emerge in Jesus' proclamation of the kingdom.

The values that are reversed are not only the material values represented in the parable of the treasure in the field; there is indication in the tale of the publican and the pharisee at prayer that one's expectations regarding religious customs and values may also be overturned by the kingdom. The element of shock remains: how is it that the kingdom is so unexpected; how is it that there is discontinuity with the past, when in fact the kingdom was so strongly and yearningly anticipated?

One might find an indication of the answer by looking at the response to the very actions of Jesus that most embodied the kingdom: when Jesus preached the radical nature of love and justice, the disciples murmured, "This is a hard saying; who can listen to it?" And after this "many of his disciples drew back and no longer went about with him" (John 6:60, 66). When Jesus related to the Samaritan woman, the disciples registered surprise, with overtones of disapproval: "They marveled that he was talking with a woman, but none said, 'What do you wish?' or 'Why are you talking with her?' " (John 4:27). When Jesus is recounted as bringing peace to nature through the stilling of the storm, the response was, "And they were afraid, and they marveled" (Luke 8:25). The more thoroughly one "knows" what the kingdom of God is to be, the less one sees of kingdom opportunities, paradoxically blinded by preconceived notions. "Justice" becomes so easily an abstract term, and in its abstraction, it is categorized and controlled. The dailiness of life translates justice from abstraction to the uniqueness of a present need in a present person. Reality intrudes upon the preconceptions, making justice as new as the surrounding needs. And we are surprised. The shape of the kingdom is concrete in the dailiness of events—for such dailiness is precisely the time and the place of justice.

Jesus preached the kingdom and embodied the kingdom; then came the disaster of the crucifixion—followed by resurrection. In the context of the kingdom message, the resurrection was a powerful confirmation of the reality of the kingdom as preached by Jesus.

The apostle Paul writes in I Corinthians 15 that "Christ has been raised from the dead, the first fruits of those who have fallen asleep." The resurrection of the crucified one, given the fact that the kingdom was to be ushered in by a general resurrection of the dead, was an astounding witness in time of that which was expected at the end of time. But the resurrection was to inaugurate the kingdom. Was the kingdom here, then, but hidden—like the treasure in the field?

The answer was both yes and no. The early Christians banded together in community, and of course a strong mark of the community was the sharing of meals: the widow and the fatherless and the sojourner participated in the community, and their needs were met from the abundance of all. Further, these people contributed of their own talents to the community, so that the ministry was one of reciprocity, and not simply a one-way giving. To the extent that the early church lived in justice, the church did indeed follow Jesus in living and proclaiming the kingdom. The most significant difference, however, was that the kingdom was now proclaimed through preaching Jesus Christ. The preacher himself had become the message, for Jesus, through his life, death, and resurrection, was seen as the inbreaking activity of God in human history, creating again a community of justice.

Like Jesus, the church proclaimed the forgiveness of sins. Such forgiveness was not at all tangential to realization of the kingdom, for sin involves the violation of God and creation, and guilt alienates the sinner from God and the community. Through forgiveness there is both judgment and salvation: judgment upon the violation as sin, much as was seen in the prophetic indictments of the Old Testament, and salvation in the inclusion in the community of God and the life of justice. "Go and sin no more" in the activity of Jesus became "Repent and be baptized" in the preaching of the church. Thus the creation of the church was a form of the kingdom insofar as the church identified itself through Jesus.

The apocalyptic understanding of the kingdom, however, was not at all eliminated. On the contrary, as the church endured persecution and suffering it identified itself with the passion of Jesus in his earthly ministry and looked for a further experience akin to the resurrection at the last days. This resurrection would take place following a second advent of the Lord: the Parousia. Paul describes this expectation graphically in his second letter to the Thessalonians: "This is evidence of the righteous judgment of

God, that you may be made worthy of the kingdom of God, for which you are suffering—since indeed God deems it just to repay with affliction those who afflict you, and to grant rest with us to you who are afflicted, when the Lord Jesus is revealed from heaven with his mighty angels in flaming fire" (1:5–7).

Thus the apocalyptic expectation of the Israelites that God would intervene in their suffering from foreign rule was transformed in the church to an expectation that God would intervene to rescue the church from its persecutions. Also involved in the expectation of the second advent was the final release from sin and death, as Paul notes strongly in some of his letters. There is therefore still a future kingdom to be expected: Christ's resurrection is the guarantee that all will be resurrected, and that the kingdom, already begun in Christ, will be brought to fruition. At that time, following the parousia, resurrection, and judgment, Christ will submit the kingdom to God, who will finally be all in all (I Cor. 15:28).

Have the old themes of justice, renewal of nature, and inclusion of the nations fallen away in the Christian reinterpretation of the kingdom? Not at all. The book of Acts recounts the phenomenal mission to the gentiles, and Romans 8 clearly shows that Paul expected a renewal of nature upon full establishment of the kingdom. Also, we must look at the witness of the book of Revelation. The last four chapters, beginning with 19:11, present the final consummation of the kingdom. Interwoven with the account are the ancient themes.

Mathias Rissi, in *The Future of the World,** gives a penetrating account of these chapters. He notes that the introduction of Christ is through the Logos identification known to the church: Christ is "Faithful and True," and the "Word of God." Between the two identifying titles, Christ is described curiously as ready for war— but he is already clad in a "robe dipped in blood" (19:13). The war has been won prior to its beginning, for the battle was precisely the crucifixion. And the war does not have to be fought again—despite the imagery of preparation for battle no war is actually described. Instead, the Lord's weapon is simply himself: the Word. Gathered for battle, the nations encounter no battle save the Word, which is Christ. That word is now a judgment that slays.

* Nashville: Alec R. Allenson, 1966.

Chapter 20 continues with a scene wherein Satan is bound. Those who are against God, whether demonic or human, are portrayed as dead or bound through the judgment of the word; following this, there is the curious account of the thousand year reign. The curiosity is simply that there appears to be no one left over whom to reign, for the saints alone are left: the general resurrection of the dead is still portrayed as future. Rissi sees in this simply a highlighting of the nature of the church's rule. *Everyone* reigns with Christ, and all are "priests of God and of Christ," so that the reign must be understood as indicative of the self-governing community of justice.

Following this millennial reign, there is another encounter with Satan, loosed from prison: the community is surrounded again, as in the days of its earthly persecution, with no help seemingly near. But as the demonic forces surround the "camp of the saints and the beloved city," fire comes down from heaven and consumes them, "and the devil who had deceived them was thrown into the lake of fire and brimstone" (20:9). Only at this point does the general resurrection of the dead occur. Death and Hades give up their dead, "whereupon Death and Hades were thrown into the lake of fire. This is the second death, the lake of fire." Death itself dies in the resurrection of the dead. Now the judgment occurs, and all are judged "by what they had done." Those who do not pass the judgment are "thrown into the lake of fire."

These events of Revelation 19 and 20—the second coming of Christ, the resurrection of the dead, and the judgment—form the prelude to the climax of the vision given in chapters 21 and 22. "Then I saw a new heaven and a new earth," writes John, and the long-hoped-for kingdom of God finally comes into view. What is it like, and how does it relate to the themes of the kingdom seen in the Old Testament and repeated in the preaching of Jesus?

The kingdom is first of all one of comfort: "he will wipe every tear from their eyes, and death shall be no more, neither shall there be mourning nor crying nor pain any more, for the former things have passed away" (21:4). "Behold, I make all things new," says the one sitting upon the throne, but the division of judgment that is proclaimed after this is the division of justice as it was from the beginning, with violators of justice destined for the lake of fire in which death dies. Then, at last, is the holy city seen—radiant with the glory of God. In imagery that calls up passage after passage of

THE KINGDOM AND THE GOSPEL

Old Testament writings concerning the coming kingdom, John describes the city. And then we have the astounding recurrence of the Old Testament themes of the inclusion of the nations and the renewal of nature. Justice is now established and, as in all the ancient portrayals of the kingdom, the inevitable consequences follow: there is the renewal of nature and the inclusion of the nations.

But how can there be a renewal of nature, since the old earth has passed away? And more crucially, how can there be an inclusion of the nations, since the nations have been resoundingly destroyed through the judgment? There are no nations left! Yet in ecstasy John concludes his telling of his vision: "And the city has no need of sun or moon to shine upon it, for the glory of God is its light, and its lamp is the Lamb. By its light shall the nations walk; and the kings of the earth shall bring their glory into it, and its gates shall never be shut by day—and there shall be no night there; they shall bring into it the glory and the honor of the nations. Nothing unclean shall enter it, nor anyone who practices abomination or falsehood, but only those who are written in the Lamb's book of life.

"Then he showed me the river of the water of life, bright as crystal flowing from the throne of God and of the Lamb through the middle of the street of the city; also, on either side of the river, the tree of life with its twelve kinds of fruit, yielding its fruit each month; and the leaves of the tree were for the healing of the nations" (21:23–27, 22:1–2).

The gates of the city are open, but in the text, the only thing outside of the city is the lake of fire, and the only ones outside of the city are those who have been consigned to that fire. Yet the renewal of the earth that is portrayed through the wonderful tree, superabundantly yielding its fruit, is also a renewal of the nations, for the leaves of the tree are for the healing of the nations. Those nations, passing through the judgment of fire, come into the city through that purification—into the city whose gates are never shut against them, and whose trees contain healing.

In the Old Testament, the judgment of God always thundered down against the wayward nation for the sole sake of calling that nation to justice, to the establishment of the kingdom of God. In this last chapter of the New Testament, we finally read, "There shall no more be anything accursed." The purging, saving judgment of God, bringing about justice, will finally triumph over all injustice, and God's kingdom will finally be established.

Clearly, the kingdom is God's triumph of goodness over evil in the ultimacy of justice. This triumph of the good is given two dimensions: the temporal and the eternal. Temporally, the kingdom of God is realized in our openness to modes of justice in our daily lives. These modes of justice must relate to the well-being of all peoples, both personally and societally; justice will bring about a positive relationship to the natural world around us, and an inclusiveness to the nations. Eternally, the kingdom relates to a resurrection of the dead, brought about solely through the power of God. This resurrection leads to immortality, whether through the imagery of the lake of fire or that city where the thirsty will receive "water without price from the fountain of the water of life." Immortality is for the sake of judgment and transformation, as all things are made new. And this transformation brings about the final establishment of a kingdom of justice where all evil is overcome, the kingdom of God.

In the long history of the church, the understanding of the kingdom of God has largely been projected to that time beyond time in an ultimate end of the age. Eschatology has been defined as dealing with that future time, called the "last things." The biblical scholarship of the last century, however, has forced the church to take more seriously the temporal dimension of the kingdom of God as we strive toward achievements of justice in our societies. Eschatology must now be understood not only as that ultimate future with God, but also as the temporal destiny in a kingdom of justice. One is forced by the scriptures to deal with the "kingdom of God" imagery with the double focus of time and eternity.

Since the kingdom has a double focus, it is important to see the interrelationship of both aspects. If God indeed brings about the kingdom in its eternal dimensions, surely God's leading of us toward temporal realizations of the kingdom cannot be dissociated from this eternal destiny. There are not two kingdoms, but one, with two dimensions. Among the unique contributions of process thought is that the peculiar metaphysics of the system allow formulation of a contemporary vision of the kingdom of God that highlights the viability of both dimensions, and that indicates the way in which both dimensions affect each other. The temporal work toward the kingdom of God is not separate from the eternal establishment of the kingdom; likewise, the eternal establishment of the kingdom affects the temporal possibilities for ways in which to live justly and with love. Through process theology both dimensions of the biblical witness concerning the kingdom of God may be recovered. When we, too, like the hearers in Jesus' time, feel the vibrancy of the kingdom's reality, then we too will hear the impact of Jesus' call to participate in the kingdom.

17

THE KINGDOM IN GOD

"WE look forward to the resurrection of the body, and the life of the world to come. Amen." So concludes the confession of the Nicene creed; these two brief clauses contain the Christian hope of God's final victory over evil. The affirmation is based upon the triumph of Jesus Christ in the resurrection. There will be a general resurrection, like his, which shall bring about the fruition of God's redemptive work.

What is "the life of the world to come"? Based upon biblical imagery, this life is one of a resurrection that leads to judgment and justice. Biblical justice was not a blind balancing of virtues and vices, but the concrete caring for the well-being of persons within society. The biblical image of "the life of the world to come" cannot be in tension or discontinuity with the biblical understanding of justice, and so that future life must be one wherein there is an ultimate attainment of well-being through the process of resurrection and judgment. In such a way, divine power enacts the fulfillment of the ever-repeated promise of justice.

Notice how much hinges upon resurrection and judgment if God's justice is finally to be vindicated. As was noted earlier in chapter 8, in principle a full justice can never be achieved in human society if justice requires a redress of evil and restoration of well-being. Examples of why this is so are painfully available: one particular woman was burned at the stake as a witch in medieval Europe. Injustice came upon her as a maelstrom, crumbling her world of meaning and well-being into a welter of panic, pain, and ashes. Five million women living in a world of justice and mutuality make no difference to that one woman's experience of fire, agony, and death. She feels no affirmation of her existence and no redress of the crime, no matter how fervently women five centuries later decry the evil of witch burning. Justice for the many does not answer the requirement of justice for her. Without "the life of the world to come," her unredeemed experience stands as a finality of injustice, mocking the power of God's justice. Without resurrection, justice cannot be complete.

Without judgment there is no justice. As we wrote about the life of Jesus, we called attention to the way in which his desire toward the well-being of Simon required him to judge those things in Simon's attitude that were against justice. Simon's false presumptions were that the woman at Jesus' feet should be excluded and condemned. His failure to care about her well-being meant that he cut himself off from relationality and justice. His true good involved him in loving care for the condition of the woman. Thus Jesus judged his smallness, revealing to him his true state and his true welfare. Sometimes through weakness and sometimes through pride, we limit the notion of well-being to ourselves or those like ourselves, just as Simon did. Like him, we too act against our own well-being. What good is resurrection if in resurrection we persist in the same sins? Only as resurrection leads to judgment is there any clear avenue toward the justice which in Ephesians is proclaimed as "the reconciliation of all things."

The issue of "the life of the world to come" that is affirmed by the church involves far, far more than the reduction to the "happy reward/miserable punishment" theme of popular speculation. It involves the full establishment of God's justice. Only through resurrection and judgment can the fullness of justice ever be realized.

But how do we express such things? The apostle Paul, in his first letter to the Corinthians, referred to that which is beyond what any eye has seen, beyond what any ear has heard, and beyond what any heart can conceive. The apostle John, as we saw in our last chapter, could only express his vision in terms of metaphors of majesty, terror, and beauty. Precisely because of the inexpressible nature of that which is envisioned in "the life of the world to come" we Christians seem to fall into several problems. Some simply discredit notions of resurrection, judgment, and justice as wishful thinking or fantasy, unfit for a twentieth-century world view. Such Christians frequently fail to see the tremendous issue of justice that stands or falls on the reality of the resurrection. Some will affirm resurrection, but with a vision too small, making "the life of the world to come" but an extension of earthly existence without frustration or pain. The depths of the biblical meaning of the kingdom receive scant due by such limitation, for well-being

means more than contentment for just a few. Finally, there are
those who loudly affirm the resurrection, but concentrate almost
wholly upon reducing the book of Revelation to a code book that
they alone can peculiarly decipher. The symbolic depths of the
book are ignored, replaced by identifying various contemporary
nations or persons as evil powers who will be consumed in an
apocalyptic catastrophe that is just around the corner. The deci-
pherers of this history, of course, are never among the unfortunate
consumed. Self-righteousness and revenge are odd entryways into
a vision of the kingdom of God.

Perhaps because of the inadequacy of the above views, there has
been a lessening of the full vision of the kingdom of God in
contemporary Christianity. If the vision is important for our efforts
to establish a finite form of justice, and if our work in the world
ultimately has an everlasting effect in God, then we cannot afford
the luxury of dismissing or belittling the Christian affirmation of
resurrection, judgment, and justice. But how do we understand the
resurrection of the dead?

The New Testament imagery refers to resurrection always in the
context of a transformation of things—there is a new heaven and a
new earth. Whatever else such statements mean, surely they indicate that resurrection cannot be understood as the extension of the
present order. We must use imagery from the present order—
witness John in Revelation—but that imagery pushes ordinary
understanding to its very limits, straining at the edges of vision.
For instance, John speaks of a river, and a tree—but the river is as
crystal, and it flows from a throne! And the tree bears twelve
different kinds of fruit, one kind for each month! Imagery is
stretched to its limit in order to become a symbol to convey that
which no eye has seen, nor ear heard, nor heart conceived. To be
faithful to the imagery is to let it break out of its confinement in
temporal existence to point to that vision beyond sight.

To use process language to express resurrection is likewise
visionary, and presses beyond itself. The metaphor of the dynamics of the actual entity can express the reality of faith's asser-
tion that God is just: resurrection, judgment, and justice can take
form in the process vision. But while process dynamics can interpret the three themes, process dynamics alone do not dictate the
themes. To the contrary, by pushing process language to express
resurrection, judgment, and justice we push its language to its
limits. But we also allow a new sense of life to pulsate into the

process understanding of God, informing it with faith, filling in the abstractions of description with the fullness supplied by faith.

The process model pushes us to say that God is heaven, and heaven is God. We must express resurrection as taking place in the life of God and through the power of God. To do so is strangely consonant with some of the oldest expressions of Christian faith, for in the biblical texts we are told that we will be made partakers of the divine nature, and that immortality belongs only to God. Early church theologians expressed the resurrection as a promotion into God and as a participation in God. Process theology must reiterate these sensitivities, and suggest that resurrection is a rebirth of ourselves in God through the divine feeling. We are made partakers of the divine life in a movement from the edges of God to the everlasting depths of God, from the consequent nature to integration with the primordial nature, from judgment to justice through a process of transformation governed by God.

How can these things be? The process term, "prehension," gives the means to discuss resurrection—and immortality—in God. In the model, prehensions refer to those feelings with which every occasion of existence begins. A prehension is a feeling of that which is other than the self. This other is also composed of feelings that have been unified into a unique subjectivity. To feel the other is to be in touch with its feelings of itself. For this reason Whitehead can speak of prehension as a "flow of feeling" from one subject into another. The connectedness that exists between one subject and another is the transition of what was felt "there," now re-enacted "here." It is as if everything exists in and for itself, and yet finds itself at home in otherness—that which is for itself is also for others; what is created "here" comes to rest "there" through the vehicle of prehension.

However, no subject can feel the totality of another subject's feelings on the finite level. This is because every subject feels not simply one other, but myriad others. The many feelings must be unified into a single feeling. As noted in chapter 2, the process of concrescence is a process of selecting, comparing, contrasting, and unifying the past in terms of that which the concrescing subject chooses to become. This selection necessarily eliminates some portion of every other's total subjectivity so that the many *can* be integrated into the new unity. Therefore, even though there is a flow of feeling, this is never a flow of the total subjectivity of one into another. Always there is selection in terms of compatibilities, both with regard to the many others that are also prehended, and with regard to the becoming subject's own feelings for itself.

There is an analogy to this issue in our experience of relating to friends. Each friend calls forth a different aspect of ourselves, so that each friendship is unique. One friend might bring forth feelings for a particular kind of music, so that there is a frequent enjoyment of each other's company while listening to this music. Another friend might share childhood memories, so that the special quality of being with that friend is the warmth of knowing each other's past as well as present. The two friends do not know each other, so that while in the presence of one, the qualities that are usually evoked in the presence of the other are dormant. Imagine that both friends unexpectedly come to visit at the same time. Won't there be a peculiar tension in the meeting? Since neither knows the other, nor that aspect that the other evokes, there is a conflict concerning which interests and which bond shall form the core of the meeting. If the relationship to the musical friend proceeds as usual, the childhood friend will feel left out; conversely, to speak about common memories with the childhood friend excludes the musical friend. The almost unconscious selectivity that operates in each friendship alone is now painfully apparent, and some wider basis of shared experience must become the content of conversation. Unfortunately, the immediately obvious shared fact is that one friend is shared in common by the other two. Relating on that basis is much less satisfying than either of the other two, so that there will be a measure of discomfort and stiltedness until deeper commonalities emerge rendering the three persons friends together. The triadic friendship, however, will have a quality of its own not found in either of the two single friendships. Selectivity and unification always utilize some but not all elements from the past, so that while there is a flow of feeling from one subject to another, the full subjectivity of the other can never be retained in the prehending subject.

This does not hold true with regard to God's feelings of the world. The finite subject must simplify the past in order to integrate all data into a new unity. Because God "begins" in the primordial nature, God "begins" with an eternal unity of all possibilities. Potentially, all actuality whatsoever can be incorporated into God's primordial experience of unity. Therefore there is no categorical reason why God cannot prehend the whole of another's feelings. The primordial nature of God is the common ground by which diverse subjects in their full subjectivity can be felt, contrasted, compared, and unified. In our finite illustration, the common ground whereby the three might know the unity of friendship had to be discovered through selectivity, sifting out those factors that were alien to the interests of each, and finding those mutual interests that could unite the three as friends. Selectivity was the basis of unity. For God, the primordial nature is the basis of unity. In principle, God and only God can feel the entirety of the other. Thus the flow of feeling that takes place as God prehends the other is a flow of the full subjectivity of the other into the full subjectivity of God. This is subjective immortality for the world in the life of God.

Is this resurrection? In the imagery of I Corinthians 15, resurrection is a transformation brought about by the power of God wherein our dead physical bodies become spiritual bodies. Our mortal nature becomes immortal; sin and death shall be no more. "We shall all be changed," says the apostle. Through the nearly two thousand years of the church, Christians have been attempting to express this Pauline vision, knowing finally that we can only fall back upon the beginning words of I Corinthians that the fullness of the vision is beyond our comprehension. In this process expression of resurrection, we simply use the metaphysics as a metaphor to express a mighty transition from a finite subjectivity which is alone with itself to that same subjectivity in the presence of God. Mortal nature becomes immortal; sin and death have no place in this transformation of our natures.

This understanding of resurrection requires that one reaffirm the creedal statement, "I believe in the resurrection of the body." Resurrection cannot be limited simply to a world of souls—God feels the entirety of the world, in all its manifold forms. In a process universe, subjectivity is not limited to human beings, nor even to all sentient beings: subjectivity is the essential reality of every actual occasion, regardless of whether it forms part of the reality of a human being or of a drop of rain. God feels *all* subjectivities in the process vision. Transformation is not restricted to humanity, but must be extended to the whole universe. There will be a new heaven and a new earth; this is the fullness of resurrection.

The resurrection is spiritual, not material. The world is not simply transposed to God, so that it exists in a sort of parallel state: the world is *transformed* in God; this is why "resurrection," which connotes transformation, is a more precise term than "immortality," which could imply simple continuance. In a process framework, one can push toward an understanding of a spiritual resurrection by remembering the discussion of God as pure spirit in chapter 5. The physical pole was defined as the means of relating to others; God relates to all others in their entirety, and hence if spirituality is understood as a depth of relatedness, God is pure spirit. A spiritual resurrection must be understood along the same lines. If a subject experiences itself as subject in God, then the new context of subjectivity is the pure relatedness of God. In God, as will shortly be developed, there is a new fullness of relatedness to all others. The finite development of subjectivity required selectivity and a clear demarcation of boundaries. The results of that demarcation remain, but the circumstances are changed. Whereas in finite existence the parameters of existence might have been the societal togetherness of many actual occasions so that a material existence developed, in God the parameters of existence are simply God. *All* relatedness, not *some* relatedness, is found in the environment of God. Therefore, the subjectivities that are resurrected in God are no longer definable in terms of material togethernesses. Materiality falls away; the conditions for materiality do not exist in the single reality of God. Resurrection is to a spiritual body.

How can this subject resurrected in God continue to experience anything at all? The basic objection being raised here relates primarily to an important qualification in process philosophy, for it is axiomatic that the "satisfaction" of a subject (or completion of a subject) cannot be added to; if there is an addition to the subject, then the subject is no longer the same subject, but another. If a subject experiences transformation in God, how is it the same subject? If a subject does not experience transformation in God, how is there judgment and justice? For resurrection alone is not sufficient to establish the kingdom of God.

The problem is technical; the attempt to resolve it is likewise technical, drawing upon the resources of process philosophy. In process thought every occasion begins with feelings of the multiple entities of the past. Concrescence is the subjective comparison and contrast of the past in light of an immediate feeling for what one can become. Satisfaction is the conclusion of the process, the determinacy of all data into just *this* subjectivity. The whole process is highly unitary: if any one part of these dynamics is not present, there is no subject. It is not even that the subject is stillborn: it is more radical than that; the subject *is* the entirety of the process, indivisibly. Nonetheless, subjectivity is process, moving from multiplicity to unity. No subject is felt by another until that unification process is completed in satisfaction. Satisfaction is the transition between concrescent creativity and transitional creativity. Satisfaction is therefore like a bridge between what one is for oneself and what one is for others. Prehension takes place as one subject feels the satisfaction of a prior subject.

God prehends the completed subject's satisfaction. Since God feels the totality of this satisfaction, God feels as well the concrescent process that resulted in just this satisfaction. But note that God's feeling constitutes a reversal of the dynamics of becoming, analogous to God's own reversal in moving from the eternity of the primordial pole toward the everlastingness of the consequent pole, and the integration of the two. God feels the finite subject's satisfaction, and consequently the concrescence. This means that the resurrected subjectivity is retained in reversal of its finite state. The satisfaction which culminates the finite state begins the immortal state. This would mean that in God the subject is always itself, but always more than itself; it is always the selfsame satisfaction, but is, as it were, turned "inside out." The flow of feeling now moves away from the solitude of satisfaction into the fullness of God's own feeling. This reversal of concrescence is the beginning of judgment and transformation.

Perhaps the abstract description might be supplemented and clarified by turning to a speculative application of the dynamics. What would all this talk of "subjective immortality" through God's "prehension" of "satisfaction" mean for someone like the woman destroyed through the unjust accusation of witchcraft? In this process understanding, resurrection takes place not upon the death of the whole person, but throughout life, as God continuously feels the occasions of the world. God continuously coexperienced each moment of that woman's existence. God coexperienced her childhood, her teen years, and every moment of her adult life. God coexperienced her fright just as she felt it when she heard the frenzy in the voices of her neighbors discussing witchcraft; God felt her own terror as she realized the accusations were directed against herself. God felt the paralysis with which she endured the humiliation of examination and "trial," and God felt the agony as the fire began its searing work: God felt her death.

Because God felt with her every moment, there is resurrection in God. This is the point where it becomes essential to realize that an occasion is not raised to immortality locked into its finite experience; hell indeed would be eternal if her fiery death were untransformed in immortality. The center of the resurrected subjectivity must be able to flow from the finite creation into the wider experience of God.

But it is God who feels her subjectivity, re-creating her. The divine concrescence now receives the finite concrescence. This means that there is a strange double subjectivity for the woman in resurrection. The focus shifts from the experience itself to the "withness" of God—for it is through God's concrescence that her own concrescence is re-enacted. The woman would feel herself in God with the copresence of God's feeling with her.

In the process model, what could we say concerning the way in which God feels the resurrected occasion? Each concrescing occasion begins with an initial aim from God, and concludes with a satisfaction which is felt by God. God is the source and destiny of every finite occasion. God's feeling of the completed occasion must include a comparison with what that occasion could have been, given the initial aim. If the woman-in-God experiences herself through the divine concrescence, then the first phase of her "more than herself" movement into God is a phase of personal judgment. She knows herself as God knows her; she knows herself as she could have been, and as she is. The first phase of judgment is the knowledge of ourselves from the divine perspective. "We shall know as we are known," says the apostle Paul in I Corinthians 13.

The second phase of judgment in God would have to take place due to the unity of God. Whitehead has a phrase, "mutual sensitivity of subjective form," which guides us in this consideration. Given the unity of the subject, all prehensions are felt comparatively. Each prehension is felt in terms of all the rest. This is the basis for the finite occasion's ability to contrast and unify all the various feelings that begin the physical pole of existence. If the subjectivity of the occasion is retained in God, flowing from the satisfaction into a coawareness of the divine experience relative to itself, then wouldn't that subject feel that mutual sensitivity whereby it was felt in relation to all of God's other feeling? And since these other feelings also retain the subjectivity of the others, wouldn't mutual sensitivity mean not only the awareness of the self from the divine perspective, but an awareness of the self as others had experienced the self? "We shall know as we are known."

Consider ways in which the woman might experience this second phase of judgment. A distinction must be made between the totality of her life experience in the unity of her personality, and the myriad actual occasions that successively formed her person. A resurrection of the total personality depends upon the moment by moment, occasion by occasion, experience of immortality and judgment through God's prehension of every occasion in her life. The "mutual sensitivity of subjective form" is the means whereby the latter results in the former notion of resurrection. God feels a particular occasion in her life, and in that feeling she, at that instant, becomes aware of the might-have-been and the actually-was of that particular instant. But the comparative feelings of God relate that instant to all of the other instances which are the self at a point in time. Through the divine sensitivity whereby each feeling is felt in relation to the others, the natural grouping of all the occasions of a life occurs in God. And the woman experiences this. So she would not only experience the momentary judgment of a particular instant but also a composite judgment concerning her total being, all through the comparative feelings of God whereby her many moments, or many occasions, are unified through God's subjecive form—a unification that she too feels in the coexperiencing made possible through her participation in the divine concrescence.

This would mean that there is a sort of "regathering" of one's total personality in the resurrection body. In our finite existence, we exist in a "stretched out" manner, one event following another, one year replacing another, inexorably moving in one direction from birth to death. The continuity is provided by the flow of feeling from one moment to the next, but always in a context of progression and loss. But in God, there is no loss, for nothing is ever past. It can't be, if God is a single entity. And God has felt every single occasion in that movement of our lives, and still feels them all. There is a composite gathering of the personality in God, and the totality is known for what it was and for what it could have been.

This is both a positive and a negative form of judgment. In God, every moment is always itself and yet flowing beyond itself. This means that the seven year old child feels the thirty-seven year old woman burning at the stake—but it also means that the thirty-seven year old woman feels again with a simultaneity the delights of other moments of her life. The regathered personality in God in the resurrection body is all ages and no age, transcending every moment of existence in the reunion of all moments of existence. This second stage of judgment is the suprapersonal totality of the self, feeling one's whole existence as copresent in God and with God, as felt by God.

But the single individual is hardly the sum total of God's feelings—God feels the world! Mutual sensitivity of subjective forms allows each, through God, to know one's composite self from the divine viewpoint, but this does not complete self-knowledge. In our finite existence, it would be foolishness to think we stopped with the edges of our skin—we are relational beings, and we are completed in and through our many relationships with others. In God, those with whom one has come in contact are also resurrected, and the relationality that bound us with these others on earth is felt as well in heaven.

In the resurrected life, self-knowledge will extend to an awareness of the way one was experienced by others. Through the power of the divine sensitivity, each is mediated to the other, knowing oneself through the heart of the other. Joys that were given will be experienced; alternatively, the same dynamics mean that pains that were inflicted will also be experienced. In the faithfulness of this experience of the self through the other, there is continued judgment.

This dynamic can be illustrated by considering not simply the woman of our earlier example, but the judge who was most responsible for her accusation and conviction. He, too, experiences resurrection in God; he, too, experiences the totality of himself; he, too, experiences his effects upon others. In God his knowledge of himself will be completed through his knowledge of how he affected the woman—he shall know as he is known. But he will know her pain along with God's judgment of what might have been, so while she might experience God's feeling of her as the compassion of shared pain, her finite judge will experience God's feeling of her as a judgment of wrath against himself for what might have been if he had only responded positively toward God's aims for himself for an alternative mode of action and being.

There are now three phases of judgment: first, the judgment with regard to the individual moment of experience; second, the judgment following from the totality of a life, and third, the judgment following from the totality of our relationships. This process of movement beyond the single subjectivity to the cosubjectivity with others through the concrescent power of God is a process of movement. From the point of view of the resurrected self, it is a movement into deeper and deeper levels of self-knowledge, with an attending sense of judgment. From the point of view of God, it is a movement into integration, whereby the many feelings in the consequent nature are brought into increasing modes of unity. The many feelings are being pulled toward the vortex of God, the depths of the primordial vision where the many are together in the unfathomable depths of unity and justice.

There are several things to be noted about this process. Notice that it is a movement toward unity according to the divine purpose. The movement is according to God's will, for freedom belongs only to God in the divine concrescence. The resurrected self *must* experience judgment; there is no freedom of option. Insofar as the will of the finite self has been conformed to God in its own finite self-creation, the finite self will feel this movement toward unity as a wonderful degree of freedom. The movement would feel like a freedom long dreamed of but frustratingly difficult to achieve in the conflicts of finite existence. Here at last, in God, there is a movement beyond the self in a feeling with others; here at last in God there is a fully realized sympathy; here at last in God is the elusive fullness of self-knowledge. But to those whose finite choices had closed them off from empathy with others, to those who denied the validity of the others' feelings, the very movement which feels like freedom to the other will be experienced as unfreedom. That which to one is heaven, to another is hell. The judge *must* feel the woman's agony, not only as she felt it but in the full knowledge of the pain and impoverishment inflicted upon society in the days and generations to come through his act. To know as he is known is pain for him in regard to this action. The inexorable movement whereby God pulls his subjectivity into that knowledge is experienced by him, not as freedom but as that which goes against his own freedom. And indeed it does. The divine freedom governs the divine concresence; insofar as one's own use of freedom is in conformity with the nature of God, one will experience God as heaven; insofar as one's freedom is against the nature of God, one will experience God as hell.

How is there redress? How is the woman requited for her agony?

And is the judge to feel the movement of God as a hell forever? The same movement by which there is judgment is the movement by which there is ultimate redemption, and therefore ultimate justice. Notice that by the will of God, the resurrected self must move beyond the confines of any one aspect of personal ego. In the first place, there is a composite ego, and in the second place, the ego is continuously growing through the increase in self-knowledge. This means that the ego, by the power of God, can no longer remain locked within its narrow structure. The finite subjectivities are being held in existence by that infinite subjectivity which is God. The mutuality with which God feels each subjectivity in relation to all others pulls each subjectivity into that coexperiencing which we have described as judgment. But hell, to remain hell, must have the reinforcement of the narrow ego. What is happening in the very process of judgment is that the ego is being opened up to that which is more than itself. The participation in the other through the power of God is not only judgment, it is the route to the transformation of justice.

Consider the woman and the judge. She is aware of him experiencing her pain within the divine nature. But her own movement is beyond that pain into transformation. The judge is not locked into her pain, any more than she is; the judge, too, experiences her transformation in God, and therefore participates in that transformation. She contributes to his redemption.

The further aspect of this follows from what it means to be completed through the other. This very completion through others is a breaking down of the limitations of the finite ego, which tends to see others as competitors or contributors to the self. In the context of divine transformation, that boundary of the ego into self-as-opposed-to-other breaks down. With its breakdown, the self becomes wider and wider. There is no longer imprisonment in the ego. The breakdown of the ego becomes the breakthrough to God. Judgment issues into transformation. In this transformation, there is an increasing identity of the self with the whole—but the whole is now God, governed by God's aim toward harmony, pulling all the multiplicities of the consequent nature into the single beauty of the primordial nature.

If one has been initially completed by one's effects upon others, this route of "beyondness" never ends in God. Those elements which have been highly valued by God insofar as they are near, not distant, to the goodness of God gain an increasing importance, and are felt by those in the process of transformation as supplementations to their own reality. The judge moves from a knowledge of himself—mediated by God—to a knowledge of himself in God, which then moves still deeper into a knowledge of God. This movement is one wherein multiplicity moves deeper and deeper into unity: the judge moves from alienation from the others toward supplementation by the others toward completion by God in a full integration with all others in God. His sorrow and pain is supplemented by their joy, his evil is supplemented by their redemption, so that the redemption of others is at the same time the redemption of himself. At the same time, the redemption of himself through the transformative power of God is given for others, who in God can in no sense consider themselves in isolation from him. In God the many become one, and that unity is the depths of the divine nature, governed by the mighty resources of God.

Judgment moves into justice. The increasing integration of the re-enacted subjectivities pulls them deeper into unity with each other and God's own primordial satisfaction. In the mutual completion, or the movement toward unity, each experiences the other's joys, each experiences the other's gratitude, each experiences the other's wonder, each experiences the other's love. These qualities are intensified since they mirror the divine ability to hold the many together in unity. The edges of God which are tragedy through the feelings of pain in the universe remain indeed the edges. The mighty center toward which we move in judgment and transformation is the overcoming of such qualities with the supplementary reality of divine goodness, love, holiness, joy. In the center of God, "the many are one everlastingly, without qualification of loss."

The vision we finally have of justice in God is simply the primordial harmony in its everlasting actualization. The reality of the world is transformed in judgment into conformity with the nature of God. The consequent nature of God is one where multiplicity moves to deeper forms of unity; this movement is the concrescence of God, pulling the prehensions of the resurrected world into the unity of the divine nature. But the dynamic depths of God are again a form of grouping, wherein there are clusters of types of harmony, all held together in the intense unity of the overarching whole: God's primordial and inexhaustible vision of the togetherness of all things, a harmony of all harmonies.

Earlier, in our discussion of the incarnation of God in Christ, we noted that since Christ *is* the manifestation of the divine nature in finite circumstances, there is little transformation needed of Christ

in God. Indeed, the whole transfiguration experience recounted in
Matthew indicates that, to eyes which could see, Jesus was already
shimmering with the glory of God in his embodiment of the kingdom. Therefore, when we speak of the depths of God as being the
actualization of the harmony of the primordial vision, sparkling in
the brightness of God's glory, we must speak of Christ in God,
transfigured rather than transformed. Further, Christ in the primordial nature is everlastingly being completed through God's reception and transformation of the church, completing the church
through its union with Christ in the primordial nature even as the
church completes Christ.

But if Christ and those who have been led to conformity with
God through him have a place in the brightness of that actualized
primordial vision, it is also so that every distinctive route toward
the realization of well-being in conformity with the harmony of
God has a place in that divine center. Each route is like a constellation in the whole sky of God, retaining its uniqueness even in the
wider sense of unity—for unity is ever a harmony of diversities,
and not the obliteration of diversities. Therefore, each constellation that has manifested the transformation into God through a
particular route retains the diversity and particularity of that route,
like a flow forever entering into God by the will and grace of God.
But still deeper than the diversities is the unity: the mutual sensitivity that begins the process of judgment and transformation continues in the depths of God, integrating the eternal and everlasting
satisfaction of God which is nothing but the beauty and holiness
and love of the divine nature. Here the beauty that is Christliness is
felt and feels itself in harmony with the beauty that is Buddhistic,
and again with Judaic ways, and again with whatever constellations have been realized through the far-flung universe as God
deals infinitely and faithfully with creaturely existence.

There is a home in God, a home for the whole universe. In that
home, multiplicity finally achieves unity; fragmentation is embraced in wholeness. The unity and wholeness receiving and transforming each part is more than the sum of them all, for the unity is
the ever-living God, drawing upon the divine resources of infinite
possibility to blend all reality into the giving and receiving of the
whole. Differentiation remains in the primordial depths of God, but
a differentiation that is divinely sustained as the most fitting actuality of unity, beauty, holiness: the kingdom of God which is the
kingdom in God which is God.

18

THE KINGDOM OF GOD

WHAT is the effect of the kingdom in God upon us? We can acknowledge that realm as our destiny, but it should be clear in a process view that we cannot dismiss such a future as irrelevant to our daily living. The reasons for this are twofold: in the most obvious instance, our actions here and now have everlasting repercussions. *That* we will be saved rests assuredly with the power of God, but *what* will be saved depends upon us. "Work out your own salvation with fear and trembling," wrote the apostle, "for God is at work in you both to will and to do the divine pleasure" (Phil. 2:12–13). In process theology, this admonition is taken with deep seriousness, for what we do matters everlastingly. We create, in our own finite freedom, the self which God receives and recreates. What is saved depends upon us. When we so pervert the will of God in our living that our distance from our true well-being is great, then the transformations we must undergo in the divine judgment are such that we shall barely be recognizable in the divine depths. "If any man's work is burned up, he will suffer loss, though he himself will be saved, but only as through fire," says the apostle Paul in 1 Cor. 3:15. On the other hand, as our constitution of ourselves in relationship to others approaches true well-being, the transformation is in accordance with the direction already set in our living. What we do and what we become matter, for we enter a resurrection life in God which, through judgment and transformation, has everlasting effects. Yet for all this, it is solely the divine activity that brings about our resurrection, and solely the divine activity that brings about our transformation, and solely the divine activity that makes our transformed selves partakers in God's justice. It is God who is at work, inexorably willing and living the divine purpose. We are saved by grace.

The second reason whereby the kingdom in God affects us here and now relates, not to what we will become everlastingly but to the creation of the temporal image of God in human society. "It is God who is at work in you," said the apostle, and the temporal side of this work is through the initial aim. What is the source of this aim? "The resources of God in the primordial nature," but now we must focus more clearly upon how those resources are made relevant to the world. That kingdom in God, developed so speculatively in our last chapter, is integrally related to why we may dare to work against any odds for reflections of that kingdom on earth in communities of justice and love. What happens in heaven has an effect upon earth.

Every moment of our becoming receives a welter of data from the past, influencing us with manifold demands. The most important datum from that past is our own immediate past self. But our present moment transcends even the moment of our immediate past, and there are demands upon our present that were not felt by our past. How do we go about putting it all together? God has felt that past, but God felt the past in judgment. The resurrected occasion is felt in terms of the divine harmony, not simply in solitariness but in that "mutual sensitivity of subjective form" whereby God feels each occasion in relation to the others. We said that God felt the world as it is, as it could have been, and as it yet can be. The "yet can be" has a double direction. On the one hand, as we developed it in the last chapter, it refers to the "can be" in the divine concrescence or participation in the glory of God. But on the other hand, this initial transformative feeling has a world-ward dimension: in light of the divine resources and in light of the divine will toward well-being and in light of all the context of the finite world, there is a "can be" relative to the immediate future of the finite world. Given *this* past, *this* present is now possible. It is still possible, until made real by the actual world—therefore it is the future of the world felt by God. God feels *how* the newly becoming occasion can unify and transcend and transform the past, and that *how* relates to the well-being not only of the self, but of the self in community. This is the effect of God upon the world; this is the lure of God for the world; this is the temporal result of the divine resurrection. God makes a way for the world to move toward its own reflection of the divine harmony: "It is God who is at work both to will and to do the divine pleasure."

How, then, do we realize the kingdom of God on earth? And since it stems from the divine reality, can we achieve a final kingdom, one that will preclude any other—is there a finality to our achievement? Do we work for a realizable future?

As we consider the first question, process philosophy makes us realize anew our dependence upon the revelation of the nature of the kingdom that we see in the biblical texts. In the very nature of the case, the process model tells us that God's influence upon us must be at the deepest layers of our being. Consciousness, in process thought, is a late development in the concrescent process of each moment—it is like the tip of the proverbial iceberg, held above an ocean containing supportive but subterranean depths. God's action upon us must be at that depth level, since God's action launches us upon our way of becoming—that is what the initial aim is all about. But if God works in us at such depths, then in principle it is a rare thing for God to be part of our conscious awareness. God is present in the mode of hiddenness.

Further, God's aim is always oriented toward well-being in the world—there is a worldward thrust to God's aim for us, so that we are pushed in obedience to that aim, not necessarily to an awareness of God but to a deeper awareness of the world. The content of the aim is toward the finite kingdom. Once again, then, God's presence is in the mode of hiddenness—how, then, do we discern kingdom orientations from other desires and influences? Cannot God reinforce the guidance?

The matter is complicated still further, since God's aim is not a pure reflection of the divine character—how can it be, since it must be fitted to the world as it is, and the world as it is may exist in perversion of the will of God? As far as that goes, how do we know it is perversion anyhow?

There is a criterion, and the criterion was briefly developed in chapter 16, "The Kingdom and the Gospel." Through the long faithfulness of God in history, the directions toward reflection of the image of God in human society are carefully developed and preserved for the generations. There are guidelines for the kingdom. But perhaps the most important guideline of all comes from the teaching of Jesus, orienting us not toward the past, but toward the future. The kingdom in God is not a static reality, it is a dynamic movement everlastingly in process, for God everlastingly resurrects a world and so intensifies and deepens the actuality of the primordial vision. The kingdom lives, and life cannot be captured in any past. "Behold, I make all things new," says the Lord in the closing pages revealing the kingdom. The worldward side of that newness is in the ever-changing shape of the kingdom. The changes are not a denial of the kingdom, but a necessarily new form of the kingdom. The guidelines are simply that: guidelines, giving us directions as from a compass rather than from a map. For the map itself must be everlastingly drawn in response to the pull toward today's form of the kingdom.

Therefore, when we look at such things as economic justice, renewal of the earth, and inclusiveness toward the nations as criteria for the kingdom, we must take Jesus' admonition as to the unexpected shape of the kingdom seriously, and not look simply to past ways of achieving the criteria as determinative. The criteria demand ever-changing actualizations. Why is this? Simply because history does not stop. New people are born, and new groupings of societies take place, and new elections take place, and new governments are developed—even when the newness is simply in the change of office. The way of the past can no more be imposed upon the present than a size eight coat be put on a size fourteen person. The fit is ill. The actualization of justice must reflect the realities of time and place—but since the world moves through time and place, the actualization of justice must ever be done anew.

What we have, then, are the revealed guidelines reinforcing for us the sense of God's directions, and the trust that God will be ever-adapting the application of these criteria through the surety of guidance at the very base of our existence. How, then, do we actualize the kingdom of God on earth? By trusting God, and looking toward the needs of the world in light of the divinely revealed criteria of justice, renewal of nature, and inclusiveness toward the nations. We must, in this trust, dare to see unexpected needs and unexpected applications of the kingdom. Our natural tendency would be to draw back from new ways of actualizing justice, for we would rather hold to the security of the past. But the kingdom as taught by Jesus does not allow us that luxury. Our trust must not be placed in our past ways, not even when those ways were enacted in response to concrete divine guidance. That would be akin to a person at age forty claiming that eight-year-old behavior was still appropriate since at that time it had been in response to God's guidance. Our trust must be placed in God, who leads us in faithfulness into the future, and hence toward continued creation of the kingdom.

Can we perceive God's guidance today? Can we tell the shape of the contemporary kingdom? How does it look, this kingdom of God on earth in our own day? And here the relativity of our perceptions and of our whole existence must shape the tentativeness of an answer, even while we trust in God and dare to formulate an answer, in order to act on the formulation. Ultimately, of course, the whole church must formulate and act on an answer, thus supplementing the individual vision with a corporate vision, drawing upon the many talents of the church. Theological vision must be supplemented with political vision, economic vision, and sociological vision for the fullness of the kingdom.

If we take the biblical criteria seriously, then we can identify several forces at work within Christianity today that seem to be pushing toward new manifestations of the kingdom: there is the focus upon liberation, so that minority groups might enter into the relationality of value and richness in the whole of world society; there is the focus upon our relationship with the nonhuman world of nature, seeing with a new forcefulness the caring that must take place in and for the whole world, and not just the human portion of the world; and there is the focus which begins to probe new modes of relationships among those in the world who have taken diverse religious routes toward realization of justice, love, and holiness. Each one of these foci demands intense energy, since each is a forging toward new modes of existence, new instantiations of the kingdom.

Insofar as the kingdom of God is mirrored on earth through the efforts of liberation, there is an increasing emphasis upon the value of each human being within the whole community. This value has always been a part of the ideology of Christianity; the newness of the value is the sense in which it increasingly values the temporal welfare of individuals and societies, and not the eternal welfare only. Indeed, in process thought, to disvalue the temporal welfare is to lessen the eternal effects—temporal evil is crucifixion, even of God. It matters to God when people are hungry, for God, too, feels that hunger. It matters to God when people shiver with cold, when there is the pain of sickness, or the sorrow of death. God feels our feelings.

In the kingdom of God, each contributes to the welfare of the whole and each receives from the welfare of the whole. In numerous ways, societies can mirror such a reality, for no one political system can exhaust such a vision of reciprocity and mutuality. Liberation theologies that focus upon political and economic oppression insist upon raising the valuation and the welfare of the many in the social community. It matters, to the good of society as a whole and to the good of God, who feels that society, that individuals comprising the society shall give and receive equitably for one another. It matters, to the good of society and to the good of God, that individuals within society be provided with opportunities to develop the potential of their lives. It matters, to society and to God, that freedom and responsibility be exercised equitably in community, that richness shall be developed for the whole society, that in responsibility and freedom all participate in the creation of a just society. The one and the many, interacting in interdependence, work toward the well-being of humanity; in doing so, the kingdom of God is mirrored on earth in justice.

When those who are outside the church say such things, they should function as a catalytic judgment upon the church. For their message is in principle the same message that Jesus proclaimed concerning the kingdom. The judgment upon the church is that we too easily spiritualized a message that relentlessly referred to the divinely instituted justice of the kingdom. Jesus preached economic justice, but in the interpretation of the church it was sometimes easy to read his teaching and action in a spiritualized way. But Jesus did not give spiritual bread alone to the five thousand—the baskets of leftovers were heavy with bread which could nourish bodies. Again, Jesus preached release for the captive. The context of his preaching was that radical understanding of the fiftieth year, the Year of the Lord. Jesus dared to proclaim his own presence as the fulfillment of that year, and the church has dared to proclaim every year of its existence as "Anno Domini," the "Year of the Lord." The root of this year means release for the captive, whether that captivity be blatant or subtle. Liberation theologians, particularly from the black community, thunder out against such injustice, calling anew for implementation of the kingdom of God.

Again, the preaching of the gospel portrays Christ as the "new Adam," and the corollary of this is a return to the conditions of creation as they are portrayed prior to the story of the fall into alienation. The vision of Genesis 2, contrary to the church's dominant interpretation, is one where man and woman live together in mutuality and openness and love. The creation of woman is far from an inferior afterthought, supplementing an already perfect reality. On the contrary, the division of the one being into two marks the culmination of creation in a togetherness in unity, akin to the divine reality. Prior to the fall, the woman is described as speaking in a way that mirrors God's own judgment upon creation, for in Genesis 2:9 the trees of the garden are described from the divine viewpoint as being "pleasant to the sight and good for food," with the further designations of one tree as the tree of life, and another as the tree of the knowledge of good and evil. In Genesis 3:6, the woman, like God, "saw that the tree was good for food," with the further designations of one tree as the tree of life, be desired to make one wise." Her fault was not in her evaluation, for it mirrors the evaluation of God; by creation, she and the man together are in the image of God.

The fault of the woman as well as the man in the Genesis 3 text was in disobedience to the divine command. The church has seldom noted that the Hebrew reading of the verse of the fall indicates the copresence of the man and woman in the fall. "She took of its fruit and ate; and she also gave some to her husband *who was with her,* and he ate also." The differentiation between the man and the woman is not divisive in creation, nor is it divisive in the sin; the divisiveness follows only as the curse of the consequence of sin. Not until the close of the drama is woman placed under the rule of man.

But Christ is the second Adam, and in Christ the curse of the fall is removed. Is it only removed for men, then? Does not Christ redeem all humanity? And if the curse is removed for women as well as for men, by what perplexity does the church use Christ to reinforce the curse, by keeping women in subordination? In Christ, is there not a re-creation on earth of the conditions of creation? Is not a kingdom established through Christ to reflect the conditions of Genesis 2 in whatever societal form is appropriate? Are we not to look to Genesis 2 to envision the well-being of man and woman rather than to Genesis 3? And so feminist liberation seeks to release the full measure of the implication of Christ as the second Adam in human society.

Political liberation, black liberation, feminist liberation, and the underlying root of all three, which is economic liberation, are the edges of the kingdom as the church pushes toward new forms of realizing the image of God in society. How society will be shaped as each form of liberation enters into the reality of history is fluid, befitting the dynamism of the kingdom. Justice, like beauty, can take many shapes. Those whose expertise is in the realm of each area will contribute their creativity to the shaping of the future as it is made present. Throughout, the kingdom that is God pulls us toward forms which mirror that divine life; the lure of God pulls us toward justice, toward the image of God, toward the kingdom of God in history. Whether or not that kingdom will be actualized depends upon our vision and our trust.

The foci of ecological sensitivity can also be understood in relation to the kingdom of God on earth. In this process universe we live in ever-enlarging circles of interdependence; everything and everyone affects all else to some degree. Therefore, there is an intense responsibility to exercise our freedom in awareness of the welfare of others. While we have clearly understood this to be the case among human beings, despite the rationalizations we have utilized to eliminate some human beings from the caring, it is not the case that we have always exercised this responsibility with regard to nature. Yet the texts from our early history speak to us now with force and clarity, and we hear anew such statements as that of Paul, declaring that all creation groans in travail as it awaits its redemption. Suddenly, in a century that sees atomic explosions in one part of the world creating dangers on the opposite side, in a century that faces in bewilderment the increasing pollution of the atmosphere, earth, and water; in a century that worries about the loss of layers of atmosphere which are essential for the protection of human life, we finally hear in earnest our responsibility to nature. We realize that we, too, are nature, and that our caring cannot be restricted with impunity to sisters and brothers in the human community but must extend toward the earth and sky.

Justice extends beyond the human community to unite with the sustaining community of nature. We are, as Heidegger said, the "shepherds of being," those through whom the world is given voice, and speaks, and finds the awesome power to participate in the creation of meaning. If we are indeed the shepherds of being, then we must exercise that responsibility, bringing nature into our caring and into our meaning. It is no longer a luxurious option, but becomes a means to our very survival. Strange that such caring is finally the requirement for survival in a world of nature! Justice, say the Old Testament texts, is the foundation of the universe. It is not so strange, then, that the lack of justice toward nature results in a shaking of the foundations that sustain us. The renewal of nature which takes place everlastingly in the recreated world in God has its own earthly analog as we take consideration of the earth into our shaping of the kingdom.

The third foci that pulls us beyond our past and yet that bears the marks of the kingdom, is that which awakens us to a new relationship to other religions of the world. This was discussed in part in chapter 15 on the nature of the church's universality, but must now be related more concretely to the contemporary form of the kingdom.

If the church is to mirror in its communal nature the character of God, and if that character is such that God values the many in the unity of the divine nature, and if it is further posited that diversity is essential to unity, even within the depths of God, then it follows that the church must rejoice in diverse modes of mirroring the harmony of God, even when those modes take place in other forms of religion. How can this rejoicing happen? Do we not push the idea of the kingdom of God too far when we relate it to an affirmation of the many religions in the world? Is not Christianity "right," and are the others not therefore "wrong"?

When there are two harmonies, each of which produces a mode of well-being appropriate to a particular time and place, how is one right and one wrong? Rather than "right" and "wrong" comparisons, perhaps it is more appropriate simply to note that they are different modes of achieving well-being. A God who takes the world seriously, fashioning aims that reflect the conditions of the world as well as the harmony of God, might even purposefully provide the world with differing routes toward harmony. God, not the church, is the ultimate source and arbiter of harmony. And if God provides initial aims to every occasion whatsoever, then the very faithfulness of God requires that the divine harmony be fitted to a diversity of conditions.

We concluded our last chapter by daring to envisage the actualized harmony of God through the metaphor of a night sky, wonderful in its beauty, lit with constellations that through their very differentiation intensify the unity of God's beauty. In God, the wonder of well-being through revelation of the incarnate character of God does not compete with well-being through insight into the nature of creativity; both reflect the purposes of God and the transformation of the world; both are given through the boundless grace of a God who wills our good. Diversity is the means toward actualization of the divine harmony. Perhaps the church is now called to reflect this in its concrete relations to other religions and peoples in the world. Competition and valuation only on the basis of conversion must give way to sensitivity to the other's welfare, and appreciation of the other's mode of achieving well-being.

To do this will be difficult. Movements toward liberation within the church and society may be simpler for the church, since anybody perceiving an illness within the self tends toward correction of that illness. As the church dares to see the call of liberation in all of its dimensions as consistent with its own dynamic identity toward justice, the church will move to create that contemporary mode of the kingdom. Likewise, in the push toward a greater ecological concern, the church can move in concert with this concern. The network of interdependent existence, as it is brought to consciousness, forces the serious consideration of our responsibility toward our environment in keeping with the kingdom call. Justice in the human community sensitizes us toward justice throughout creation. But the movement toward acceptance of the other religions in the name of the kingdom might carry a new shaping of the church beyond that which is implied in the kingdom of God as realized through liberation and ecology.

To relate to the other affirmatively means to be open to the influence of the other. To be open to the influence of the other involves us in changes that are not within our immediate control. If we can speak of changes occasioned through liberation as analogous to the self-healing process of the body, the changes occasioned through openness to other religions are more akin to the changes that are wrought in an individual through love of another. The risk involved in loving another is that one's welfare depends to a high degree upon that other; the interdependence which is always operational is highlighted and strengthened in intensity through love. In a sense, the other gains power over one, for the sorrows of the other become sorrowful to oneself; the joys of the other become joyful to oneself. Further, there is the risk that whereas, apart from love, one determines one's own future and one's own path as much as possible, with love there is a joint working out of the path.

If Christianity heeds the call to love the other, to manifest the nature of God with regard to the other, then the shape of Christianity will be changed through the dialogue which takes place in that love. Those things that cause sorrow to those of another religion will be felt as hurts by the Christian as well; those things that bring joy will be a cause of gladness. We will begin to feel the others from the inside, as subjects, and not simply as the other, the stranger, the object. We will begin to feel others on earth as we will eventually feel others in heaven, albeit the intensity on earth must

perforce be much less. But we will be called to action here on earth
as a result of such love, either to alleviate the cause of sorrow
insofar as we can, or to celebrate the triumph of joy. In such
openness to the other's welfare, the path of Christian realization of
the kingdom of God on earth will be affected by its relations to
other religions. The freedom of "how" those changes will take
place will ultimately remain within Christianity for Christianity,
just as Buddhists alone will determine the "how" for Buddhists.
Each religion, whatever its name, remains itself in responding to
the other, responsibly moving and changing in the dialogue. The
content of the changes will follow from the openness to other forms
of religion, other ways of achieving well-being.

Can we trust God's wisdom to guide our response to such a
situation? Can God guide us in our becoming Christianity even
though we risk loving others not like ourselves? The preaching of
the kingdom of God consistently calls for that kind of trust and
that kind of love; the church, being ture to its nature, will take the
risk.

All we can do here, from the viewpoint of theology, is to discern
the directions of the church today that suggest a deepening of the
ancient values—justice, renewal of nature, inclusiveness toward
the nations. We can call the church to evaluate the opportunities,
and join the church in exploring the future set before us. The
details of following through are, fortunately for all of us, more than
theology can undertake, for the movement into the future is the
task of the whole church: the economist in the church, the historian, the political analyst, the student of other cultures. Only as the
church utilizes the diversity embraced in our own unity can we
fully respond to the leading of God to create in our own time that
future which is the kingdom.

The caution that must ever be sounded, however, is that the
shape of the kingdom can never be finalized. The source of the
kingdom is God, leading the church, leading the world through the
transformation that takes place in the kingdom that is God. Therefore there is no stopping point, no time when a temporal kingdom is
complete. The kingdom, as the reflection of God, is ever complete
and ever in the process of completion. Needs of the future cannot
be met by the maps of yesterday; always, the map is being created
through the fulfillment of present responsibilities. No sooner do we
achieve the kingdom than we must critique the achievement, for
the kingdom moves on. We create the kingdom in faithfulness to

our particular task, sharing its benefits with the width and breadth of the community, so that the community likewise might share with yet other communities. Individually and collectively, we form the church and create the kingdom of God—only to look to God and the needs of the world anew, and see how our creations may yet be surpassed.

19

THY KINGDOM COME

THE call to the kingdom is so great: economic justice, renewal of the earth, openness to the nations of the world for the peace of the world! How can we as individuals possibly answer the magnitude of the call? We can only be involved in a portion of the world and one aspect of the work, and our effectiveness seems terribly small. Do we simply concentrate on our own task, and hope others will take responsibilities elsewhere? In bits and pieces, will the kingdom come?

The kingdom of God is the reflection of God in human society: that which is contained in the beauty and justice of the divine nature is to be mirrored in our own circumstances. In God, the many are one everlastingly, each contributing to the others and receiving from the others in the unity of God. If this image is to be duplicated within human society, then the fragmentation of each doing a task in isolation from the others is antithetical to the kingdom. It is not enough to confine oneself to one's own task; one must contribute to others and receive from others throughout the breadth of the work. But how can this be?

Prayer is vital to the coming of the kingdom. Through prayer, we enlarge the effectiveness and scope of our work in the entire task; also through prayer, we bring to conscious realization the unity that belongs to all Christians by virtue of our identity in Christ. Finally, it is primarily through prayer that the future kingdom that is our destiny in God is pulled through to our finite realizations here and now. Is there a kingdom of justice in God? Does this kingdom await us? Does it call us? As we respond to that call, our destiny interacts with our present reality. The call comes through the initial aim of God; prayer can heighten our attunement with that aim, and aid us in its actualization. Thus prayer is the avenue of union between the kingdom of God which is God, and the kingdom as it is reflected on earth.

How do we enlarge the effectiveness and scope of our work through prayer? Every moment of our existence begins with an initial aim from God. This aim is directive, guiding us toward a best mode of action in our given circumstances. This touch of God is at the deepest levels of who we are, below the layer of consciousness, and therefore, while it certainly offers the material and the impetus toward consciousness, the touch itself remains hidden. The orientation of the aim toward the world around us and the distractions and needs represented by this world serve to reinforce the hiddenness of the aim. That the directive force in our lives comes from God is more a matter of faith than sight.

Frequently through meditative forms of prayer we can quiet ourselves, screening out the distractions of our surroundings, centering in toward the depths of who we are. We can direct our consciousness inward toward the place where God touches us. The Christian tradition of prayer has often cited the paradoxical claim that the way "outward" to God is the way "inward" to ourselves; such a way begins with a focus upon the self in order to break through the self, first to God and then to immediate service in and to the world. Prayer is that inward step, seeking the strength of the guidance of God as it is given through the initial aim. God is faithful; the aim is ever given, and it is a grace-laden gift. The direction of God is based upon our fullest realities, and therefore is a direction which is really possible for us. God's will *can* be done, else how could we pray "thy will be done"? As we allow ourselves to become more open to God's aim in the quietness of prayer, that specific guidance from God will become more apparent to us.

Prayer is the road to renewed confidence in the guidance of God as we work for the reflected image of God in our lives and in the world. The confidence that comes from prayer is strengthened also by the conformity between what we perceive as God's guidance for us, and the normative guidelines of the kingdom as seen in the biblical witness. Can we see the personal guidance received in prayer as a mode of enacting the justice which is the foundation of the kingdom of God? Does the action that is before us have some positive effect upon this earth, affirming or renewing its sustaining capacities? Does the guidance received through prayer break through some false barrier erected between peoples and nations? The faithfulness of God means that there is a consistency to divine action, so that personal guidance is always consonant with the wider purposes of God that are revealed in the themes of the kingdom. While the actions of any individual will seldom embrace all three of these great themes, there will be a resonance with the redemptive spirit of the kingdom, and a movement which is in some way reflective of at least one of the themes. The inward guidance of prayer and the outward guidance of revelation combine, and our confidence is strengthened.

This confidence is the means, gained through prayer, whereby we enlarge the effectiveness and scope of our task. Without such confidence, we might grow discouraged by the weakness of our singular work. With it, we know that God's guidance of us fits in with the larger task of the whole; our weakness is supplemented by divine strength; our singularity is complemented by the many others who are also colaborers with God in the kingdom. And no action is without effects in a process universe: that small task which is before us will have repercussions that can be useful for the wider work; God can weave those effects into the total fabric of the kingdom. The confidence gained through prayer increases our vision and hope; consequently, we act with more zest. Our effectiveness increases.

Through prayer we participate in each other's work, thus actualizing the unity that belongs to the church through identity with Christ. In addition to that mode of prayer which is a centering inward in order to focus upon God's guidance in the initial aim, there is also intercessory prayer, through which we participate in God's aims for others in a direct way.

Consider an example of this. John lives in a small town in Pennsylvania; he feels a responsibility to work for alleviation of severe health risks that endanger the workers in a factory in his community. His background in industrial hygiene fits him for this work, and his sense of God's guidance in the direction of justice leads him toward this form of action. But there are many factors involved in the complexity of the dangerous working conditions, and much resistance to the kinds of changes he thinks must be made. John is just one individual; what can he do against the status quo of these long established practices?

Joan lives in Cincinnati, and her own work is in a quite different area. But John is her friend, and she feels his sense of helplessness. In fact, she feels it herself, for apparently she is powerless in this situation. How can she help? Her only resource seems to be prayer—is it a weak resource? What happens as she prays for John?

Remember that God works *with* the world, *for* the world. The initial aims God gives to John are woven from the realities in John's situation, together with what is now possible given those realities. Imagine that the realities in John's world include a sense of hopelessness on the part of the workers themselves: it has always been this way, and it always will be; my parents worked in these conditions, and so will my children. Hopelessness goes hand-in-hand with complacency, since it reinforce the nonnecessity of change. God must reckon with these attitudes in fashioning the really-possible aim for John. The odds *are* great. And Joan prays. All that this means is simply that against the negative realities in the world, suddenly a positive reality vis-a-vis this particular situation is introduced. There is not only John, who is a potential agent for change, but there is also Joan, who in the action of prayer molds her own concerns to John's situation. God can work with the material of Joan's praying, for in fact her praying changes the world. She is a part of the world; as she directs herself to John's concerns, she becomes a part of his world, a part of his particular situation, and therefore that situation is qualitatively different than it would be if she neither cared nor prayed. By prayer, she adds to the material world with which God works in providing redemptive aims. Hope supplements hopelessness; a desire for change supplements complacency. Because Joan prays, John can receive possibilities through initial aims that will be stronger than they could have been if Joan did not pray. Thus Joan participates in John's work through prayer.

Prayer changes the world. The statement is not metaphorical but literal. In a process universe, everything that happens in the world matters. God works with what is, in order to lead the world toward what can be. To pray is to change the way the world is by adding that prayer to the reality of the world. Because prayer is added to the world, the reality of what-can-be changes. Redemptive possibilities that might have been irrelevant, and therefore inaccessible to the world without prayer, can be released by the power of prayer. By no means is this because God begrudges those redemptive possibilities to the world, and must be peculiarly persuaded to release them. Far to the contrary, biblical texts indicate that God yearns for our redemption, cares passionately for our well-being and, in fact, prompts us to pray. As we pray, we change the world by changing ourselves in our deepest orientation. And with that change, we alter the total situation with which God works. Prayer releases the power of God to lead the world toward the kingdom.

Notice the implications of the fact that through prayer we change the world first of all through a change in ourselves. Joan prays for John. At first her general sense of helplessness may form the content of the prayer; she knows of no specific direction to pray, simply that her deepest concern is to be for John through God in prayer. It is enough that divine wisdom will utilize her prayers for John's good. But in the course of her praying, Joan might find that she does indeed become more specific as she directs herself to John's good. This can be simply through God's leading her toward this mode of specificity as she is open to such leading in prayer. Also, Joan's openness to God and to John's welfare in prayer creates a readiness in her for further action. There will be a quiet prompting in her life directing her to this or to that activity with regard to John's situation. Prayer is a form of action that yields still further forms, and these further forms are an extension of the prayer. God will use Joan's prayers not only in direct reference to the kinds of initial aims that can be offered to John and those others involved in that whole situation, but God will use Joan's prayers to extend her own involvement in other areas of her life.

This means that Joan participates in John's work, even though she is hundreds of miles distant. John works for his community, not only for the sake of those in need, not only for his love and responsiveness to God, but for Joan as well. John is Joan's representative in the work. When John, in turn, prays for Joan, she is his representative in her own form of work. The underlying unity which they both share in Christ is actualized through prayer, and their bondedness with each other is a participation in each other's work.

Apply this principle on a wider scale. One Christian is called to be a minister, another is called to work in a mill. Through prayer, each participates in the other's work: the millworker represents the minister, and the minister represents the millworker. When the unity of all Christians is manifested in prayer for one another, then the tendency that afflicts us of valuing one form of work and devaluing another can be overcome. Instead, we can understand that each works for all, and all for each. What sense does it make to value this and devalue that in such a unity? When both forms of work are in response to God's leading toward the kingdom, then both forms are necessary. The unity underlying the diversity *is* the mark of the kingdom, and all alike share in the value of the kingdom.

Jesus gives a parable that might illustrate this reality. In Matthew 20, the kingdom of God is likened to a householder who hires laborers for his vineyard. Some are hired early in the morning, with the promise of a specific fee. Every three hours during the day the householder hires more laborers, each time with the promise of the same payment. When evening comes, to the surprise and dismay of the earlier workers, everyone receives the same payment. "Do you begrudge me my generosity?" asks the householder. In our own application, we wrongfully tend to ascribe a high valuation to some forms of work, and a low valuation to others. But if through prayer each participates in the work of all, then we are what we are for each other. Finally there is but one value, the value of the whole kingdom of God. From this value, by the grace of God and through the power of prayer, we all receive.

How is it that in prayer the future kingdom in God finds realization in the present? Perhaps the best illustration that this is so comes from the Lord's Prayer. The prayer is for the coming of the kingdom, which is immediately followed by the petitions for bread and for forgiveness. Both petitions, however, have reference not only to the immediacies of the present but to the future as well. The petitions are not separate from the prayer for the coming of the kingdom but are in fact avenues for that coming.

The gospel understanding of the final coming of the kingdom was communicated through the imagery of an eschatological banquet. There was to be a meal, a wonderful meal, at which we would sit with the Lord and rejoice in the abundance of our redemption. This meal-which-was-to-come was foretold in the feeding of the five thousand; it was also foretold in every humble meal that Jesus shared with the disciples. Daily bread was an image for the bread of life; the one was temporal, the other eternal. In no sense was the daily bread considered simply a poor substitute for that final spiritual banquet; rather, physical needs and spiritual needs were integral to one another, so that the daily feeding was an apt portrayal of that everlasting sustenance of life in the world to come.

"Give us this day our daily bread," says the gospel petition. Some scholars see in this wording a request today for that which is ours, not only today but everlastingly. Not only today's supply but tomorrow's and tomorrow's—but if tomorrow's supply comes today, the future is made present. The kingdom comes as that reality in our future, our destiny in God, affects our present action. The results of this action will be well-being for the wholeness which is ourselves, body and soul in human society, living in the light of that everlasting kingdom which is God.

The second petition likewise pulls the future into the present through the asking for forgiveness. "And forgive us our debts, as we also have forgiven our debtors." In the Aramaic language in which Jesus gave this prayer, the word for debt was also the word for sin, so that the petition is for the forgiveness of sins. But why should God's forgiveness of us appear to be contingent upon our own forgiveness toward others? What can this mean? For we know that God acts toward us from grace.

In a process universe, each affects all; the well-being of one has an effect upon the well-being of the others. God works with what is to bring about what can be. When we retain attitudes of hostility or resentment in unforgiveness toward another, that attitude has a real effect upon the other. We refuse to allow ourselves to become part of the redemptive reality of the other, wishing instead that the other experience a negative judgment. But remember that God feels the world in every moment of its completion; God feels the other and ourselves together in the divine nature. In chapter 17, "The Kingdom in God," we drew a vision wherein we each knew ourselves through the other, as the other experienced us. This mutual participation in each other forms the basis for our own judgment and for our transformation. In the final unity of divine justice, the redemption of one is felt by the other, so that God is the reality of reconciliation. In the kingdom which is God, we move toward acceptance of each other.

When we block that acceptance on earth, we act against the eschatological reality. Further, our own lack of forgiveness puts us in the position of needing forgiveness ourselves. The petition, then, reflects that circular interaction between what is so in God and what is needed on earth. In recognition of that divine reality of forgiveness, both in the transformation that is our destiny and in the acceptance of our whole selves by God which makes that transformation possible, we ask for and act from the forgiveness of sins. The prayer for forgiveness invokes that which will be in the eschatological reality of God into the present order of our existence. The future is made present through prayer.

All prayer is finally a variation on the theme of the Lord's

Prayer. Through prayer we open ourselves to the divine will, that the guidance fashioned for us in heaven might be felt and effected on earth. We change the world by molding the world toward the divine concern for well-being in justice, renewal of nature, and openness and peace among all peoples. As these changes are effected through prayer, always the note of gratitude must sound. It is from God this glory comes, and through God this power is released, and by God's faithfulness these modes of redemption are made possible.

Through prayer, we risk being open to the advent of the kingdom of God. The conformity with the purposes of God that is sought in prayer brings upon us the startling possibility of revaluing our ability to work in a significant way for the kingdom. Prayer is a means whereby we open ourselves for conformity to God's purposes for the well-being of the world, for the reflection of the image of God in human society. Prayer is a catapulting activity, pushing us to appropriate action in the world. Prayer is a unitive activity, through which our fears of fragmentation are put to flight in the deep reality of the togetherness of the kingdom.

The kingdom of God places before us two destinies, blending into unity. On the ultimate level, there is the kingdom which is God, our everliving destiny. It does not now appear what we shall be, but we shall nevertheless be transformed, reconciled with all creation in the depths of God in a justice that is inexorable love. This destiny undergirds and empowers our efforts for the second, which is the kingdom of God on earth, reflecting the divine justice in whatever way is appropriate to the goods and evils of our specific time. Prayer is the union of the two modes of the kingdom, the avenue whereby we open ourselves to the power of God for the world. And the whole church is called to be the embodiment of the ultimate prayer, "thy kingdom come."

CONCLUSION

20

GOD FOR US: TRINITY

WE have spoken of God as presence, seeing this presence exemplified supremely in Jesus of Nazareth; as wisdom, understanding this wisdom as the providence of God experienced by Christians in the history of the church; and as power, interpreting this as the triumph of God over evil, ultimately in the divine nature and persuasively in the world. Presence, wisdom, and power: are there grounds for extending the discussion of these three divine attributes into an understanding of the trinity? To follow this route is to develop a doctrine of the trinity that is based on the human experience of God. It is in the gospels that we know of God's presence in Jesus, in the history of our church that we know of God's providential wisdom, in our experience and in our hope that we dare to speak of divine power. We are in the position of saying that the actions of God for us indicate the very internal nature of God. What God is for us, God is in the depths of the divine being. If God is presence, wisdom, and power for us in our human experience, then God is presence, wisdom, and power internally and everlastingly. But if the ground for saying God is presence, wisdom, and power rests in our human experience, then we are understanding God's inner nature through our own experience.

The legitimacy in this procedure is in the assumption that God cannot be less than that which God can do. The cause must be sufficient for the effects. The actions of God bespeak the nature of God; if God's actions are experienced in a threefold way, and if each way always seems to point back to an initial unity responsible for the ways, then the unity that acts so powerfully must be triune in nature.

On the other hand, a caution must immediately be introduced: we experience each other as being present to us, as influencing us, and as having both internal and external power. In fact, we have given a philosophical analysis that attributes such qualities to every existent reality whatsoever. We do not, however, call every existent reality triune. The most that can be said is that we experience these qualities in varying degrees of intensity, naming the most intense—the human world—as personal. Could it be that the argument for God as trinity, when based on the experience of intensity involved in God as presence, wisdom, and power is reducible to an argument for God as personal? Such would seem to be the logical result of an argument that God cannot be less than the effects which result from divine action.

However, there are philosophical reasons for maintaining that God is not only personal, but also triune. In process thought, this follows from the qualitative difference between God and finite actuality because of the reversed concrescence as discussed in chapter 5. To exist is to be in relation, and internal relations presuppose external relations: the many become one, and are increased by one. Relationships signify strength of being. God is the ultimately related one, because of the reversed concrescence: God and only God relates positively to every single element in the entire universe; only God has such power. Furthermore, this relation to every element in the universe involves the gift of resurrection for all the world in God. God's subjectivity contains and transforms every other subjectivity that has ever existed. If there is sufficient ground for positing such a wonder, and process philosophy provides that ground, it means that God is many and one in a way totally different from anything in our experience. Metaphor and imagination must come to our aid to express such a reality.

Imagine a symphony, in which each note is intensely alive. Each note in this symphony of fantasy would feel itself in relation to all the others, feeling its place in the whole and the whole as well. The life that sustained the lives of the notes would be the symphony as a whole. Posit a deeper locus of awareness than the aliveness of the notes in that life which is the whole, the symphony itself. A living symphony, sparkling with awareness of its own beauty both from the perspective of the whole and from the multiplied perspective of each part—the single beauty is intensified through the multiple awarenesses merged into the unified awareness of the whole. This is fantasy, obviously, and if it is hard to imagine what such a symphony would be like in its own nature, it is still harder to imagine how one outside that symphony could be attuned appreciatively to such a complex beauty. Imagine that every listener becomes a participant in the symphony, adding a new note, and

that the symphony is everlasting, ever deepening, ever intensifying—infinite, inexhaustible beauty. A fantasy, surely, for no symphony is like that. Yet if it could be, it would be something like the
process notion of God. God infinitely relating to the entire universe, bringing that universe to resurrection life within the divine
nature, unifying it within the divine experience—we fumble our
way into the fantasy of a living symphony, but even that metaphor
is not sufficient to describe the amazement of God. The fantasy is
but a dim way to project what such a reality could be like. We, in
our human experience of personality, are but the dimmest
reflections of such an awesome reality. But the reality of God could
be something like that.

How, then, shall we name that infinitely complex, infinitely
living reality? "One" is accurate, for it is the single unity of God
which accounts for that living symphony: God's is the beauty,
God's is the adventure, God's is the joy. And God is one. But
complex! The unity of God is of a complexity far transcending that
which we can experience, pushing us to the edges of our imagination to fathom what it must be like. This awesome complexity of
God is preserved for us through the notion of trinity, for otherwise
we might fall into the arrogance of thinking that God is but humanity writ large upon some cosmic screen. The degree to which God
surpasses our own experience creates a qualitative difference in
kind, for the leap between God and ourselves in intensity of experience is vast.

Yet God incorporates the world into the divine life; the world
becomes the complexity of God in an apotheosis that is participation in the divine life. The hearers become the singers in the
symphony; the fantasy becomes a lived reality. And the embracing
reality of the divine life is an ever-increasing divine complexity in
unity. God as trinity becomes a symbol to indicate the sense in
which the unity of God embraces a complexity of a magnitude
greater than which none can exist.

If we thus retain the term trinity to indicate the infinite complexity in unity of the divine nature, we push the word far beyond its
traditional meaning of threeness. It is so, of course, that in the
process doctrine of God we must speak of God in the threefold way
of primordial nature, consequent nature, and what Whitehead
called the superjective nature, by which he simply meant that
aspect of God that provides the initial aims for the world. The
reason against utilizing these terms as an interpretation of trinity is

simply that the terms are abstractions for our understanding, ways of describing the reality that is God. If we wish trinity to name the subjective reality of God's own experience, we cannot use abstractions. We must instead look for an expression signifying the infinite richness of the divine life. God is the subjectivity of subjectivities, the many who are nevertheless one in living unity, without loss of individuality nor qualification of the integrity of the whole; God is the supremely complex One. If trinity can be expanded beyond its traditional use to indicate this mighty complexity in unity, then it retains a symbolic appropriateness in its designation of the inner nature of God.

"Trinity" denotes the magnitude of the divine power that accomplishes the vision of the divine wisdom, all within the everlasting unity of presence. Presence, wisdom, and power: those qualities we perceive in our own experience of God for us can be understood in reference to the divine nature itself when that nature is expressed as complexity in unity, trinity. Thus "trinity" is a symbol that faces in two directions: there is the God-ward signification, wherein the symbol expresses our sense of the divine subjectivity, and there is the world-ward direction, wherein the symbol bespeaks our own experience of God.

Traditionally, that which we are developing as presence, wisdom, and power has been expressed through the names of Father, Son, and Holy Spirit. There are strong consistencies between the traditional formulation and that developed here. Our christology was developed under the rubric of God's presence for us in history through the revelation of Jesus Christ. The ecclesiology developed in these pages followed from an understanding of God's wisdom in creating, guiding, and sustaining the church, and of course this is the traditional interpretation of the work of the Holy Spirit. Our eschatology rests upon an interpretation of divine power, centered in the depths of the Godhead: does this not bear analogy to the doctrine of God as Father? While the trinitarian names of Father, Son, and Holy Spirit have not been used thus far, the trinitarian work of God usually described through Father, Son, and Spirit has been pervasively present in this process theology. Far from eliminating any understanding of the trinity, the development has been profoundly affected by an understanding of the trinity. God is trinity in presence, wisdom, and power in the dimensions of our human experience. The deepest way to say this is that God is for us. "God for us" thus expresses the trinity and the gospel simultaneously.

That the trinity and the gospel are both indications of "God for us" is seen most clearly in the fourth gospel. The third chapter recounts a discourse between Jesus and Nicodemus. Background to the chapter is the contrast presented in chapter two between the believing disciples at Cana who receive the sign of the wedding miracle, and the unbelieving crowd in Jerusalem, to whom no sign is given. Nicodemus comes to Jesus from the crowd, neither believing nor disbelieving, but wavering in the dilemma of doubt. He identifies himself with the crowd, but comes out from the crowd, as would a disciple. Haltingly, he begins to question Jesus, asking who he is, and what he is saying. The evangelist presents Jesus' answers as revealing the nature of God in terms of what we have come to call the trinity, and the gospel. Jesus first speaks of the nature of God as Spirit, bringing us to birth. He then speaks of the passion of the Son, lifted up and drawing all humanity to God. Finally, in the culmination of the passage, he speaks of the transcending, sending Father: "God so loved the world that he sent his only Son, that whoever believes on him should not perish, but have everlasting life." In this text, the gospel writer concludes the triune presentation of God with what will become identified as the most concise expression of the gospel. God as triune is God for us, and God for us is the good news of the gospel.

The fact that God is revealed as Spirit, Son, and Father in the context of being "God for us" has tremendous implications for our understanding of the trinity. It means that God as Spirit, Son, and Father refers to the world-ward direction of trinity. As world-oriented, the words are inexorably reflective of the distinctiveness of the time and place in which the words were given. To take the words out of the historical context and push them to the transhistorical description of God carries certain dangers.

To speak of these terms as historically relative is in no sense to speak of them as false, it is simply to speak of them as conditioned by particularities which are not always shared by all peoples. The terms have a particular and not a universal meaning, and therefore must be constantly translated for changing places and times if one is to be faithful to the intent of the original meaning. God fashions aims for the world which must take account of the particular past and the real possibilities relative to the world there and then. In no sense are aims somehow false because they are not universal; on the contrary, their truth is dependent upon their absolute relativity, their conditioned and therefore appropriate nature. Likewise with revelation: that which God reveals and manifests for us is conditioned as much by us as it is by the divine nature. Frequently revelatory aims are far more reflective of our condition than God's. The inexorable implication of this is that a revelation of God as trinity in its world-ward orientation will always be suited to the conditions in the world, taking its coloration from those conditions. This means that the world-ward expression of God as triune is not exempt from historical relativity: it *must* partake of historical relativity if it is to be a true manifestation of God for us. Precisely because this is so, we cannot absolutize any historical sense of the trinity.

If God as Father, Son, and Holy Spirit is a specific way to speak of God's power, presence, and wisdom toward us, for us, and with us, then there are serious considerations for moving today toward emphasizing this trinity as power, wisdom, and presence rather than as Father, Son, and Spirit. The consideration is simply in the historical relativity of the terms. They no longer convey that which was implicit in the words in their initial use.

For instance, use of the term "Father" for God comes to us from the lips of Jesus, and we assume that what we mean by father today is precisely what he meant by Father, for does not father mean first and foremost the relationship of physical generation? Yet the biblical scholar Joachim Jeremias has extensively studied the meaning of the word "Abba, Father," as used by Jesus. In the culture of that day the fundamental importance of the relationship between father and son was the transmission of wisdom. A father taught his son the secrets of his trade, training him to carry on the work of the father. For Jesus to call God Father connoted first and foremost the intense intimacy whereby Jesus knew God's work and did God's work. Given the fact that what God does is in deep consistency with who God is in the divine character, for Jesus to do God's work was, for Jesus, to reveal God's nature. Thus the use of the word "Father" to indicate his relationship to God was intensely appropriate for Jesus in the usage of his day. Today, however, we no longer consider "Father" in the sense of a transmission of knowledge; rather, we tend to think of the term in the sense of male progeneration. Maleness rather than work or character tends to define the word for us, and we attribute our own meaning to the intent of Jesus. But this confuses the reality of the meaning of Jesus. We only confuse the issue further when we take that historical meaning and push it to the ontological understanding of the inner nature of God.

Likewise with the word "Son." Through sonship, Jesus draws us to God. How can we understand this all-important sonship? And what does it say about the nature of God? How was Jesus "Son"? Consider the fact that two of the gospels recount incarnation in the context of the virgin birth, and that one of the earliest incarnation passages of the epistles, the hymn of Philippians 2, speaks of incarnation in the form of a slave. What do these things mean, and how do they affect our notion of God as Son? Incarnation is historical, fitted to a particular time and place. In the Jewish culture of ancient Palestine, there was a strong sense of social hierarchy: the king was the highest social position, and a slave was the lowest. Further, all humanity was divided in terms of social value: men were highest, followed by women. Legitimate sons, who would carry on the patrimony of Israel, were valued next, followed by legitimate daughters. Below the legitimate daughters in ranking were the illegitimate daughters, and lowest of all were the illegitimate sons. The daughters could receive a name in Israel through their marriage, but of course the boys could not. Unable to carry on the patrimony, the illegitimate sons were lowest on the social scale.

Whatever else the doctrine of the virgin birth means, it surely also indicates the social status of Jesus of Nazareth. If Joseph is not his father, then Jesus' social ranking is that of the illegitimate son. Further, the ministry of this son in his adult life continues the theme of lowliness, for he calls himself a servant and does such work as washing the feet of the disciples—the work of women and of slaves. Ultimately, the church associates him with the Suffering Servant of Isaiah 53. Illegitimate Son and Servant, all within the context of incarnation: what can these things mean? What other meaning can be read into the situation than that the incarnation embraces the whole of humanity, and renders our caste systems meaningless?* The highest becomes the lowest; in becoming lowest, the designation of lowest is surely annulled. The lines that

* I am indebted to Nelle Morton for this insight. She first called attention to this implication of the virgin birth narratives in "Holy Spirit, Child Spirit, Art Spirit, Woman Spirit," published in *Women's Caucus—Religious Studies Newsletter*, Summer 1976, p. 8.

220   GOD-CHRIST-CHURCH

divide humanity into "higher" and "lower" are no longer valid. If they are broken down by God in incarnation, how can we still raise them up in the name of incarnation? Had incarnation—the revelation of the nature of God for us—taken place through a woman, the incarnation would not have embraced the lowest dregs of our human attributions of value, and the lowest of the low would have been left out of incarnation and the revelation of God for us. As it is, however, we have the amazing inclusion in the gospels of an emphasis upon virgin birth, and of the servant function of the Son. The deepest meaning of God as Son in incarnation is not at all the maleness of Jesus or even the Sonship of God, but the inclusiveness of incarnation, embracing every form of the social divisions of humanity. Today, however, when we hear the designation of the trinity as including "Son," we tend to overlook this fullness of scope to the incarnation. Instead, we use it as a basis for attributing the restrictions of maleness once more to God. By doing so, we violate the fullness of the revelation of God for us given through God in Christ; we make the revelation small. Through our foolishness we build up again the partitions that God broke down, and dare to say that the prejudices are ultimately affirmed by the inward nature of God! We use God as Son to deny the work revealed through God as illegitimate son and slave in the history of humanity.

"Spirit" does not fare much better in our contemporary milieu. Even here, there has been an evolution of the word toward an unbiblical emphasis upon maleness. Originally, the word conveyed the wisdom of God in the ordering of the church. Such precision is lost to our contemporary world, for our use of the word "Spirit" lists where it will, blowing with every contemporary wind of preference. "Spirit" can become a means of declaring degrees of holiness within the church, such that "higher" and "lower" again become divisive marks of prejudice and value. Alternatively, "Spirit" has been taken in an anarchal sense defying modes of order. Given this option, there is some irony in the fact that a still further perversion of "Spirit" appeals to God as Spirit in a legalistic sense to declare a preferred way of doing things as God-endorsed and therefore unchangeable. How do such interpretations of God as Spirit indicate to us the all-embracing grace of God, empowering and guiding our redemptive living in the world? How do these interpretations of the trinity convey to us the deep richness of the gospel?

The further theological difficulties with such distortions of the trinity through our failure to look at the words Father, Son, and Spirit as historically relative expressions of God for us is that we push the distortions back into the nature of God. With regard to maleness, we encounter the difficulty of saying on the one hand that God is not anthropocentric, that God transcends sexuality, or mere maleness and femaleness, and yet on the other hand we insist that God is indeed a male, and that only another male can properly represent "him." We reinforce this confusion by insisting that all of our language concerning God be portrayed through masculinity, bewailing the fact that we "must" do so, for how else can we speak of God? We hope this book will indicate that we can quite easily speak of God without recourse to masculine-bound words, so that the full deity of God can come to expression.

The problem, it must be emphasized, is not in the initial revelation of God through use of the words "Father," "Son," and "Spirit," but in the fact that the historical relativity of the words is lost to view. The initial context of the revelation is lost in our contemporary sensitivity, so that we are in the topsy-turvy position of using the same words equivocally, conveying a meaning far removed from the intention of the revelation of God in Christ as God for us.

We advocate, then, that the triune nature of God for us be expressed directly through the understanding of God's presence with us and for us through Jesus of Nazareth; through the wisdom of God whereby God brings the church to birth in each generation, guiding it through divine providence in its manifestation of apostolicity, unity, and holiness; and through the power of God, bringing the world to justice within the transformation of the divine being and guiding the finite world toward societal forms of justice. This is "God for us," in the world-ward orientation of the trinity. In no sense is it discontinuous with the God-ward orientation of the word, for it is the reality of God that is revealed in Christ. It is the nature of God's integrative wisdom that produces the aims of divine providence, and it is the internal nature of God that achieves the fullness of justice and love in an everlasting dynamism of beauty. The complex unity which is the God-ward designation of trinity issues into our experience of God as presence, wisdom, and power in the world-ward designation of the trinity. We know God as trinity by knowing God for us.

One further implication of the trinity as God for us should be noted, and that is the sense in which the phrase itself contains both the transcendent and the immanent and the relational elements of the meaning of trinity. "God" transcends the world in divine power, working with the world according to the divine will and purpose. Yet this God is "for" the world, relating infinitely to the world, both through receiving the world and guiding the world, curing the world and caring for the world. The very word "for" conveys the intensity of the divine love; God is "for" the world in relationality and covenant. "Us": the world is not abstract, not universal, not some generalized reality, but the world is as concrete and as particular and as peculiar as "us." Through the relative provision of initial aims, the transcendent God is immanent in the world for us and for our good. In the everlasting reciprocity of the process, the immanence of God returns again to the transcendence of God, as God receives the world. Receiving the world, God fashions for it, in its next moment of becoming, an aim that will lure it toward harmony. "God for us" conveys the trinity; "God for us" conveys the gospel; trinity and gospel are finally just this mystery: that God is for us.

If the traditional formulation of the world-ward direction of the trinity was historically conditioned and therefore relative to time and place, it is certainly true that the present development partakes of the same relativity. A theology developed through process thought must underscore the relativity of its perception. It is finally not at all a photograph of the way things are between God and the world in Christian experience: it is but a vision of reality, a way of expressing from a particular perspective in time and place how we may interpret our experience of God through Christ and the church. The purpose in stating the vision is simply that our vision of reality matters. In itself it becomes a part of our redemptive experience. How we think about reality enters into our attitudes toward others, toward God, toward ourselves. When the vision of God as seen through the divine presence in Christ is such that it inspires our love, then that lovingness opens us more deeply to the influence of God and hence orients us as well toward God's caring purposes in the world. When the vision of God bespeaks the wisdom of God, given in faithfulness through divine guidance in every moment of our existence, then through the vision God evokes our trust. In trust, we dare to move into a future which takes us beyond that which we thought could be achieved on the basis of the past alone. And when the vision of God is such that it expresses the divine triumph of justice, then it elicits a catalytic hope with regard to the achievement of justice in forms of our earthly society. If God cannot overcome evil, how can we? But if God's overcoming of evil in the depths of the divine nature is in fact a call to our own efforts to overcome evil in our finite sphere, then there is every reason to work for social justice, every reason to open ourselves to conversion from personal forms of evil, every reason to live in the joyfulness of a community dedicated to holiness. How we think about reality matters; our expressions of a vision of reality are part and parcel of that life which we call redemptive and Christian.

That the vision is relative is essential to the openness of the vision and to the redemptiveness of the vision. Because it is relative, one can hear the different expressions of others in openness rather than fear, learning from the richness of another how better to perceive reality from one's own perspective. Because it is relative, there is freedom in the expression—the tight burden of being able to say what is so absolutely from a perspective where we see only relatively is lifted, and one can play with the vision, measuring it always with that vision which is a beauty just beyond sight, yet felt. Finally, perhaps, the expression of a vision of reality which is relative to our time and place is simply a mode in finitude of what might finally be an everlasting dialogue, each sharing with another a vision of beauty from a particular perspective, yet keenly and gratefully and joyfully feeling the depths of beauty from which all our visions spring.

GLOSSARY
OF
PROCESS TERMS

Actual Entity: Each unit of process is called an actual entity; it is a drop of experience which comes into existence through the creative process of concrescence. Actual entities are the "final real things of which the world is made up." They are the building blocks which, through an essential interconnectedness, make up the composite world of rocks, trees, and people.

Actual Occasion: This phrase is almost a synonym for "actual entity," with the one distinction that the word "occasion" implies a locus in the spatio-temporal extensiveness of the universe. Thus "actual occasion" refers to a finite reality. "Actual entity," on the other hand, is not so limited. God is understood to be in some sense nontemporal; therefore, God is always referred to as an actual entity, and never as an actual occasion.

Concrescence: This refers to the activity of becoming; it is the unification of many feelings into the single actual entity. In concrescence, feelings are contrasted and evaluated until they are integrated into a final unity, called the "satisfaction." The activity of concrescence is the self-production of the subject.

Consequent Nature: Whitehead refers to the physical pole in God as the Consequent Nature. This is God's feelings of the world. It is "consequent" in a twofold sense: first, it follows from the primordial nature in God, and second, it follows from the actual happenings in the world.

Creativity: "Creativity," "many," and "one" are ultimate notions for process thought. Every actual entity is an instantiation of the process whereby many feelings are creatively unified into one determinate subject. Creativity proceeds in two forms: concrescent creativity is the process of becoming, and transitional creativity is the process of influencing another's becoming.

Initial Aim: This is the connectedness between God and the becoming actual occasion. From the point of view of God, God's knowledge of the becoming occasion's entire past is integrated with God's own purposes. This yields a particular possibility for what the new occasion might become, and this particular possibility is the initial aim. From the point of view of the becoming occasion, the occasion feels the aim of God's purpose for itself.

Mental Pole: Every actual entity has both a mental and a physical pole. The mental pole is the grasp of possibilities relative to the subject's own becoming. This grasp of possibilities guides the way in which the feelings of the physical pole are integrated into subjective unity.

Negative Prehensions: Every item in the universe is felt; these feelings are called "prehensions." A negative feeling is one in which the particular item felt is excluded from positive incorporation in the concrescent process.

Objective Immortality: Every actual occasion affects every successor. The effect is the transmission of its own reality into the new reality by way of transitional creativity. This can only be a partial transmission from the point of view of the finite actual occasion. No one occasion can feel another in its entirety.

Physical Pole: This is the means by which a becoming occasion feels all the influence of its past through "prehension." It inaugurates concrescence.

Prehension: The feeling of others is called "prehension." Prehensions involve emotion, purpose, and valuation. Because of prehension, there is connectedness in the universe.

Primordial Nature: This is the equivalent of the mental pole in God. The primordial nature is God's grasp of all possibilities. This grasp involves an ordering evaluation of possibilities into a harmony which is called the "primordial vision."

Satisfaction: This constitutes the achievement of unity whereby a subject is itself. It is the goal of conscrescence, and completes the occasion. Full unification of the occasion is called "satisfaction." Because of the reversal of poles in God, satisfaction in God relates to the primordial vision, and therefore is everlasting in God.

Sensitivity of Subjective Forms: In the process of concrescence, every prehension is felt in light of all other prehensions. This is the basis for the contrasting activity which is the creation of unity. It is sometimes referred to as "mutual sensitivity of subjective forms."

Superject: To be something for oneself necessarily entails being something for others. "Superject" refers to the sense in which an occasion has an effect beyond itself. This is not optional; it is simply a matter of fact. Whitehead underscores this frequently by calling an actual entity a "subject/superject."

Subjective Form: Every prehension is felt with a certain positive or negative value from the point-of-view of the feeling subject. This constitutes "how" the other is felt.